D1168998

Secrets of...
The "A" Game

By Logan Edwards

Secrets of the "A" Game

Published by
Sweetleaf Publishing
Los Angeles, CA

www.sweetleafpublishing.com

ISBN: 978-0-9776505-1-4

Printed in the United States of America

Cover and Interior Design: Printmedia Books and Chad Perry

Editing: Chad Perry
Copyediting and Proofreading: Jessica Keet

Cover Illustration: Audrey Botha

Interior Illustrations: Audrey Botha, Chih Hang, Anastasiya Igolkina, Paola Condreas, Stefan Wehrmann, and Alexandra Mikhnevich

Prologue

I have a confession to make. When I was growing up, from junior high all the way through college and beyond, I wasn't successful with women. I wasn't good looking, popular, wealthy, athletic, or particularly intelligent. I wasn't cool in any sense of the word and I knew it. I accepted that I just wasn't attractive to women and even though there was occasional interest and even a girlfriend or two, I was in no way successful with women in the way I truly wanted to be. I felt powerless when I met women and at the time I firmly held the belief that if any woman was ever attracted to me, I should feel extremely fortunate.

During my formative years I went out a lot and tried to meet women, but the vast majority of them simply weren't interested in me. In high school I joined the tennis team, spiked my hair, bought new clothes, and even threw massive parties when my parents were out of town—anything I could do just so girls would notice me. What I would have said to them if they had actually noticed me I couldn't begin to tell you, because they *never* did. Essentially, I was a computer nerd when no one had computers and I spent my free time playing Dungeons and Dragons and watching TV.

My college experience wasn't any better than my high school experience, with the exception that I drank so much I wasn't able to dwell on how unsuccessful I had become with women. Even with all the social activities I was involved in, including sporting events, mixers, house parties, study groups, and more, I *still* wasn't attracting women. I went through some dark periods because I was learning more about the world and more about myself, and I realized that I wanted women to be a part of my life, but remained clueless on how to make it happen.

After I left school and got a job I spent a lot of time thinking about why I couldn't attract the kind of women I desired. Unfortunately, since I had a decent job, all of my solutions revolved around buying the designer clothes, expensive furniture, and fancy cars that I was *positive* would reverse my fortunes. After all, from all of the commercials I watched, magazines I read, and music I listened to, if I just owned these products I would be surrounded by women. Of course I wasn't surrounded by women even after buying all of these things and it completely shattered me. Happiness never came to me and by my mid-twenties I was beginning to think that it never would.

After working so hard on having all of the right possessions and flashing a lot of cash, I found I was only marginally more successful with women and it depressed me to no end. I thought to myself, *I'm buying all of the things I'm being told I need to have in order to attract women and it's not working.* Because I was trying everything I knew how and it wasn't working, I felt like a complete loser. I was just a few years out of college and I was depressed and isolated because I tried and failed at something I knew was important to my long-term happiness.

Does my life story and lack of success with women sound familiar?

Do you find yourself going out to bars to meet women and end up sitting alone the entire night? Do you see attractive women you want to talk to, but always talk yourself out of approaching? Do you see other guys and think they look better, have more money, and act cooler than you and because of that you could never compete with them? Do you get nervous and forget what to say or say stupid things when you meet women? Do you think everyone is looking at you and think they'll laugh if a woman rejects you? So did I. I was confused, frustrated, depressed, angry, sad, and ultimately...alone.

Like most others guys, I believed all of the myths that the media, society, and Corporate America continue to perpetuate to this very day. I thought that as long as I was nice to women and did everything they asked, they would fall madly in love with me. After all, women always say they want to find a nice guy, and my friends and family always told me to "just be myself." Because I did what I was told and followed everyone's advice, I ended up living a life of failure and rejection.

I stopped going out. I stopped looking at women. I stopped thinking about what I would say if I ever had a chance to meet women. I gave up on the prospect of *ever* finding someone special. Finally, I started to think about how I could find happiness in a life of near solitude, just so I didn't have to face rejection and the fact that I wasn't attractive to women. My days became filled with video games, reality TV, fast food, alcohol, porn, and a job I hated. But no matter how hard I tried to fill the void where companionship, laughter, love, and sex should have been, I couldn't do it—the emptiness never went away.

Then one day, something happened... something changed.

I wish I could tell you I met a legend or I almost died or some other weird twist of fate that unequivocally changed my life forever, but it wasn't anything nearly as dramatic. Since I had given up and stopped participating in society, all of the pressure that caused me to believe in the myths that had ruled and ultimately ruined my life, faded away. Eventually, since I was completely alone, I was left with only one person who I could listen to—my inner man. My inner man had drastically different ideas on how to get things done and as it turned out, those instincts were precisely what I needed to meet and attract women anywhere, anyplace, anytime.

In a sense, the very phenomenon of how women become attracted to men completely eluded me, until one day I was walking from the parking lot to the office I worked at and I saw a cute girl walking toward me. To this day, I can't tell you why I acted against my usual routine, but instead of keeping my head down and completely ignoring this young woman, I slowed down a bit, made eye contact, and smiled at her. Almost instantly, she smiled back at me, so I slowly raised my arm, gave a very relaxed wave and said, "Hi." At the time, what came next shocked me—she slowed down and said, "Hi" and then I watched her as she walked past me.

I smiled and said "Hi" to a woman and she responded positively—something that hadn't happened in a long time. I knew that if I had stopped and talked to her, we probably would have had a really nice conversation and perhaps we would have met later for a drink. At the time, I'm not sure how I would have pulled that off, but for the first time in a long time, I saw possibility. I realized that if I could be happy with myself and my life, women would pick up on it and would be open to talking and possibly more. I figured out that it wasn't the car I drove or the clothes on my back that created attraction, but my own attitude. Of course, this was only the beginning and I had a lot of learning to do, but I was determined that I would eventually be successful with women, no matter what it took.

It's amazing how something so simple and natural made me completely re-evaluate my attitude on life and women, but that's exactly what happened. From that point onward I started following my instincts—that initial drive that seemed to occur a split second before self-doubt and insecurity reared their ugly heads to somehow convince me that I shouldn't bother. Now I follow my instincts—my ego, reputation, past experiences, and heartbreaks be damned. It was by far the best decision I've ever made in my entire life.

I'm going to share with you what I've learned after years of following my instincts, my inner man, and learning from both the successes *and* the failures I had to endure in order to become successful with women. Success started with a change in attitude because for many years, I had a bad attitude and a poor self-image, yet I expected women to treat me as though I didn't. I suppose I thought women would see through all of the negativity and "save me," but now I see why that very attitude doomed me from ever attracting great women.

Over time, the phenomenon of how women become attracted to men no longer eluded me. While I had always assumed that women use logic to determine whether they are attracted to someone, I realized that they follow their emotions—their inner woman—and rarely "decide" whether someone is attractive. It became crystal clear that being nice all of these years never set off any romantic feelings in the women I met. I was always nice, pleasant, and non-threatening—all very good qualities for a friend— but not attractive qualities for a boyfriend. I figured out that while nice wasn't an initially attractive quality—I already possessed other qualities that women *do* find attractive.

At first I felt even more lost and bewildered as to how I could create attraction based on how I made a woman feel. However, over time and through a lot of trial and error, I realized that attracting women was much easier than I imagined. Instead of buying more clothes and constantly upgrading my car, I started to open up and talk to more and more women, and eventually learned the specific qualities they find attractive in men. At the same time, I looked at myself in the mirror and realized that I already had a lot of the traits women look for, but after years of self-delusion and media manipulation, I had forgotten what they were.

I finally figured out that women don't always want the guy with chiseled good looks or a huge bank account. Most don't care about the fancy cars, designer clothes, or expensive dinners. What they want is a man who follows his instincts, has confidence in everything he does, sets and meets the goals he creates for himself, and ultimately makes a woman feel understood and respected and, most importantly, safe and secure. I evolved from a guy who tried to give women everything I thought they wanted, into a man who could give the right women, the ones *I* found most attractive, what I knew they needed.

Armed with a completely different set of ideas on what really attracts women, I started to make different lifestyle choices. Now that I knew what women really needed and was confident that I had many of those qualities, I needed to show women that I had what they were looking for. That meant no more evenings in front of a screen, no more junk food, no more feeling sorry for myself, and no more keeping my head down and acting as though I didn't exist to the world. I started finding new and interesting ways to meet women in places I never thought possible, by doing and saying things I never would have thought would work when I was growing up.

I started to consider myself a salesman, giving woman only a taste of the goods and offering them an opportunity to obtain the deluxe package... *if* they behaved themselves. I changed my frame of mind from thinking of women as the "goods" that I might eventually, through a lot of false starts and missed connections, end up in a sexual relationship with, to viewing myself as the one to be pursued, the catch, the prize. I never aggressively pushed this frame of mind because I knew that if a woman didn't "get it," then she was going to miss out and someone else would "win" the prize.

Some women hated hearing about this change in attitude because it brought to the surface their own attitudes regarding men and courtship. Of course most women don't consciously think they're princesses surrounded by frogs, but that attitude is still ingrained through millions of years of evolution. It's the standard Victorian-era view of men only wanting one thing from women, who must protect themselves from single-minded men and save themselves for only the most worthy. The difference now is that I view myself as someone special, someone who saves himself for only the most worthy women.

Even though I no longer bought into the notion that only women are allowed to play hard to get, I didn't blame them for trying. I realized that it's built into their genes and bombarded into their brains by today's mass media. Instead, I began to acknowledge a woman's game, but also let her know that I didn't *play* hard to get, I *was* hard to get. Eventually, that kind of confidence created a level of success with women far greater than "just being myself" ever did.

I didn't really want to be hard to get when it counted, but I held that attitude long enough for a woman to recognize that I was different than most men she encountered. I made it a point that women should understand that I know what they value in men, that I have options, and that I represent a challenge that women can't easily find. Although some women felt it was unfair that I had this unique insight on the male/female dynamic, most came to appreciate it, especially when they considered the alternative.

I already understood that a woman knows, subconsciously or not, whether she would ever sleep with me during the first few minutes we meet. But it took a while to realize that acting desperate and horny, or simply being nice and wimpy yielded nothing but rejection. I also recognized that once a woman felt she wasn't attracted to me, no amount of pursuit or persuasion was going to change her mind. Because of that, I was finally liberated from dead-end crushes and trying to use logic to convince women to like me. Now I could easily move on from a woman who wasn't interested in me without feeling sorry for myself.

I continually learned from my rejections and adjusted my attitude and behavior so I didn't repeat the same mistakes again and again. I left my wimpy, desperate habits behind and became a confident, interesting man who loved his single life. I continually refined myself until I had a product the "market" demanded, instead of trying to convince the market that they needed my product. I eventually had my choice of women because I knew I had a lot of attractive qualities, I knew where I could go to show them off, and I knew how to quickly demonstrate those qualities to gauge whether or not a woman found them attractive. These are the skills you are about to learn...

Contents

Introduction

Welcome to *Secrets of The "A" Game!* Like a lot of guys, you probably wish you were more successful with women, but you don't know how. Realizing that you need help with women and doing something about it is difficult for most men, largely due to ego and stubbornness. Because you've embraced the idea that you *can* learn how to attract beautiful women and are willing to make changes in your life to make it happen, you should start by congratulating yourself. Not only are you going to learn how, but you're going to put that knowledge into action and achieve a greater level of success with women than you ever thought possible!

In case you still think it's just you who's clueless when it comes to dealing with women, it's not. There are millions of single guys who don't know how to talk to or act around women. Without question, men are at a disadvantage because women can always consult their friends, watch *Sex and the City*, and read *Cosmo* whenever they need help with men and relationships. Men, on the other hand, have very few resources to turn to—ever ask your friends for advice on women? How did that work out?

Of course, there are romance guides at the bookstore and thousands of articles on the Internet purporting to teach men how to date women, usually providing such valuable tips as what kind of flowers to bring on a first date and ways to act nice and polite. The advice tends to be either completely obvious or utterly useless because, for starters, it ignores the fact that you first have to meet and attract women before you can date them. Plus, as you will soon learn, traditional dating is on life support—dinner and a movie are out!

You may have also noticed a growing industry of books and courses based on bedding women using complicated techniques that create far more confusion and frustration than success. Whether through hypnosis or outright manipulation, these methods *may* work, but they're unnatural and sometimes difficult to comprehend. Meeting and attracting women shouldn't require a degree in psychology, which is why you won't have to wade though a sea of jargon and psychobabble just to make sense of *The "A" Game*. I've written the entire book in an easy-to-read style without acronyms, charts, and dense theories on mating and courtship.

The "A" Game isn't a fad or a "get laid quick" scheme. You won't learn how to manipulate women or get permission to treat them poorly. Women aren't evil and they aren't the enemy. In a way, women are after the same thing you are—to be with the most attractive (looks, wealth, personality) person they possibly can. Women maintain highly evolved social defenses to thwart guys who don't meet their standards and most do a very good job of it. Starting now, you're going to maintain your own high standards and present yourself as a challenge—the same way women challenge men. Women admire and seek out that which is hard to get, like diamonds or Jimmy Choo shoes, and you're going to learn why women find men who present a challenge, who are genuinely "hard to get", extremely attractive.

Instead of a system that you have to commit to memory and follow slavishly, *The "A" Game* is a toolbox of concepts and tactics you can choose to use based on a given situation. Whether at the mall, during the day, approaching a beautiful woman who's shopping for shoes or at a bar, late at night, approaching a group of men and women, *The "A" Game* explains how women become attracted to men and how to accelerate that attraction. Regardless of the circumstances, attracting women is a dynamic interplay of verbal, visual, and emotional stimulation that requires a dynamic approach, which is exactly The "A" Game is all about.

So what is The "A" Game and why should you learn it? For those of you who don't already know, the term "game" is slang for being skillful at charming and flirting with women. The term "A" Game is often applied to athletes and means doing your best and giving your all—however, it's not just applicable to sports, but to anything you do in life. In this case, "A" Game is a combination of the two—developing your best self and applying it to the art of meeting and attracting women.

Imagine being the kind of guy that women are drawn to, who make them smile and laugh with ease. Imagine being able to build enough rapport with a group of women so you can easily walk away with one of their friends. Imagine being able to build enough comfort and trust with a woman to get her phone number, bounce to another bar, make out, or even take her home, all in the same night. Whether your goals include finding the right woman to create a long-lasting relationship with, or bedding a new girl every night, you can now stop imagining and start realizing these possibilities!

Bringing your "A" Game means meeting and attracting women efficiently with confidence, style, and class all the while maintaining your dignity and personal standards. Through a blend of psychology, sales techniques, and my own personal research, you're going to gain a better understanding of how women think and feel and how to work with their needs and desires instead of against them. Not only will you gain valuable, practical insight that can instantly change the way you approach and interact with women, you'll also have an edge over guys who still place women on pedestals and find themselves forever stuck in the "friends" zone.

You have every reason to get excited about learning how to better meet and attract women, but it's going to take more than just reading a book; it's going to take a commitment to changing your life. Reading this book is just the first step in what could be a lengthy journey from chump to champ. For some, just a few minor tweaks is all it will take to help elevate their game, while others may start completely over, rebuilding themselves from scratch into the ladies man they've always wanted to be. Regardless of your skill level and where you want it to be, you not only have to be willing to learn, but also willing to make the necessary changes and apply what you learn until it becomes instinctual.

For many of you, real change requires some amount of "bottoming out", where you're pissed off and ready to throw in the towel, much like I was when I hit rock bottom. If you've reached a point where you've become disgusted with what your romantic life has become, don't despair, because this is where real life-altering change takes place. If you haven't already, now is the time to say *enough is enough* and channel that energy—the anger, the frustration, the loneliness—into a passion for meeting and attracting the women you've always wanted, no matter the obstacles, the setbacks, the rejections. You have the power to change your life as long as you really want it.

At this point you might still be stuck dwelling on your obstacles or past rejections. You might be thinking that *The "A" Game* is designed to help good-looking guys attract models and actresses—that you don't look good enough, make enough money, or you're just too boring to take advantage of this knowledge. This is your innermost fear talking and over time, it's become your reality because you allowed it to be. As long as you hold the frame of mind that you're not good enough to meet the kind of women you find attractive, you never will. You're going to learn that women aren't nearly as superficial when it comes to looks and money as you think they are, because they're driven by their emotions. If you can find out what kinds of emotions a particular woman desires to feel and then help stimulate those feelings, most will look past any real or self-perceived flaws you have. This is the power of *The "A" Game*.

Throughout the book you're going to learn new concepts and ideas, but also specific things to say, tactics for dealing with various situations, and "canned" routines to help get you started. Once you understand the basics, you can often figure out what to do on your own, using a little critical thinking. If you hit a snag, like finding yourself talking to many women, but never attracting them, you can always refer back to the book until you've overcome any minor obstacles preventing you from advancing your interactions with women.

Structurally, *The "A" Game* is arranged into four sections, each helping to develop and elevate your inner and outer game and applying it to a variety of real-world situations. The following overview describes how the book is laid out and what types of information you'll find in each section.

Myths and Rules

We'll start by examining some of the myths that prevent men from meeting and attracting women, from the classic *Just be yourself* to the more subtle *Guys can "convince" women into liking them*. Demolishing these myths will help open your mind to the rest of the material in the book, beginning with rules on meeting and attracting women. The rules fully explore the foundations that the rest of the concepts in the book are based on. Before you dive into any other chapters, start by reading the myths and rules because they're crucial to everything else you want to learn.

Inner Game and Outer Game

Once you have a firm grasp on the fundamental rules on meeting and attracting women, we'll focus on your attitude toward yourself and toward women. "A" Game starts from within so it's important that you have a positive outlook on how you see yourself and the world around you. When it comes to attracting women, confidence is king, so you'll want to make sure you have what it takes to approach and Open women you've never met. You'll also learn about personal style and grooming habits to ensure that your general appearance isn't an obstacle to meeting the women you desire.

Understanding Women

While you may feel it's impossible for men to ever understand women, in this section you'll gain just enough insight to recognize what they find attractive about men, what they despise, and what they notice about you when you approach. You'll also learn about different types of women so you can build your own profile of the kinds of women you desire and those you should kick to the curb. As you'll learn, holding and maintaining these standards builds confidence and helps attract a better class of women. Finally, you'll get a brief run-down on all of the great places you can go to meet women, including the best times to go and what kind of success you can expect.

Five Stages of the "A" Game

While the first half of the book is dedicated to the "prep" work involved in meeting and attracting women, the latter half focuses on applying that knowledge in the real world—the real "meat" of exactly how to meet and attract women. Each of the five stages of The "A" Game: Open, Hook, Attract, Connect, and Close flow from one into another and provide a comprehensive framework for meeting and attracting women. From walking up to a group of women and Opening them, gaining their approval and Hooking them, breaking away from the group with one of the women and Attracting her, building comfort and rapport by Connecting with her, then finally escalating the attraction into something sexual by Closing her, these chapters cover everything you need to know to make it happen.

In case you were wondering, all of the information in this book has been thoroughly tested, not just by me, but by countless others across the world. Regardless of their looks, wealth, or previous experience with women, they were able to incorporate some or all of the information into their daily lives and elevate their game in ways they never thought possible. I have no doubt that you will find similar success if you commit to putting this knowledge to work on a consistent basis.

Everything you need to know to meet and attract women can be learned, or unlearned as the case may be. You won't have to undergo any plastic surgery or extensive training and counseling. In fact, you probably already have most of the skills and knowledge you need to attract women, but forgot it all because of years of self-deception and insecurity. A lot of what you're about to read will seem like common sense, things you already know, which will make these concepts, tips, and tactics easier to remember and eventually apply when you see a woman you want to approach.

I passionately believe that every shy, insecure, self-conscious, and heartbroken man can learn how to improve their ability to meet and attract women. My goal is to provide you with all of the tools you need to make it happen, and to help change your attitude toward women so you never fear rejection again. If anything you just read in the Prologue about my life as a lonely guy who wasn't successful with women, who convinced himself he was unattractive, and who gave up on ever meeting great women, sounds familiar, this book was written for you. If you are interested in changing your life, like I did, so you become a confident man who knows what he wants out of life and how to get it, including meeting and attracting beautiful women, this book was written for you.

Finally, I sincerely hope that you have as much fun learning and applying this knowledge as I have. As long as you're dedicated to improving your skills—preparation, presentation, communication, escalation, and more—you will eventually master the ability to meet and attract women just like any other skill. However, before diving into the specific methods, qualities, and attitudes you need to refine, there are myths that you probably still believe in that will prevent you from opening your mind to this new way of thinking. We'll begin by demystifying many of the reasons you may have built up that prevent you from being successful with women, so you can tackle the rest of the book with a fresh perspective.

Now, let's have some fun!

Chapter 1

Myths

In this Chapter

★ Understanding why "just being yourself" is bad advice for attracting women

★ Discovering why you don't have to be rich or handsome to meet women

★ Learning why you can't use logic to "convince" a woman to be attracted to you

Myths about meeting and attracting women

1. *Just be yourself.*

2. *Be nice and women will be attracted to you.*

3. *Women don't want men they don't know to talk to them.*

4. *You have to be a millionaire, athlete, or model to attract women.*

5. *Women know what they're looking for, so they'll find you.*

6. *Meeting women takes lots of time, energy, and money.*

7. *Guys can "convince" women into liking them.*

8. *Women have it easy because guys are always talking to them.*

9. *Women only want boyfriends and husbands, not just sex.*

10. *You're no good with women and you aren't going to get better.*

Myth #1: Just be yourself

If you've ever asked a friend, typically a female relative, how you can be more successful with women, you've probably been told that once you meet a women you're attracted to, all you have to do is be yourself. This supposed conventional wisdom, which has endured for decades, is probably one of the reasons why you bought this book in the first place. You probably followed the advice they gave you, but women seemed even less interested in you than before. Eventually, many men are forced to look at themselves in the mirror and realize that even though they're trying to be whoever it is they think they're supposed to be, it isn't working.

The problem isn't with who you are and whether you're attractive to the opposite sex; no matter what your status in life is, how good you look, or how much money you have, there are qualities about every man that women find attractive. There are also qualities within every man that women find, at a minimum, unappealing. Unfortunately, most men never stop to think about how women interpret what kind of man they are when they are "being themselves."

The problem also isn't the advice you've been given—when most people tell you to "just be yourself" they're essentially telling you not to lie to a woman with the hopes of bedding her through a series of convoluted half-truths and outright deceptions. The problem with this advice is how you interpret it. Instead of just being yourself, you have to focus on being your *best* self. Ideally, you want to be your best self in all situations, but for the purposes of this book, you have to focus on being your best self whenever you are around women.

Most men are "themselves" all day, every day, with little thought given to being anything but themselves. If you hope to increase your success with women, you have to start by learning what qualities they're attracted to in men, as well as what traits they find objectionable. Once you understand what women are attracted to, you can start to cultivate and ultimately demonstrate qualities that you already have, while downplaying some habits that might turn a woman off. Ultimately, you're being yourself, but you're putting your best foot forward instead of in your mouth.

Everything you're about to read promotes the idea of being your best self over being your average self who never seemed to get much attention from women. You don't have to fundamentally change to be your best self. However, some guys might want to take on that challenge after realizing that they've set themselves on a course for loneliness. Instead of trying to transform yourslef into some you're not, you'll learn what women like and don't like, so you can examine your own behavior for similar traits to highlight or de-emphasize.

The elements that fundamentally create attraction between two people are already inside of you, but were perhaps buried by an unhappy childhood, destructive relationships, or the media's ability to make you feel like less of a man. Throughout this book you're going to realize that you've had everything it takes to meet and attract women all along. Starting now, you're going to learn how women feel, how men think, and how you can bring two strangers together so sparks can fly.

Myth #2: Be nice and women will be attracted to you

It happens thousands of times every day—a nice guy meets an attractive woman, but before he can make any progress as a potential suitor, he finds himself in the "friend zone." Nice guys have always wondered why they finish last, but never seem to find the answer. It's interesting, because most men understand that nice guys finish last, but since don't know any other way to act, so they continually revert back to being nice, or slowly turn into bitter assholes.

Nice guys grow up believing that the best way to attract women is to be as nice, pleasant, and unoffending as possible. If that didn't work on a particular woman, most guys think it was because she didn't think they were good looking, rich, or important enough and there isn't much they can do about it. After all, it makes logical sense that a woman should be attracted to a guy who treats her well, is sensitive to her feelings, buys her nice things, and more. However, women, for the most part, are not logical creatures but emotional ones. So while being as nice as possible makes logical sense as a means to attract the opposite sex, it just doesn't work that way with women.

Eventually, most women want to end up with someone nice, someone who loves them for who they really are, but before they can get to the nice guy, they need to be attracted to his more interesting qualities, "nice" not usually being one of them. It's difficult to know what each woman is thinking when she says she wants a "nice" guy, but when it's time to deal with the personality traits of a "nice" guy, they simply aren't interested. When guys try to be nice, they usually come off as boring and predictable, which is great when you're married, but it's a complete turnoff to the majority of women you're trying to attract.

If you want to increase your success with women, you have to shake the notion that you need to *try* to be nice. After flirting with a woman for five minutes, you don't want her to walk away thinking about how nice you are, but rather how funny, charming, mysterious, and unpredictable you are. This book is devoted to helping you shed the notion that being nice means being attractive. You will instead learn how to exhibit all of those playful qualities that women find irresistibly attractive, even when they don't know why.

Myth #3: Women don't want men they don't know to talk to them

A lot of guys see women they want to approach and start a conversation with in everyday circumstances like coffee shops, bookstores, and gyms, not just at bars and clubs. Unfortunately, one of the biggest excuses guys use to talk themselves out of approaching a woman is the nagging feeling that by talking to someone they don't know, they're interrupting her or putting her in an awkward position. In a weird way, most people are unconsciously seeking permission to do everything they want to do in life, but if you want to be successful with women, you have to learn to give yourself permission to talk to whoever you want to talk to.

Every guy can think of a few absurd rationalizations they've come up with in order to give themselves an "easy out." Are you worried that the singular act of introducing yourself will cause her to think you're a pervert? Or maybe she'll turn you down and everybody will make fun of you. Maybe you can "just tell" that you're not her type. Or she'll think you're a jerk for interrupting her day. Do any of these sound familiar? One or more of these thoughts go through every guy's head when he wants to talk to a woman, but only confident men shrug it off and approach anyway. The rest let her walk away, never to be seen again, or watch as another guy makes his move.

The best advice is to start caring more about what you want and less about the hypothetical situations you construct in your mind. At some point, every guy gets tired of watching other guys do all the approaching. It's time to be the guy who talks to the women he wants to talk to. If it's what you truly want, you have to stop being so thoughtful and start adopting an "I don't care" mentality. Whoever she is, once you see her, approach instantly and stop worrying about what you're going to say, how you're going to keep the conversation alive, or what the outcome is going to be.

Men think in logical terms, so most believe there is a specific step-by-step procedure for breaking the ice. These isn't, so if you're new to approaching women, stop caring about what reason you need to have to talk to her; just walk up to her and say "hi." Admittedly, if this is all you have to say, you're not going to get very far at first. What you will accomplish is getting over your fears that something bad is going to happen just because you grabbed a woman's attention. From there you can start working on your Openers, then your conversational skills, and then your ability to Close, but if you can't even say "hi" to an attractive woman, you're stuck in neutral.

As for thinking that women don't want to be approached, sometimes it's true and sometimes it isn't, but you should find out every time because it's what you want and possisbly what she wants too. You can learn more about why guys always have to approach in Myth #5, *Women know what they're looking for, so they'll find you*, but the take-away is that nothing is going to happen unless you make it happen and women fully expect men to make things happen.

Myth #4: You have to be a millionaire, athlete, or model to attract women

If you can learn to stop being nice all the time, the next issue you have to resolve is the constant need to put women on a pedestal. Men can be so confident and cocksure about themselves when it comes to everything they do, *except* talk to and attract women. When some guys are confronted with attractive women that they want to talk to, a little voice rears its ugly head just to let them know they shouldn't bother, that they aren't good enough. Unfortunately, because of self-doubt, men miss out on meeting a lot of great women and vice versa.

All of this insecurity is centered on the belief that a guy with average looks can't attract a beautiful woman. By building up a woman into a goddess in their own minds, they're also tearing themselves down and as a result, they don't talk to the women they're attracted to. It's important to take women off the pedestals in your mind and treat them as equals. It puts a woman at a disadvantage when you treat her as superior to yourself simply because of her looks. It's unfair to her and it's unfair to you, because when you treat yourself as inferior, she has little choice but to treat you accordingly.

The majority of men believe that very attractive women are only interested in guys with comparable good looks. This belief is rooted in the fact that men view women superficially, and assume women view men in the same way. Of course women prefer a traditionally good-looking man, but that's just one attribute of many that can attract a woman. Most women are far more interested in the way a guy makes her feel than how he looks. It only takes a few bad relationships for a woman to realize that beautiful- looking men can also be really big assholes.

It's true that having money or power or good looks helps men attract women. However, with the exception of the most cynical and jaded women, girls look for guys with charm, humor, chivalry, wit, charisma, and none of these qualities cost a dime or years in the gym. You're a guy, she's a girl; anything else that prevents you from talking to her are concepts in your head based on years of negative conditioning. You have to be able to ignore your doubts and walk up to women, look them in the eyes, say what you have to say, and let the chips fall where they may.

Myth #5: Women know what they're looking for, so they'll find you

Somewhere, in the not too-distant past, in the days of old-fashioned values of *Casablanca* and *Gone with the Wind*, men were expected to approach women and make the first move. These values have been ingrained into people's minds, specifically women's, so it's expected for men to be the initiators while women sit back and do what they can to look as attractive as possible. So while women don't always require a knight in shining armor, they like romance, or at least the feeling that they're being pursued or courted.

Not too long ago, we in the Western world entered into a period of relative equality between men and women. We live in a society open-minded toward independent single mothers, career-driven women, and women elected to the highest echelons of government. Given all of these advances in female empowerment, you might wonder why women haven't become as aggressive in their pursuit of relationships with men as they are with most other aspects in this new era.

Without a doubt there *are* aggressive women who call their own shots and seek out men whom they desire, who compliment their lives, who they believe will meet their needs, but these women are a rare breed. Despite all of the opportunities women have to advance their careers and all of the choices they can make now, they still believe in inequality when it comes to meeting guys and the courtship they expect should follow. In other words, despite all the talk of "equality," when it comes to men and women, guys need to make the moves while women do the selecting.

Women feel they can tell a lot about a man by the way he approaches. Is he insecure, confident, or arrogant? In a woman's mind, the way you approach: the walk, the talk, and the body language, are all indicators of your personality. Women want to put men to the challenge of approaching so they can see these characteristics in action, which gives them a better sense of who they're dealing with before they get involved with them. If women made the first move, they would lose this advantage, so they usually put their energy into making themselves attractive and approachable. As a guy, if you find what she's displaying to be attractive, you have to be proactive and pursue her without exception.

Most women have a crystal clear idea of who their "ideal" guy is, but that doesn't mean she'll chase him if she finds him. As unfair as it seems, guys have to do most of the work in meeting women and they fully expect you to make the first move and usually the next twenty moves. Even when women go out together to meet guys, they'll usually still sit back at a table and wait to be approached. The point is that with most things in life, if you want it you have to go for it, fair or not.

Myth #6: Meeting women takes lots of time, energy, and money

There's an old joke that perfectly encapsulates the potential costs and payoffs of dating. It involves a poor college student who saves up his money to take a first date to a fancy restaurant. To his dismay, she orders all of the most expensive things on the menu from appetizers to lobster to champagne and more.

As she's about to order dessert, he asks, "Does your mother feed you like this at home?" "No," she says, "but my mother's not looking to get laid, either."

Meeting women can definitely take a lot of time and money, but it doesn't have to. When it comes to dating, men are always expected to pay for the first date, if not for a few subsequent dates before a woman offers to pay. This is just one of the many reasons why traditional dating is discouraged throughout this book. However, meeting and "hanging out" with women doesn't cost much at all, and usually provides a better way for people to get to know one another compared with having dinner and watching a movie.

If you just go to bars and clubs, you can easily spend hundreds of dollars a month and still not have much to show for it. Bars and clubs can be the best and worst place to meet women, depending on your style. You can just as easily meet women at cafés, malls, video stores—everywhere you normally go. You don't have to buy the latest fashions, rounds of drinks, and cab rides just to meet women. Women are everywhere and they are even easier to approach at places other than clubs and bars.

Also, consider what you currently spend your money on and whether it's bringing you the long-term happiness you desire. Would you truly rather play video games or buy expensive collectibles than have a cool girl to hang with who enjoys having sex? Expensive toys can give you immediate, yet temporary, satisfaction, but are you just buying things to fill the void in your life? Are you really avoiding meeting people because you think it's expensive or because, up until now, you haven't had much to show for the effort?

After you read this book, think about the solitary hobbies that you budget your money toward and for at least the next few months, devote that money to the cost of socializing. Socializing includes the clothes you wear, the places you go, the drinks you buy, and so on. Consider it an investment in yourself as if it were a tuition fee for learning more about talking to people, meeting women, and how to calibrate your game so you become more successful with women. Reading this book alone will not get you the results you want unless you put yourself out there and yes, invest a little time, energy, and money into meeting the types of women you've always wanted to.

Myth #7: Guys can "convince" women into liking them

One of the unfortunate side effects of overcoming Myth #2, *Be nice and women will be attracted to you*, is that once a guy realizes he doesn't have to be nice all the time, he instead fills the void by trying to impress a woman by talking about his status. Guys naturally want to talk about their car, their job, their expensive clothes, or other attributes as a way to convince a woman of how wonderful they are. In fact, the qualities don't even have to be superficial, but any *logical* explanation for why a woman should like him, go to a different club, go on a date, have sex, and so on.

You simply cannot convince a woman to be attracted to you because men and women don't "choose" who they're attracted to. Imagine if you were really hitting it off with a gorgeous woman and while she was laughing at one of your jokes, she thought to herself, *Wow, this guy is smart and funny… he seems like he's just my type. I think I'll feel attracted to him.* Obviously it seems absurd when you read it, but men still act as though if they continue talking about themselves and keep explaining all of the great things about themselves, that a woman *has* to be attracted to them.

For women, attraction works at an unconscious level as an automatic response to visual and emotional cues. For guys, attraction occurs in response to mostly visual stimuli, namely a beautiful face and a shapely body. Attraction usually occurs in seconds and minutes, not hours and days, so you should concentrate on building attraction from the very beginning of every interaction. Your job is to demonstrate, not explain, your attractive qualities and then follow her signals accordingly.

Finally, even though a guy can't use logic to convince a woman to feel attraction toward him, attraction itself has a certain logic to it. For instance, it's logical to say that if you exhibit attractive qualities to a large number of women, the chances that one or more of them will become attracted to you will increase. The point being that you must focus on demonstrating, not explaining, the attractive qualities you possess and allow attraction to occur organically, not logically. For more information on which qualities women are and are not attracted to, refer to Chapter 6, "What Women Want."

Myth #8: Women have it easy because guys are always talking to them

As you've already read, again and again, men have to do most of the work to meet women and advance their relationships. There are some exceptions to the rule, but on the whole, a man has to do the approaching and women get to choose based on how attracted they are to a guy's look, personality, and the feelings he generates within her. Without a doubt, there are usually a lot of steps that need to take place between meeting a woman to waking up next to her, and guys are responsible for making most of these steps happen, but that doesn't mean women have it easy.

So, while you're responsible for "making it happen," realize that you get to make all the decisions on who you approach, when you want to approach, and what you want to do when you invite her to hang out sometime in the future. If you can't make an effort to do the small things it takes to demonstrate to women that you know what you want and you know how to go about it, you won't be very successful with women. You have to take responsibility for all the steps involved in meeting women and guiding them toward the kind of relationship you want, whether it's a one-night stand, a long-term relationship, or something in-between.

No gender has it easy when it comes to meeting that special someone. A guy can spend an entire evening building up the courage to talk to just one woman and when he gets shot down, he's done for the evening, his confidence in tatters. A woman, on the other hand, spends time finding the right clothes, getting her hair styled, applying makeup and countless other rituals before going out, and then she has dozens of guys look at her who never approach. By the end of the night, these mini-rejections are just as disappointing as the single rejection a guy gets because in the end, neither got what they wanted. Remember that guys get to choose who they want to talk to, so they make their choice from the very beginning.

Myth #9: Women only want boyfriends and husbands, not just sex

Guys who think that all of the single women of the world are desperately seeking a husband, a house in the suburbs, and 2.5 kids generally find women exactly like that, or none at all. This is the reality that some men create for themselves, that of manipulative women with an agenda and men who fear getting snared by one of them. It's unfortunate, because there are a lot of great women from all walks of life and every age range looking for something lighter than a serious relationship, including casual sex.

Truth be told, there are lots of women who have an agenda to get married as soon as possible, and men who fear commitment, but if that's all you see, that's all you're going to get. Most men don't take any responsibility for their role in this state of affairs; they gingerly play along and suppress their apprehension. Taking responsibility means owning your attitude and in this case, not assuming that all single women want to get married as soon as possible.

Most men have no idea what a particular woman is looking for on any given night, because they never attempt to find out. Most women *do* want long-term relationships, but maybe not tonight. Maybe she just got out of a long relationship, maybe she's dating around, or maybe she's getting back at her ex. You never know what frame of mind a woman is in until you take the risk in talking to her, which is no risk at all. A woman usually has no trouble letting a guy know what her status is and what type of relationship she's looking for—you just have to pay attention.

Myth #10: You're no good with women and you aren't going to get better

I can tell you this isn't true, but you really must read this book and go and try things out; as long as you don't give up, you'll find yourself constantly improving. There is no risk to anything other than your ego when trying to meet women. For every approach you are either going to succeed or you're going to learn something. You might learn something about yourself, about a particular girl, a particular situation, or about women in general. By putting yourself out there, never giving up, and learning as you go, you *will* get better.

Chapter 2

Rules

In this Chapter

★ Understanding why loving your single life is crucial before women can become attracted to you

★ Discovering why you have to approach within seconds of seeing someone you're attracted to

★ Learning why being interesting and playful is far more attractive than being a nice guy

Rules on Meeting and Attracting Women

1. *Love your single life.*
2. *Own your attitude.*
3. *Look and feel your best.*
4. *Act fast, never hesitate.*
5. *Keep an open mind.*
6. *Don't be nice, don't be a jerk, always be interesting.*
7. *Don't trade your status for a woman's approval.*
8. *Focus on her, not on yourself.*
9. *It's always your fault.*
10. *Never give up.*

Rule #1: Love your single life

Many men, and women for that matter, view romantic relationships as something to fill the void in their lives. They think that once they get a girlfriend they will "have something to do." If you have this mindset, everything you say and do will drip with desperation rooted in the fact that you have no life, or one that you don't enjoy. Loving your single life means that you have friends and hobbies you enjoy, and consider having a woman in your life as something nice to have, not a must-have. Guys with a vibrant single life are very attractive to women who want to find out "what he's all about."

Guys who haven't been successful with women for most of their lives usually aren't very happy with other aspects of their lives. Over the years, guys can get caught in a vicious cycle of letting themselves go, physically and mentally, until they have very little chance of attracting the types of women they prefer. After a few initial failures with women, some guys retreat entirely from any form of social interaction, preferring to play video games, eat fast food every night, and addressing only the bare minimums of personal hygiene.

Guys who let their lives deteriorate to hermit status can't simply memorize an Opener and expect it to work. It takes more than a well-delivered Opener to catch a woman's attention, and it starts with loving the life that you're currently leading. True, there *are* people who absolutely love playing video games all night, by themselves, surrounded by takeout containers. However, since you're reading this book, you probably don't fall into that category, and hopefully you have the capacity to admit to yourself whether you're enjoying life or think that your life could use some improvement.

If you don't really like the life you're leading at the moment, all is not lost. There are steps you can take, small and large, to improve how you view yourself and your circumstances. Whether or not you have a lot of disposable income, the goal is to completely fill your life with so many activities you enjoy that you have to figure out how to fit a woman into your life. You want to be in a position where you *choose* to get involved with someone because it might make your life *even better.*

Whatever you love to do, might love to do, or used to love doing are all areas you should explore in your community. Log off and open an alternative weekly paper from your area and find people, places, and events that match your interests. It can be difficult to connect with random people, but it can be significantly easier if you stack the odds in your favor by frequenting the places in which you enjoy doing what you love to do.

Loving your single life gives you much more confidence when meeting women. Since you already love your life, you aren't looking for a woman to "complete" you, so you won't be desperate for any particular interaction to lead to a phone number or more. When you're living and loving your life, women notice and they're curious why you have such a good time doing everything you do.

Rule #2: Own your attitude

Owning your attitude means accepting reality, your place in it, and your ability to define how you feel about it. Nobody *makes* you angry or sad or happy, you have complete control over how you feel. By accepting this, you can always approach women with a confident, yet playful attitude regardless of how your last ten approaches went, or your big breakup or whatever issues are "making" you treat a fresh face as anything other than an opportunity to get to know someone new. If you already love your single life, it will be much easier to own your attitude.

One of the best ways to know whether you own your attitude is how reactive you are to the events around you. When something "bad" happens, like getting rejected by a woman, how do you respond? A lot of guys internalize their reactions, especially negative ones, when things don't go according to plan. Instead of dealing directly with a situation and trying to determine how they might have contributed to the problem and how they can improve their situation, they blame others. They might blame a woman, their friends, their parents, or this book, because it's easier than dealing with problems and inadequacies head-on.

Owning your attitude is about taking complete responsibility for how you feel and act. Once you take responsibility, you start to appreciate how liberated you are from the natural ups and downs in life by realizing that your emotions don't have to follow the same roller-coaster ride. Shit happens, but it's up to you to determine whether it's truly "shitty" or just "one of those things you learn from." This applies not only to meeting women, but to every facet of your life. Next time something bad happens, try not to internalize any negative feelings or lash out at people, but calmly remind yourself that you're just along for the ride.

Another important aspect of owning your attitude is being honest. Some very successful seducers get away with making up entire life stories to suit a situation. However, that approach can eat away at your confidence and you begin to lose respect for yourself, because you've lost the "real" you. In the long term, honesty truly is the best policy. Honesty doesn't mean telling a woman she looks fat in those pants. Rather, it means being upfront with people about who you are and what you're looking for when it comes to sex and relationships. Not only are you owning your attitude, but owning up to your word.

Rule #3: Look and feel your best

With so much competition out there from other guys, it's no secret that you have to make a great first impression to attract a woman's attention. First impressions happen every time you meet someone and it's those impressions that influence how women will view you for as long as you know each other. Even if a woman forgets the particular circumstances of your first encounter, the feeling you left her with, if any at all, drives her future expectations of you. For example, if you made a woman laugh during the first few minutes you met, she'll tend to think of you as hilarious, even if you don't make her laugh the next time you see each other.

First impressions are largely based on two things—how you look and how you act. For a lot of guys, how they look directly influences how they act—if they feel they look really good, they have a lot of confidence in themselves, but if they feel they don't look very good, they're insecure and hindered by self-doubt. If you want to be able to talk to women everywhere, you have to be primed at all times, both in how you look and how you feel. People meet each other in the strangest and most unexpected of places, so you'll never really know when to look and feel your best. With that said, you should aim to look and feel your best as much as possible.

Of course not everyone is blessed with a model's genetics, but you can still make the best of what you've got. Whatever your greatest attributes are, you have to learn how to make them shine like diamonds. It also helps to bring your perceived weak points up to a reasonable standard, so they don't mentally drag you down. Looking your best also includes holding a confident posture, maintaining your hygiene (showering, brushing, nail clipping), eating well, exercising regularly, and getting enough sleep. It usually takes more than nice clothes to feel your best, so consider a healthy diet and occasional trips to the gym as a foundation for the positive, playful attitude you need to attract women.

Looking good means different things to different people, but what it means to *you* determines how you feel about yourself. Some women like thick stubble on a guy's face, while other women prefer the neat, preppy look. It's impossible to cultivate a look that attracts all women, so you should concentrate on clothes you like to wear, that you look good in, and also work well in the places you frequent.

First impressions mean a lot and you don't want pit stains or dirty nails preventing you from meeting a wonderful new woman. It's sometimes just the little details on an otherwise decent-looking guy that can make or break his ability to meet and attract women. From head to toe, even if you aren't wearing the latest fashions, make sure what you wear looks good on you, but doesn't distract women away from your fun personality. As with the other rules, this one applies anytime you leave the house, because you never know when an opportunity might present itself.

Rule #4: Act fast, never hesitate

Most men give far too much awe and admiration to women they hardly know based solely on their looks. Guys get so intimidated by beautiful women that they literally freeze in their tracks like a deer caught in the headlights, because they place more weight on talking to women than they should. Some guys think they have to impress a woman within the first few minutes of meeting her because they've built up a conversation into a momentous "make or break" event. In actuality, it doesn't always matter what you say, as long as you say something.

Acting before analyzing is a major sticking point for most guys. One or more of the Myths usually preoccupy a guy's mind while he contemplates whether or how he should approach someone. In the first few seconds that she notices you looking at her, you've missed a great opportunity. You want to catch a woman by surprise by approaching and Opening before she has a chance to analyze you and your intentions. The best way to make sure you approach instead of stare is to employ the three-second rule.

The point of the three-second rule is to avoid hesitating by encouraging you to approach women fast enough to keep you from talking yourself out of it. You do not want a woman to see you hesitate because the longer she notices you hesitating, the more insecure and creepy you seem. Also, hesitation creates an added sense of nervousness to your mental state and gives a woman time to size you up and possibly decide not to talk to you—a personality trait you do not want to portray when approaching women.

The three-second rule essentially states that once a man spots a woman he's attracted to who gives him eye contact or a smile, he has three seconds to approach and Open her. If you wait any longer, because you hesitated, your chance of successfully Opening is greatly diminished. Once a guy misses his "window of opportunity" he'll have a difficult time coming across as a sincere guy who is approaching out of attraction. Instead, the longer he waits and stares and shuffles, he looks more like someone on the prowl looking for the first woman who might say "yes" to him.

Of course it takes more than merely approaching in three seconds to successfully Open a woman. It definitely matters what you say after those three seconds, but in the event that you have nothing to say, say anything! You'll either succeed or you'll learn until you've learned so much that you almost always succeed.

Rule #5: Keep an open mind

Keeping an open mind is essentially about staying outcome-independent and enjoying the ride that life offers. In practical terms that means talking to people just for the sake of talking to them and having a good time at it. If anything interesting or exciting spawns from talking to someone, it should be considered an additional benefit, not a given.

Keeping an open mind means not only treating the beautiful women of the world as regular people, but also treating everyone else, including unattractive women, as regular people. Talk to everyone, have fun, and don't burn bridges just because you don't see immediate payoff. In other words, keep yourself open to any and all possibilities.

Some guys, when they find themselves talking to a woman who isn't very interesting or good looking, treat her poorly so they can quickly move on to someone "better." Someone who is open-minded about the situation may not be attracted to a woman, but might ask her to introduce him to her cute friends. If he likes what he sees he might invite her and her friends along to the next club, and from there the possibilities are endless.

By talking to everyone and keeping your mind open to the possibilities, you can find yourself in fun and interesting situations you might never have expected to be in. For instance, the average-looking woman that you joked around with might invite you to a party she's having that's swarming with her single girlfriends. Or she might introduce you to her cute friend across the bar. Or she might grab you and her bisexual girlfriend and take you home for the night. You can always turn down these options, but they're certainly nice to have.

Another good reason to have an open mind is to keep your confidence up when you get rejected. Even the most gifted seducers get rejected, but instead of dwelling on what they might have done wrong, they assume it must have been the circumstances that were off. Maybe she just got fired or failed a class. Perhaps she lost a family member recently. You could remind her of her last boyfriend or maybe she still has a boyfriend. She could have been approached by ten others guys that night. There are thousands of reasons why your rejection had less to do with how you look or what you said than with a woman's frame of mind.

If, after a rejection, you still have difficulty keeping an open mind, always remind yourself that women love men just as much as men love women. Women also love sex just as much as men do and if they have to find someone to have fun with, it might as well be you. And no matter how hard of a shell women put forward to prevent themselves from getting hurt, they all have a soft spot inside that they desperately want found.

Rule #6: Don't be nice, don't be a jerk, always be interesting

There's a fine line between being confident and being cocky and you need to toe that line at all times. Instead of being nice or being an asshole, aim for enthusiastic, entertaining, spontaneous, charming, edgy, or countless other attractive and memorable qualities. Nice guys tend to blend together and are instantly forgettable. Assholes certainly stand out, but for all the wrong reasons. You want your personality to be unforgettable so that no matter how many other guys she talks to that night, she'll remember you for days.

If you don't think you're very interesting, where do you begin? Have you ever thought about why you're here? Not why *we* are here, but why *you* specifically are here and what it means to you? A lot of guys don't think much about it, but women sense immediately when a guy they're dealing with has his life on track. After college, the more clarity you have about who you are and where you're headed, the more attractive you will seem to women who are wondering where they're headed as well.

Most women look for interesting guys who have their life together and understand themselves on a deeper, more introspective level. One of the ways to become more interesting is to spend some time illuminating your own path: who you are, where you're going, and why it's important to you. The specifics aren't nearly as important as the fact that you've spent time thinking about it and you're actively working toward your goals, whatever they may be.

If, while having a conversation with a woman, you find yourself running into uncomfortable silences, try to be a better listener so she isn't just talking *at* you. Engage her in conversation topics that interest most women, or even better, topics that interest her specifically. You should try to lead the conversation, while still allowing her to do most of the talking. However, you can pick up on little hints that tell you where she wants to direct the conversation by listening to her responses to your questions. While you do that, it also doesn't hurt to crack some original jokes about the situation, analyze her words, and playfully throw them back at her as a challenge, and anything else that keeps things fun and lightweight.

Finally, being interesting and engaging is always attractive, but it also helps to be original and creative in the way you interact. After you approach, never let her get comfortable with her expectations of you by keeping her guessing what you'll say or do next. By keeping her on her toes, you set yourself apart from all of the other chumps who do and say pretty much the same thing. Make yourself a mystery that has many layers that must be peeled away by just the right type of woman. It's an intriguing challenge that most men don't offer, but women can't resist.

Rule #7: Don't trade your status for a woman's approval

When you first meet a woman, consciously or not, she tests you to find out what kind of man you are and what she can get away with. She might ask if you're gay or make fun of your hometown, or she might ask you to buy her a drink or watch her jacket/drink/seat while she talks to other people. These are tests that women use to find out how well you stand up for yourself. Women look for a man with confidence who doesn't allow himself to be used by anyone, including her.

You have to learn to answer a woman's ridiculous tests with challenges of your own. It's difficult at first because you've already approached and Opened, so you feel like you need to meet her demands in order to continue talking to her. In truth, if you actually need to meet these challenges to continue, you should walk away, because the requests only get more expensive and time-consuming. Be the alpha male and never let a woman's "tests" tear you down.

If you're unfamiliar with the term alpha male, you probably aren't watching enough Discovery Channel. In many species, there is a dominant male who protects and has sex with all of the females in his group, while the other males have no sex and have to wait until the alpha male dies or becomes too weak to lead. In these social structures, most males never become alpha males, never have much sex, and rarely produce offspring. In our own society, you can easily find examples of men who have their choice of women, and those with no opportunity for sex whatsoever. The dominant male, or leader, of a group of humans is considered the alpha male.

So how does this lesson in zoology translate into something you can use? Think of it this way: The alpha male dismisses any sort of female "tests" thrown his way, while other males attempt to pass the tests and fail by virtue of playing such games in the first place. The point of being an alpha or dominant male isn't to take advantage or control other people, but to position yourself so that you're never taken for granted. Men who have a lower perceived value are typically taken for granted by women because they make themselves available at all times and generally do everything that's requested of them.

Alpha males know that women like to be around them, so they don't shy away from approaching and meeting new women. Being an alpha male is all about your attitude and projecting an image of someone who is fun to be with, someone who women want to be with. Being an alpha male is self-perpetuating—the more you believe you're an alpha male, the more you become one.

Rule #8: Focus on her, not on yourself

By default guys seem to focus on themselves much more than the women they're talking to. It's sometimes difficult to get your mind off of how nervous you are, what you should do to meet someone, and what you should say when you meet them. Subconsciously, when you're talking to a woman, she's wondering what you want from her and the answer is usually obvious. You must forget about your nerves and what you want to accomplish for the time being, and focus on her immediate needs, such as her boredom or her self-esteem.

When guys worry about what they should be doing or saying when they meet someone, they aren't paying attention to the woman they're talking to. Does she look bored or drunk? Is she alone or with her friends? Is she smiling or does she seem upset? Most importantly, does it look like she's romantically involved with someone around her, or is she wearing a wedding ring?

When guys forget to focus on a woman's state of mind and her present circumstances, they're not talking *with* her, but *at* her. You want to be conversational and friendly in your approach, so she lowers her defenses. Women can quickly determine whether a guy is nervous and self-involved, or if he's having fun and enjoying himself by chatting with people around him. Even after you approach a woman and start a conversation, you have to pay attention to what she says and, more importantly, her body language.

You may not be able to figure out what a woman wants based on what she says, but her actions are a pretty reliable indicator of her intentions. Body language rarely lies, so if you can learn to focus your attention on what she does, you can calibrate what you say and how you act. Does she look interested or is she just humoring you? Does she look around while you talk or does she look you in the eyes? Does she touch you when she talks or does she aim her body away from yours? These are just a few of the things you have to pay attention to and react accordingly.

You should react to her body language by doing whatever you can reasonably do to make her feel good. It may sound obvious, but by changing her state of mind and helping her to feel curious, happy, and attractive, you've done more than most guys who try to impress a woman or buy her time with a drink. Any guy with ten bucks can buy a woman a drink, but turning her frown upside down costs nothing and can mean everything. By subtly providing her with what she needs, she'll be drawn to you.

Rule #9: It's always your fault

Although you can never have control over the emotional baggage a woman brings into a conversation, such as losing a job or having a boyfriend, if a woman is single and receptive and things didn't work out, it was your fault, not hers. Although it's a difficult pill to swallow, it's one that will help you learn and grow even when your initial reaction is to blame everything but yourself. As long as you point fingers at the venue, your friends, the woman, and anything else, you'll use those as excuses for not learning what went wrong and how you can fix it in the future.

Think about the last few times you talked with a woman and it didn't work out, meaning you never asked for her phone number, you got rejected, or the conversation got awkward. For instance, maybe you saw a woman you wanted to talk to who was out with her friends and you waited until just the right moment when she was by herself and walking away from the bathroom to talk to her. She was receptive to talking to you and for a minute or two everything seemed like it was going well. Then, all of a sudden, her girlfriends come out of nowhere and drag her away from you. For most guys this means they just got cock-blocked by a "bunch of bitches."

Unfortunately, blaming a "bunch of bitches" is exactly why you get cock-blocked time and again—because you don't accept any responsibility for your failure. It's like leaving a freshly roasted turkey on the kitchen table and then leaving the room with your Labrador still in the kitchen. You return just a minute later to find that the dog ripped the turkey apart and ate it. You could blame the dog, although it's done nothing more than be a dog, or you can could blame yourself for knowing how dogs act around food. The same principle applies to women because you already have an idea of how they act—they act like women.

It does you absolutely no good to blame a woman's friends for "rescuing" her even if she didn't need or want to be rescued. Similarly, it's senseless to blame a woman for failing to notice how attractive you are. Your personality can overcome just about any obstacle, as long as you realize that you can only control your own actions and reactions and no one else's. Anytime something fails to happen the way you thought or wished that it would, use these episodes as learning experiences so you can work to ensure that those same issues never trip you up again.

Rule #10: Never give up

Before you can walk into any situation and confidently Open one or more women, you have to be able to conquer your fear of rejection. The more you put yourself out there, the more inevitable rejection becomes—whether you're a regular guy or a master pick-up artist. Since rejection happens and is bound to happen more frequently the more comfortable you get with approaching, you have to train yourself not to let it affect you. Of course you could give up and avoid approaching all together, which eliminates the possibility of rejection, but then you're right back where you started.

As with most of the things people fear in life, the best way to overcome fear of rejection is to demystify it by familiarizing yourself with it. However, dealing with rejection isn't something you can learn from a book; it's something you have to deal with head-on through experience. Besides, you don't have much to lose by being turned down. Your pride may get bruised in the beginning, but after a few rejections, even that fades. Just try not to get too attached to the results of your Opener or your conversation. Instead of aiming to get a woman's phone number or take her home, try to make her laugh. This is a great way to take the pressure off of you. If your interaction goes any further than a few laughs, take it as a bonus.

Once you get used to the occasional rejection—easily the most difficult part of mastering your game—the fear is behind you. You'll see that meeting women isn't terrifying and that if someone doesn't spark to your style, your ego can handle it. Most importantly, you'll start to see patterns in the way women react to you, so you can continually improve your approach. If you look at rejection as a tool for learning more about yourself and about women, you still might not enjoy being rejected, but you probably won't mind it as much either.

There are literally billions of women in the world and you've hardly met any of them! Whenever you go out, whether to a bar or a library, make it your mission to talk to as many woman as possible, young and old. You'll create so many opportunities for yourself that you'll never let a rejection get you down. No matter what happens, there is always a new night in a new situation with new people, so leave yesterday's baggage behind you. Everyone deserves to be with a wonderful girl that suits them perfectly and there is absolutely no reason to settle for less. The only way to find her is to meet, learn about, and have fun with as many women as possible.

Chapter 3

Adjusting Your Attitude

In this Chapter

★ Exploring why guys don't approach women they're attracted to and how to overcome it

★ Mastering your confidence level when it comes to meeting and attracting women

★ Building a positive and playful attitude whenever you're around women

Adjusting Your Attitude

Improving your ability to meet and attract women involves not only the things you do and say, but also who you are as a person and how you see the world. Almost anyone can read a book and mimic some new tricks that give them a few advantages they didn't have before. However, to truly be able to think on your feet, move past the basics, and succeed with women beyond what you thought was ever possible, you have to examine your attitude toward, and behavior around, women.

Most men live their lives thinking that their looks and the amount of money they have are the two biggest factors in determining whether women are attracted to them. It's true that for many women these factors are a *part* of the overall set of qualities they consciously look for in men, but they aren't the only factors or even the most important. What most men fail to realize is that attraction is a feeling, not something a woman consciously decides on. Women *feel* attraction, they don't logically think through why they should be attracted to someone. Once you understand this, you begin to realize that there are many other avenues to creating attraction beyond flashing cash and having pretty-boy looks.

Because men are so caught up in having the possessions they think will attract women, they get frustrated when they obtain these status symbols, yet never achieve the success with women they believe should go along with them. It doesn't take long before a man feels he has the possessions it takes to attract women, yet doesn't attract them, and consequently begins creating elaborate justifications for why an approach didn't work, or why he should never approach in the first place. Every guy has different reasons for limiting his own success, so you have to start by examining your attitude, not your possessions or lack thereof, for why you aren't as successful with women as you think you should be.

Following that, you should examine whether or not you lack confidence around women. Confidence is a trait that every woman, from homely to supermodel, believes is critical for even a modest amount of attraction. Without confidence, and specifically confidence with women, you aren't likely to be taken seriously and even if you successfully meet new women, you'll often find yourself in the Friend Zone as in "let's just be friends." Ultimately you have to be honest with yourself about your level of confidence and be willing to make changes in your single life, so that you can learn to love who you are, whether you're single or not.

Why Guys Don't Approach Women

Every guy has his own reasons for not being able to approach women, whether he knows what they are or not. Fear of the unknown, fear of embarrassment, fear of what other people will think; no matter what the reasons are, almost all of them ultimately point toward a fear of rejection. If your fear of rejection or fear of making social mistakes is deeply ingrained and impossible to shake, you might need help from a professional, such as a therapist or counselor. Before you take such drastic measures, let's examine some of the common reasons why men don't approach and strike up conversations with women they find attractive. This section will help you demystify any fears you might have of approaching women. In fact, you'll learn why it's actually a social mistake *not* to talk to people to whom you're attracted.

1. You don't know what to expect.

Most guys like to feel they're in control and they don't like surprises that might risk the control they *think* they have. Coming up with something interesting or funny to say, saying it to a complete stranger, and hoping she'll find you attractive gives guys the feeling that they aren't in control. If this applies to you, you have to stop thinking that approaching a woman causes you to lose control, because you never had control of the situation—you only have control of your own attitude and actions.

Control is mostly a state of mind when it comes to attraction. You don't have any real control over anybody else, but you *do* have control over your expectations, so you need to manage them appropriately. If you expect every woman you talk with will be charmed by everything you have to say, you have unrealistic expectations. If you expect women to be different from one another with different states of mind and different desires in life, you'll understand that even a 50% success rate is unrealistic.

With some guys, a certain panic sets in when they feel they're putting themselves on the line and that the outcome is completely out of their hands. Most guys never get rid of this feeling of panic—even some of the smoothest operators get that queasy feeling in their stomach right before they approach. Regardless of that fear, they still approach, even when they're faced with self-doubt, hurt feelings, and a knock to their reputation.

The only way to be comfortable with "losing" control is to keep putting yourself out there and talking to as many women as possible. Eventually you'll stop expecting a particular outcome when you talk to a woman, but instead enjoy and learn from the interaction and if something comes of it, great. If nothing comes of it…move on to someone else.

2. You care what other people think.

Do you think everybody in the club is watching you as you make an approach? Do you think *anybody* is watching you? Sorry, but you probably aren't important enough to merit that kind of attention and you should be comforted by that fact. When you worry what the strangers around you think about what you're doing, you're already assuming that you're going to do something "wrong" or "bad."

You will always care what other people think, but you have to become more selective about whose opinions really matter to you. You might have friends who sit back and never approach women the entire night, but have no problem laughing as you get turned down nine out of ten times. If you're stuck with these types of people, tell them exactly what you said, what happened, and then ask how they would have handled it differently. If they don't have any good answers, it might be time to make some new friends.

One of the reasons to go out with a group of guys is for their support and advice. If you aren't getting either, you should find new friends to go out with because your current "friends" will hate and cock-block you at every turn. Alternatively, you can go out alone so you don't have to consider what your friends think or how a rejection might affect your reputation.

Once your confidence and your game are up to speed, you should expect women and men to watch you. Except instead of watching you because they think you're going to fail, they watch because you're having fun and making girls laugh and they wonder what you have going for you. This is the kind of attention you should strive for, because people always remember the superstars of the night and they never remember some guy who got turned down, because there are dozens of those guys in every bar, club, and lounge in the world.

3. You don't want to get rejected.

Rejection is one of, if not *the* biggest, reason why guys don't approach women. Rejection stings some guys longer and harder than a punch in the face, the loss of a job, an argument with a best friend, and most other forms of pain and embarrassment. However, you have to understand that given the fickle tastes of both men and women, attraction isn't always forthcoming, even if you try everything in the book to make it happen.

For a lot of guys, when they only approach one woman a week and she turns them down, they feel they've completely struck out for the entire week until they rebuild their courage and try again. However, if you approach ten women every night you go out and all but one turn you down, you'll only remember the one who laughed at your jokes and gave you her number. Some clichés always ring true, attraction as a numbers game is one of them. Aim to attract the entire bar, not just one woman in it.

Most guys fear rejection because they think it only happens to them and they can't take the hit to their ego. You have to be able to view attraction as a numbers game and understand that rejection is inevitably going to occur. If you try to approach more women, you will get rejected more often than if you didn't approach at all. Consequently, you will have many more opportunities to succeed when you approach and Open as often as possible.

Every guy has been rejected at some point in his life and women have done plenty of rejecting in theirs. If there were no rejection, the world would be one big orgy, which, come to think of it, might not be so bad. However, in the real world, guys get rejected all the time and so will you as long as you keep putting yourself out there. Dealing with rejection is just a matter of not taking it personally. Why would you care if a woman you don't know, who knows nothing about you, rejects you? She is rejecting you for her own personal reasons, not because of you. Your mantra should always be "her loss."

4. You don't know what to do or say.

Maybe you never had any sisters or never knew any women who were true friends. Maybe you've just gotten out of a long relationship and now you've completely forgotten how to talk to attractive women. Or maybe you draw a complete blank when faced with a woman you're interested in. Whatever the case may be, you look and act like a deer in the headlights anytime you're confronted with talking to a woman you don't yet know.

Not knowing what to say ranks only second to fear of rejection as to why men don't approach more women. A lot of men put an excessive amount of importance on the first few things they say to an attractive woman. While first impressions are always important, the words that come out of your mouth make up only a small portion of the overall package you initially present to someone. Your body language, tonality, eye contact, personal style, grooming, and overall attitude make a far greater impact than the words with which you Open.

Note that what you Open with does make an impact on the woman you're approaching, just not as much as you think. Eventually you'll be able to come up with seemingly original things to say every time you need to approach and Open a woman or group of women. In the meantime, you can always start by confidently saying "hi," "hello," or just "hey." It may sound stupid to you when you say it, but it's better than saying nothing at all and letting an opportunity pass you by. Unfortunately, there is no perfect line you can use that works for any woman in every situation, so say something, anything, if only to get her attention for a moment so you can move on and talk about something else.

5. You don't believe it will work.

It seems too easy to read something out of a book and say it to a random woman in a bar, only to find out that it *does* attract her attention. Whether you don't believe the material would work for anybody or that it won't work for you, the problem lies in your confidence, not the specifics of what you say or do. Having confidence in what you say is the first step in making it work for you. If you don't have confidence in what you're saying, no one else will either.

All of the advice and techniques in this book have been thoroughly tested by dozens, if not hundreds, of guys. It's easy to blame the material in the book when you try it one time and it doesn't work for you. When you read something, try it one time and it doesn't work for you, it's easy to blame a book and not your body language or eye contact, or any of the other aspects that are a part of the entire package you present when you first meet someone. Never depend on a good Opener to do all the work for you, but always have confidence in your words, no matter what they are.

Remember that the Openers themselves aren't the only thing you need to have working for you. As you already know, your attitude, style, level of confidence and many other traits need to "work." You can never expect a few lines in a book to do all the work for you, but as long as you show confidence when you Open, you don't have to worry as much about what you say. This book provides the "what" and "how," but you have to believe in the material and your ability to make it fun and interesting.

6. You don't want to bother her or her group (upset her, offend her...)

When talking to your mom, sister, or niece, how much time do you spend worrying about whether you're annoying or upsetting her? Most guys never worry about saying the "wrong thing" when they talk to their female relatives, so you should apply that same frame of mind when talking to any other women in your life. Women sense hesitation when you're contemplating whether you'll be bothering them, and they translate that into you being afraid. If she gets just a hint that you think you're too boring or simply not good enough to talk to her, she'll tend to believe it and you won't likely stand a chance with her.

If you truly think you're a catch, a guy who really has something to offer just about any single women out there, you must let the women you find attractive know this by approaching them without hesitation. Women want to meet great guys who have something to offer, so if you ignore them, you're denying them this opportunity. If you believe you have something wonderful to offer and you approach with that mindset, she'll pick up on it and you'll stand a much better chance at attracting her.

Men go out with the express purpose of meeting women and although it may come as a shock, women go out with the same purpose in mind. The difference is most women don't act or appear nearly as desperate as the average guy on the make. If you're confident, intelligent, and playful, then you're not bothering her; you're giving her a break from her boring day to meet someone interesting. That may not always be the case, but more often than not, if a woman makes eye contact with you, she wants you to talk to her.

7. It seems unnatural for a man to walk up to a woman and start a conversation.

Compared to instant messaging, personal ads, and blind dates, asking for an opinion or making a playful joke to a stranger is completely natural *if* you act natural about it. Thinking that it's unnatural to initiate a conversation with someone you're attracted to is another ludicrous rationalization men use for not having the balls to talk to women they find attractive.

Men and women meet in the most unexpected ways millions of times a day. Sometimes there's a lot of context to two people meeting, like at a party of mutual friends, through a college class, or on the job. It's usually easier to meet and get to know people through your existing network, but then you're only meeting those people passively. In other words, you should try to take an active role in meeting women outside of your limited circle of friends and acquaintances.

Instead of meeting women in a "take what you can get" fashion, you should actively seek out women you find attractive and find out whether you would make a good match. Even if it feels unnatural, you'll find it adds a little more "control" over with whom you spend your time. Ultimately, meeting new people, romantically or otherwise, extends your network and increases you chances of meeting more people "naturally" at parties and other social functions.

8. You have poor self-image/confidence/self-esteem.

We live in an image-conscious culture that places a lot of weight on unrealistic ideals of beauty. Marketing plays a big role in teaching men that if they buy a particular product, they will attain the beautiful women associated with that product. It's a vicious cycle because you start believing that if you only looked a certain way or owned a certain status symbol, you *should* get the women that you want, but you rarely do.

In actuality, women place a lot of value on their emotions—the way they feel— even if they don't know it. Sometimes those emotions get displaced and attached to material goods, but if you can be the guy who cuts through that bullshit and strikes an honest emotional chord with a woman, you'll elevate yourself above the fray as a guy with integrity who has something to say, something that stirs the heart and the mind.

Your goal then, when you're meeting and attracting women, is to create an emotional response. Ideally you want to create a *positive* emotional response, but anything that catches her attention will do, at least initially. No matter what you look like or where you're at in life, you have the ability to create a positive emotional response in the women you meet. Your clothes and your bank account rarely have this ability, and you should always keep this in mind whenever you lack confidence.

Every guy has qualities that women find attractive, but many don't know what those qualities are, or how to effectively demonstrate them. In Chapter 6, "What Women Want," you will learn that women don't mind being with a good-looking guy with power and money, but you will also learn about all the other qualities you can demonstrate that attract women. No matter what you look like, there are women, plural, who want to meet a guy like you. I must note here that if you have extreme self-esteem issues you should consult your general physician or seek therapy, because the problem most likely affects all aspects of your life, not just meeting women.

9. You make it too important.

If you're only approaching one woman a week and you still feel your manhood rests on the success of just one approach, of course you'll think it's important. To break through that mindset, you have to cast a wider net and start to understand that you can't be all things to all people. If you don't regularly talk to women and you treat each encounter like it could be your last, people will pick up on your needy, outcome-dependent behavior.

Consider the guy who spends an hour sipping his cocktail while building up the courage to talk to the woman he's been staring at. He finally gets the nerve to approach her, but for some reason, it just didn't go anywhere. The guy's confidence is shattered, so he starts to drink heavily and give up on women for the night. What he didn't know is that the woman had just gotten into a fight with her mom and she was waiting for her friends to arrive and cheer her up.

Some guys place far too much importance on talking to women even though they aren't in complete control of the interaction. In this previous example, the guy stopped talking to women for the rest of the night because he focused on talking to one woman, and placed far too much importance on the outcome. He took it personally when she wasn't interested in him, even though her issues had nothing to do with him. He should have considered the interaction as practice and quickly moved on to someone else until he found some mutual attraction.

Always keep in mind that you have to keep approaching and stop assigning importance to something that lasts two minutes. Also remember that you have no control over a woman's state of mind, only your own, so focus on being your best self and demonstrating your attractive personality. As long as you don't stress about impressing or pleasing anyone in particular and just enjoy yourself, women will be attracted to you and your positive energy.

10. Because you can't control the fears that stop you.

Unfortunately, this issue can't be rationalized away. If, after reading this book, you're still afraid to ask a stranger for her opinion or just say "hi," you need professional help, no joke. If you're serious about mastering this aspect of your life, visit your doctor and explain the issues you're having, so he or she can refer you to someone who specializes in these types of anxieties.

You should also consider putting this book down until you feel more comfortable in social situations. This book promotes the idea of pushing social boundaries in order to meet and attract women. If you don't feel comfortable around people you don't know, it could do more harm than good to force yourself to do things that you genuinely fear without having the right support system in place.

Male Sexual Confidence

Despite what women say and how much they might object, they want a man who acts like a man. Nature intended men to be strong, assertive, bold, and sexual, but society and the media in particular, have convinced men that these are the wrong traits to display to attract women. Men today seem afraid of saying the "wrong thing" when a woman is around, presumably to protect her from his natural sexual interest in her. There is also the fear of being rejected, humiliated, and scorned, all of which boils down to men being afraid of being their true selves.

How billions of years of evolution have been subverted in just a few decades is beyond the scope of this book, but it's happening. You're probably reading this book because you found yourself trying harder and harder to make your personality as pleasant as possible to women, but it didn't work for you. Your lack of sexual confidence has turned you into a wuss. A wuss caters and panders to women in the hopes of getting their approval and ultimately doing whatever is requested, in the hopes of getting some form of sexual access.

The intent is not to turn you back into a Neanderthal, but to give you permission and encouragement to let your inner man out and be proud of it. The entire book, but especially this chapter, is devoted to helping you stop apologizing for being male, to celebrate your inherently sexual nature, and to reclaim your sexual confidence. You have to stop thinking so much so you can be a man, she can be a woman, and you can both let attraction and nature take its course.

The concepts in this chapter are some of the most difficult to digest, because they require more than just memorizing an Opener and trying it out in the field. You're going to be asked to really examine your mindset and your behavior. In order for the rest of the material to work well for you, you have to admit that you need to make changes in yourself and be willing to make them. Let's start by finding out whether you have sexual confidence with women.

Do you have confidence when it comes to women?

Sexually confident men aren't afraid to be themselves and allow their natural sexuality to flow freely. They love the company of women and treat them well, but they don't let society tell them how to act, and consequently, women love them for it. Answer the questions below honestly to determine whether or not you have sexual confidence:

1. Are you nervous, insecure or overly nice around women?

2. Do you obsess and over-analyze everything a woman says and does, looking for clues as to whether she might like you as more than just a friend?

3. Do you initially act like a woman's friend in the hope of being able to convert your friendship into a relationship?

4. Do you make yourself available to women anytime they need friendly, comforting male company, like after fighting with their boyfriends?

5. Are you clingy or needy, calling the same woman every day or even several times a day?

6. Do you tolerate a woman's rude behavior or her flaking on you?

7. When you are in a relationship with a woman, is she generally in control of your free time?

8. Are you constantly afraid that if you do the "wrong" thing she'll immediately leave you?

9. Do you grovel or beg for sex or do women reward you with sex for behavior they deem "good"?

10. Do you feel shameful and guilty if you let it be known that you're a sexual kind of guy who enjoys being with women, sometimes just for sex?

If you answered "yes" to any of the above questions, you probably need help with your sexual confidence.

Once you start breaking through all of the male-sexuality-bashing you've endured through the years, you can rebuild your confidence and become secure in your masculinity. When you can assert your independence and individuality, you become more comfortable with your self-image. You also start to view yourself as someone of value who takes an active role in choosing your partners, instead of just accepting what falls in your lap. It's extremely liberating to be a man's man and not change your behavior to fit society's expectations of how emasculated males should act.

While reading the above questions you probably noticed they didn't mention looks or money, but all involved your attitude and behavior. You may not have an athlete's physique or a stockbroker's bank account, but you don't need either of these things to be sexually confident and attractive to women.

What is confidence?

★ Confidence begins with having control over yourself. It's important to realize that the factor you have the most control over is your mind and your actions. You have to stop believing that your success or failure with women rests on anyone else's shoulders but your own. Take control of your attitude and own your behavior, and then you'll be in a position to confidently charge into interactions with women without holding them responsible when they aren't interested.

★ Confidence isn't just a state of mind; it's a state of being. When confident men look in the mirror, they see someone to whom women are attracted. Confident men don't dwell on the negative, only on their positive aspects—what they expect women to notice when they first meet. Confident men don't focus on being confident, they focus on doing well with whatever it is they want to do, like their job, their sport, or their relationships with women.

★ Confidence comes from within, including your body language and how you speak. Confident men believe they're great guys with a lot of good qualities, and they express that with the way they move, before they ever begin talking. Once they start talking, the tone and speed of their voice portrays someone who is sure of himself and what he's saying.

Gaining Confidence

As any woman will likely tell you, confidence is one of the most attractive personality trait a man can possess. But how do you gain confidence? It can't be bought or faked and you just can't suddenly decide that you're confident. You can, however, help develop your confidence by incorporating the following tips into your life. You can start utilizing any or all of these ideas to become more confident, not just with women, but with everything you do in your daily life.

Look and feel good

Looking and feeling good has such a tremendous impact on your confidence that I have devoted an entire chapter to helping you improve your style and grooming. Looking your best includes positive body language, good grooming, and finding your personal "style." If you can master all three, you won't only look good to the women you meet, but you'll *know* that you look good, which is a powerful way to boost your confidence.

Men who know they look good "beam" a positive, sexy vibe that women notice. Not only should your clothes look good on you, but your body language should catch a woman's eye. From maintaining eye contact, talking in an even and unhurried tone, and carrying yourself with a confident posture, you'll be amazed what a few small improvements can do to boost your self-image and your success rate with women.

Remind yourself that you're a catch

After months or even years of getting shot down, most guys have issues with their confidence and self-image. Guys are pretty hard on themselves when it comes to failure with women, and they find it hard to give themselves credit for their other successes in life. If you don't have anyone around to give you an ego boost, there's no shame in doing it yourself.

Start by getting a piece of paper and listing all of the reasons why you're a great catch. Maybe you have a great job that you love. Or you could be hilarious once you break out of your shell. Or you may even have a skill or hobby that you're really good at. Whatever makes you get up in the morning and makes life worth living are usually qualities that women love. Before you go out to meet people, think of your list and of all the great things that make you who you are.

Unless you know what your best qualities are, you'll never have them in mind when you meet people. If you recently thought about the great qualities you possess, you'll be likely to talk more confidently and communicate more effectively. Women may not know why they perceive you as confident, but it's not the specifics that turn them on as much as the mere fact that you're confident and it shows.

Lead, don't follow

It takes confidence to be a good leader, so if you want to boost your confidence, you need to be able to effectively lead a group or at least lead yourself. Become the "man with the plan" and don't be afraid to make decisions on the fly. When it comes to what you're drinking, eating, wearing, playing, watching, and more, have an opinion, make it known, and fight for it if you have to. You should always have an opinion and be willing to back it up if you feel strongly about it.

Leadership is especially important when it comes to trivial matters between men and women. Women put a lot of time and effort into making themselves look good, presumably for men such as yourself. As a result, women generally want men to devote their efforts to handling the decisions, big and small, regarding what you do together. If they happen to disagree with you, they will let it be known, but until that happens always take the initiative in determining where you go and what you do. Don't *ask* what to do or *tell* a woman what to do, but inform her what you plan to do, and assume she will want to do it as well.

If you're new to taking charge of your own life, you will find it extremely difficult to command a group of people, but that should be your goal. There are literally hundreds of books on various forms of leadership, but each covers mostly the same ground. If you have trouble taking control of your own life or you're too shy to speak your mind, find some self-help books to boost your leadership skills. It doesn't take long at all for small strides in leadership to translate into increased self-confidence.

Treat women as equals

A lot of men view women they meet for the first time as a collection of hot or not body parts and thus treat them according to the same superficial scorecard. If a woman is extremely attractive, they treat her as a goddess before she even has a chance to exhibit her personality. Based solely on looks, a guy will try to determine what his relative value is to the woman in whom he's interested. This usually translates into stilted conversations and awkward worship at the pedestal onto which he's projected her.

Confident men treat women the same way they treat their friends or their kid sisters. In fact, some guys think specifically of the way they teased their sister when they were kids when talking to attractive women. Women, especially if they have older brothers, find this approach very disarming.

While most guys brag about themselves or hopelessly grope for common ground, confident guys playfully tease and mock the women to whom they're attracted. When you do this, you send the signal that you're comfortable talking with beautiful women and aren't worried about offending them, which demonstrates confidence.

Stay outcome-independent

Guys who aren't used to interacting with women often find themselves in a constant state of worry over what they're saying, how the conversation is going, and whether or not the woman is into them. All of this thinking translates into nervous behavior, which women pick up on instantly. One of the biggest turnoffs for women are insecure guys who can't hold a normal conversation because they're too worried about how the conversation is going.

By talking with as many women as possible, confident guys don't have to worry about any particular conversation "working out" to their benefit. Confident guys know they have attractive qualities and as long as they keep a positive attitude and show off those qualities as often as possible, women will be vying for their attention. Confident men aren't dependent on the outcome of any particular interaction with a woman for their validation as a man— they are outcome- independent.

Next time you find yourself getting nervous before you approach or while you're meeting a woman, try to relax and just enjoy the fact that you're out having a good time, casually meeting people. Don't think about getting phone numbers or making out, just try to have fun. The more laidback you are when talking to a woman, the more confident you will seem and women will naturally be attracted to you.

Talk to many women

Confident men focus on talking to as many women as possible at the same location. Most men spend a lot of time building up their courage to talk to a single woman and if they get shot down, they don't try to meet anyone else for the rest of the night. If she does show interest, they hang around the same woman for the rest of the night until they get a number or she gets creeped out and walks away. You want to focus on talking to as many women as possible the moment you enter a new location, and avoid hunting for one woman who might be attracted to you and then never leaving her side.

Sometimes sticking around beyond your natural shelf life can work for you, but all it usually does is force you to awkwardly talk about yourself much more than you should. A confident man typically approaches, Opens, and walks away after a few laughs. Then, he moves on to another group and does the same thing and then another group and so on. As he make his rounds, women who were initially attracted to him keep their eye on him as he charms and entertains every other attractive female in the area. Most guys would assume that a woman who witnesses a guy flirting with other nearby women would turned off by his behavior, but it actually demonstrates that he's a catch, which makes her want to secure his attention even more.

If you can hold yourself to light, fun interactions lasting five to ten minutes before politely moving on, women you originally approached will find ways to talk to you, and women you have yet to meet will make sure you do. Confident men walk away from women they've just charmed because they know they can do it again and again. They also know that if things don't work out with one particular woman, they'll have options on which to fall back.

Take the high road

Finally, taking the high road means doing what is right as much as humanly possible. Confident men stay confident because they respect themselves, and this self-respect comes from establishing a reputation as a good person who does the right thing. So even if you must break from the pack, always try to do what's ethical. Whether you believe in karma, the law of attraction, or the golden rule, they all boil down to "what goes around comes around" so you can either stay on karma's good side, or eventually learn the hard way that negative energy comes back to haunt you.

Everyone has opportunities to lie, cheat, steal, and more, but the majority of confident men choose the high moral ground. They may do this for its own virtue or because they know that the feeling they get from doing what's right translates into an attractive quality that helps them become more confident and successful with women. Being honorable isn't a lost art and although it may get in the way of a good time every now and then, in the long run it's going to help you meet and attract more women.

Confidence Exercises

You may have a better understanding of what confidence is, but a mere definition isn't going to help you much. You have to leave your comfort zone and discover your confidence in the world around you. If you weren't confident to begin with, you might need to take baby steps and work your way up.

The following exercises will help train you to stop hesitating when you see someone you want to meet. By setting goals and replacing deliberation with action, you will force yourself to approach and Open women without thinking about it. If you're still having trouble with one of the exercises, keep at it until you feel confident enough to move on to more advanced Openers.

Exercise 1: "Hi!"

This is a simple exercise and is intended only for the severely shy, who aren't yet up to actually speaking a sentence to a woman they don't know. It's pretty simple, actually—all you have to do is walk down a busy street, through a mall, or anywhere with a lot of foot traffic, make eye contact with every woman who walks past you, and then smile and say "hi." It may seem weird at first, but you're doing nothing wrong. In fact, you're just being friendly and as a bonus, learning that there are no negative repercussions for being outgoing. Being able to say "hi" to anyone at anytime is the first step in building your confidence with women. Once you're comfortably saying "hi" to women and noticing them smiling and saying "hi" right back at you, you're ready to move on to Exercise 2.

Exercise 2: Numbers Game

Now that you're comfortable at least saying "hi" to women, it's time to set a goal to approach between five and ten women each day. However, instead of just saying "hi," you should use an Opener and prepare yourself to hold a conversation. To make the transition a little easier, consider approaching women who are slightly less attractive than you would normally be interested in, so you don't feel intimidated. Since you're likely to generate more interest because you're aiming lower, you'll have many opportunities to practice your conversation skills.

If, after a little chatting, you decide that you're not interested in exploring things further, you have the option not to pursue it. This shouldn't make you feel as though you've used a woman, because all you've really done is introduce yourself and talk for a few minutes. If you do decide to walk way, thank her for the chance to meet her and leave things on a positive note.

Exercise 3: Wingman Bets

Instead of looking at meeting women as the last game of the World Series, you should consider it more as batting practice. With batting practice, as with approaching women, you can miss many times, but you won't strike out. One of the best ways to reinforce this is to go out with a wingman and give each other $200 in $20 bills, or whatever amount you feel comfortable with. Then, as you approach a woman and get rejected, your friend gives you one of your twenty dollar bills back. If you get rejected ten times in a night, you've earned all of your money back. If you fall short of your goal, your wingman gets to keep the rest and vice versa.

These types of little games actually make getting rejected fun and worthwhile and along the way, you'll meet a lot of other women who *don't* reject you. It completely turns the tables around when you start thinking of getting rejected as a goal, and getting a phone number or a kiss as a bonus. Eventually you stop betting, and having fun and meeting people becomes your main goal, but getting phone numbers and making out are still bonuses.

Exercises like this help you overcome your fear of rejection by forcing you to get rejected to win your money back. They also stop you from being outcome- dependent—you stop caring about whether you succeed with a woman because you've turned the idea of "success" upside down. Whether you make back twenty bucks or find a cute girl to have some fun with, you win either way. That's exactly the mentality you need to have before you stop using these confidence exercises—you're having fun, so no matter what happens you win.

What These Exercises Accomplish

Conquer your fears

Learning to approach and Open, even in the face of fear, is a powerful way to boost your confidence. From now on, if you start to feel fear when you think about or talk to a woman, consider it a call to action. Fear should be your signal to kick your game into high gear. For instance, if you sense yourself hesitating when you see an attractive woman you want to talk to, consider it a sign to stop thinking and immediately walk over and talk to her. Or, if you're hesitant to call a woman who gave you her number, stop thinking and immediately pick up the phone and make the call.

By pushing yourself to continually do the very things you fear, you'll not only overcome your fear, you'll also get a sense of accomplishment from triumphing over these challenges. Each time you succeed with an exercise, you'll notice a boost to your self-esteem. Just as importantly, when you move to the next exercise, women will start to notice and react to your newfound confidence.

Practice makes perfect

If you want to become a world-class race car driver, would you drive around the track once a week? No, you would drive that track all day, every day, for as long as they would let you. You should apply the same attitude toward meeting women. If you want to improve your skills, you have to commit yourself to following through on each exercise. By devoting yourself to overcoming your fears and learning new skills, you will naturally develop more confidence around women.

Talking to a new woman once a week is like driving a race car around the track just once a week and expecting to win races. If you want to take your game to new levels and experience fun and interesting people that you normally wouldn't, you have to decide to do something radically different with your frame of mind. By the time you complete the exercises, you should be able to chat up women every day, no matter where you are. Take every opportunity to meet new people and try to interact with as many women as possible, regardless of the circumstances. With each interaction, your confidence will continue to climb and you'll find each approach easier than the last.

Success breeds success

It's been said that repetition is the mother of skill, but it can also be said that skill is the mother of confidence. As you complete the exercises, you'll find some techniques that work really well for you and become almost second nature to you. Once you start accumulating near bullet-proof techniques, you can eventually Open like you're on autopilot, while also developing new techniques as you continue practicing the old ones. Once you realize that you've developed a new skill that requires very little effort or forethought, your confidence will naturally skyrocket.

Attitude Checklist

Try to be mentally prepared before leaving home because you never know when you'll see someone you want to meet. Your attitude and energy level tells a woman a lot about you, so she'll use this initial impression to determine whether she should keep talking to you. Use the list below to make sure you are in the correct frame of mind before walking out the door:

★ **Body Language:** You're comfortable in your body and physically relaxed. You can high-five an entire bar if you have to, and would have no hesitation touching a woman's arm or shoulder if you're both laughing.

★ **High Energy:** When you see a woman you want to approach, you can quickly switch from relaxed to high energy. You're ready to be playful and fun and no minor bumps slow you down.

★ **Spontaneous:** You're relaxed, but ready to launch into high energy at any time, you also need to be ready for anything. If you get invited to go somewhere new, be willing to run with it.

★ **Friendly:** You look in the mirror and you see an honest, friendly guy, prepared with fun and interesting things to talk about. You can look anybody in the eye, walk over and chat them up if you want to.

★ **Sexual Self-Confidence:** All women want you, or at least you believe they do. You know deep in your heart that when women are looking around, they're looking at you and they're "inviting" you to talk to them.

★ **Smiling:** You can walk out the door smiling, not a fake smile, but a genuine smile. If you have all of the above going on and you're about to hit a party or a club or whatever, you really have something to smile about. You can hold on to that smile for the rest of the night, no matter what happens.

Chapter 4

Style and Grooming

In this Chapter

★ Understanding why first impressions are so important when meeting women

★ Navigating essential grooming techniques so you don't stand out for all the wrong reasons

★ Examining fashion basics and the finer details that help you stand out

Style and Grooming

Think about some of the most handsome men that occupy the fantasies of women around the world. If you broke down their features, part by part, they probably wouldn't be as good-looking as you initially thought, but women are still attracted to them. However, they're not attractive *just* because they have good genetics; two other factors also play a role—a great personality and world-class style. You learned about confidence and personality in the previous chapter, so now we're going to focus on developing your personal style.

Since plastic surgery or years in the gym aren't practical or desirable for most guys, the following chapter concentrates on something you can easily work with—your style. You might not have an army of stylists at your disposal, but you do have this book and maybe some men's fashion magazines and a few females in your life that can help guide you. With all three in hand, you can make a few small adjustments to make a big impact on your self-image.

While you read this chapter, don't get freaked out about drastically altering your appearance just to please women. If you feel like you look good, the people around you will probably feel the same way. When you're comfortable in what you wear and with how you look, you can relax and allow yourself to be the all-around fun-loving, friendly guy to whom women are attracted. Remember, you want to dress and groom well so you can be your best self, not because you feel you have to be somebody you're not.

First Impressions

The Western world lives at an accelerated pace compared to just a few decades ago. To remain competitive, we make instant assumptions and snap decisions regarding who we talk to, what we buy, how we get where we're going, and thousands of other major and minor life decisions. When it comes to sizing up potential romantic interests, women are no different in their decision-making.

With the variety and speed of today's communication—cell phones, e-mail, instant messaging—people now treat live interactions with the same immediacy. Very few people indulge in the time it takes to fully assess another person's character before deciding whether they should form any type of relationship with them. Instead, we rely on our first impressions, rarely second-guessing the notion that what you initially see is what you get.

Given today's fast-paced realities, first impressions are as important as ever. Your grooming and personal style shouldn't deter you from approaching women, nor should it deter them from talking to you. The first few moments of contact between two people can set the tone for their entire relationship—if there is one—so you have to be willing to put some time and energy into how you look.

In just a few seconds, a woman forms an instant, usually everlasting impression of what type of person you are. Are you making a good first impression? I hope I've illustrated how important it is because there are no second chances in this game. You should strive to make a memorable, even extravagant, first impression because almost everything that follows depends on it.

Start off on the right foot

Before I dive straight into the do's and don'ts of men's style and grooming, understand that there is no silver bullet or perfect formula that allows you to impress and attract every woman. Every woman has her own experiences and upbringing that helps shape her tastes and expectations. However, there are some basic grooming fundamentals and style tips that are almost universally applicable. At the very least, while you may not be the perfect guy for every woman, you will feel confident and comfortable in social situations by following my suggestions.

If you want to improve your appearance as much as possible, you have to start by taking an honest look at yourself and how you dress. Over the years, you may have really let things slide, especially when it comes to the clothes you wear. Maybe after you got out of college you dove headfirst into an all-consuming new job, forgetting that those short sleeve button-down shirts you wear to work aren't appropriate for clubs. Or you may have been in a long relationship where it came to a point that you didn't have to dress well very often and now you're back on the market, clueless as to what looks good.

Whatever your circumstances, just about every guy could use a refresher course on how to groom and style himself, so his looks never become a distraction to the new women he wants to meet. It may not be your looks that are holding you back, but to find out, you need to ask yourself whether women are attracted to your style. If the answer is "yes," you might not need to change a thing. If the answer is "no" and you find yourself constantly getting turned down, although you feel like you said and did all the right things, you most likely aren't making a good first impression and your personal style might be the reason. If this is the case, you need to look at yourself objectively in the mirror and analyze what you have going for and against you, and be willing to try new things.

The best way to start is to read through the following sections on style and grooming, then examine yourself and put all of the elements discussed into two categories—the things you really like about yourself and the things you think could use improvement. You may even need to seek outside help if you thought you had the goods all this time, but were in fact style-challenged. Once you have your list of plusses and minuses, you can go about prioritizing the list of minuses in terms of what can be easily remedied, like clipping your nails, to what can take months of hard work, like losing weight. Plus, you can start looking at all of your plusses and find new ways to highlight what's already working for you.

The point of all this is not to radically change yourself so you look like a plastic television personality, but to help you find your best features and scrub your worst, so you can walk out the door knowing that you look and feel the best you possibly can. Your goal is to eliminate any self-perceived image problems so you aren't held back or distracted by them when you meet new people. By the end of this chapter you should have a good idea of what works for you and how to make it shine, and what doesn't work for you and how to tone it down.

Grooming

Ultimately, no matter how good you are at your game, women make the decision about how far they'll take a sexual relationship with you. It's usually done subconsciously and you never know exactly when that sexual switch will flip on. Although women don't like to admit it, most judge a man on his outward appearance when they first meet him. Therefore, one of the first steps in upping your game and accelerating sexual attraction is to develop your image into something that appeals to women's eyes.

You don't want to take any chances when you leave the house and you think you might see women you want to meet. As you get ready to leave, you have to pay attention to what you're wearing, how you feel, how you look, and how you smell at all times so you don't ruin your chances before you even begin.

The last thing you want is to meet a beautiful woman only to have her focus on your dirty fingernails instead of your attractive personality, for example.

The previous chapter detailed the mindset you need to have in order to have confidence when talking to women. This chapter covers all of the so-called superficial aspects, namely your style and grooming, to help you make a great first impression. By learning more about style and proper grooming, you can fully prepare yourself in advance and avoid potentially embarrassing situations. Let's start by covering all of the grooming basics and then move on to how to wrap up your nicely scrubbed self in the right clothing for the right occasions.

Grooming Basics

The competition for women of quality is fierce and those who succeed understand that one of the most fundamental aspects of creating attraction is a man's hygiene. Of course these guys also realize how much more is involved in creating attraction, but a lot of men don't even understand the basics, or they just don't try. If you think that simply showing up is enough to impress the ladies, you have greatly underestimated how demanding women are when it comes to grooming. Most women put a lot of time and effort into their "look," so they expect the guys they meet to put at least a fraction of the same effort into their own appearance.

The following section is not a guideline, but basic rules for getting yourself ready to go out—there is nothing optional about brushing your teeth or taking a shower. It may seem like a lot of effort and it can be at first, but if you want to make a great first impression and carry that through to future sexual encounters, read and follow these grooming basics closely. After that, you can think about building on your personal style and killer Openers, but start by nailing these grooming essentials first.

Hair

Make sure you have a hairstyle that looks good on you. You can find out by asking your friends' girlfriends or splurge and go to an actual salon and have professionals give you their honest assessment. The style you had ten years ago and still have today may be doing you a lot of harm, so don't be afraid to try something new. Besides, no matter what you do, hair grows back...usually.

Beyond your hairstyle, also make sure that your hair is free of grease and dandruff. It should disgust you if you've got either going on, so imagine her reaction when the both of you are laughing and little flakes float to your shoulders. A bad haircut is one thing, but a greasy or flaky scalp is a deal breaker. If you can't solve the problem using over-the-counter shampoos and conditioners, consult a doctor.

Finally, if you're going bald, you need to come to grips with it and decide whether you're at the point where whatever is left needs to come off. If you're combing over a few loose strands to cover an increasingly larger bald spot, you're well past the point when you should be shaving your head. It may seem like a drastic measure, but it can actually create a powerful and attractive impression. Many women find men who are completely bald much more attractive than guys who appear to be going bald.

Teeth

A bright smile can help win over a girl time and time again, but teeth that are stained, yellow, or show visible signs of plaque are sure to send her in the other direction. Always remember to brush your teeth every morning, every evening, and after meals. You should also floss regularly for the health benefits as well as keeping bad breath at bay. If you think you might have bad breath, you probably do. If you aren't sure, ask a relative or close friend because nobody wants to talk to someone whose breath smells bad.

If you want more than just clean teeth and good breath, consider whitening your teeth, either at home or by visiting a professional. Women find clean, sparkling white teeth very attractive and more and more people use bleach treatments to get unbelievably white teeth. Even if you can't pull off a decent Opener, if you flash a gleaming smile and bat your twinkly eyes, you might be able to distract her from your mumblings until you say something funny or interesting. Regular brushing always helps, but if you want a smile you can see from across a room, visit a dentist to find out about bleaching and other treatments.

Finally, if your teeth look like a buzz saw, you might be self-conscious about it and probably don't smile as much as you should. The importance of eye contact and smiling cannot be overstated, so if your jagged teeth are holding you back, you should visit your dentist to find out your options. If you have a crazy set of teeth and you smile just the same, it might put off a few women, but what do you care, you're already smiling. Luckily, most people have fairly straight teeth with maybe one or two not lining up where they should, which isn't worth worrying about.

Skin

Throughout the book, you will come to understand why you should touch early and often in an interaction. Because of this, you should concern yourself with how your skin looks and feels. How your skin should feel actually depends on where you live and what you do for a living. In some areas, women expect their metro men to have the same baby-smooth skin that they do. In other areas, a guy with soft hands would seem less than masculine because women expect rough and tumble guys to have meaty, rough paws.

If you're unsure about what type of skin women around you prefer, or if you're just in need of an Opener, you can ask women their opinion and then ask them to feel your hands and tell you how you rank. Just remember to give it some context by telling her that your sister/niece/cousin told you that your hands are too soft or too rough and you wanted to get another female opinion on it. You can end up having a five-minute conversation about soft versus rough skin that involves a lot of touching and caressing, not a bad way to start things off.

Unfortunately, some guys have much bigger skin issues to deal than whether they have soft or rough skin. One of the biggest confidence destroyers out there is greasy and/or acne-prone skin. Acne simply isn't attractive and never will be and severe cases can cause a lot of psychological damage. If you have a mild case, keep your skin clean using over-the-counter medicated pads and creams. Also, when you're out meeting people, check yourself in the mirror every few hours and gently wash away any excess oil. If you have severe acne, it's a medical problem and you should see a doctor. There are high-powered medications you can take to clear up almost any case of acne.

Odor

Do flowers wilt and die as you walk past them? Do people gag when you raise your arm? If you stink, you're out of the game and unless you have a medical problem, there is no excuse for body odor. Women love anything that smells good, especially themselves and the guys they're with. A shower, some deodorant, and yes even a splash of cologne and you've knocked this problem out.

As for the majority of guys who already have their body odor in check, you should concentrate on which colognes and aftershaves you use. Wearing aftershave and cologne are easy ways to subtly increase your attractiveness.

Women pick up the slightest scent; aftershave, in particular, really grabs their attention. Women also often know the names of popular colognes guys wear and like to tell guys they know what it is, so consider this when you're buying new cologne.

Cologne has multiple uses beyond just smelling good—it's also a great topic to bring up when you're talking to a woman. Pick two of your favorite colognes that don't clash with each other and spray one on each wrist and then pick just one to dab on your neck. After you've been talking for a minute, tell her you were testing colognes that day and ask which of the two she likes best. Whatever she chooses, agree with her and compliment her on her good taste.

Specifics

You dress well, you have a decent haircut, your teeth are always brushed, and you smell good. If you have all of these things going for you, you're in great shape and in most parts of the world you are well ahead of the competition. But maybe you live in a big metropolis where competition is fierce, or you just want to up your game so you can aim directly for the hottest women in the room. The next section covers the finer details you can attend to that can really put you in a class of your own.

For some guys, the suggestions below will seem far too high maintenance and even effeminate, which is a normal reaction. However, for guys who are competing against actors and millionaires, every little detail that gives you an edge is worth exploring. It doesn't hurt to at least skim the list in case you find a personal trouble area, like a unibrow or ear hair, which needs some attention. Remember, if you notice it, she will notice it as well, and you don't want something like long fingernails to prevent you from meeting an attractive woman.

Facial Hair

There are no hard rules that say you should or shouldn't have facial hair. The fact is, a lot of guys look better with two days worth of stubble than when they're freshly shaved. Conversely some guys try to grow facial hair and it comes in as thin little patches of baby hair and looks horrible. You probably know by now whether facial hair looks good on you or not, but it never hurts to ask a friend.

Whatever you decide to do, clean shaven, stubble, or a full beard, pick one and go with it. A week's worth of growth on most guys just makes them look like bums, so unless you're an artsy type who can get away with it, keep things trim and try to maintain the same amount of growth from day to day. Also, keep things clean; you don't want food in your goatee when you're talking to a woman.

Eyebrows

Most women don't expect men to maintain finely shaped eyebrows like they do, but they definitely don't get turned on by a unibrow. If you happen to have more than just a few errant hairs between your eyebrows, do what women do every day—use tweezers to pluck them out. Don't get too crazy and start shaping your eyebrows, but clear out the spot in between them and check every week or two and keep it clean.

Nails

Whether you have soft or rough hands, you need to keep your nails trim and clear of dirt. You don't need to get a weekly manicure to keep your nails in good shape, but you should clip them and smooth out the rough edges.

Consider where you expect your hands to go if everything goes according to plan. The state of your nails can play a factor as to whether you get that chance.

Feet

Feet can play a much bigger role in the summer months when people are wearing sandals and flip flops. Women love to look at a guy's shoes, but in absence of that are your toes, which you should keep in decent shape, much like your fingernails. Any athlete's foot, ingrown toenails, or foot odor must be dealt with if your toes are going to be exposed. If you can't take care of this normally hidden body part, she might assume that you don't take care of your other hidden parts.

Ear/Nose Hair

Would you ever kiss a woman with a visible moustache? Hopefully not, because hair doesn't really belong there and it's bound to distract you every time you see it. The same holds true for your ear and nose hair. It could be said that it does in fact belong there, but since women view it as a turnoff, you should remove it anyway. It only takes a few seconds to do the job using electric clippers designed specifically for nose and ear hair. As a guideline, if it protrudes from your nostrils or you can see the hairs in your ear in the mirror, trim it.

Back

A nice muscular back can really be a turn-on for women who like athletic men, but not if it's covered in pimples, skin flakes, and even worse, thick hair. If you have light acne on your back, buy over-the-counter body wash made specifically for blemished skin, preferably with exfoliate to help remove dead skin. If you only have a small amount of back hair, it's perfectly natural and should be left alone. However, if you look like you're wearing a wool sweater after you take your shirt off, you might want to visit a salon for a wax, or at least avoid shirtless situations outdoors.

Pubic Hair

Although the state of your pubic hair probably won't be an issue when you first meet a woman, it should be included as part of your grooming rituals. Most guys like women who keep their pubic hair well trimmed or even completely waxed, usually because it makes things easier to find and generally cleaner. The same can be said for a guy's pubic hair; if you expect her to keep her pubes trim and accessible, you should return the favor. You don't need to shave, but break out the scissors and clear out the excess and you could be well rewarded for the effort.

Conclusion

Remember, although these are grooming rules, there are always exceptions out there who have hairy dads and must absolutely be with a gorilla-type for a boyfriend. Some women grew up as tomboys with ten brothers, so a little dirt under your fingernails would be right up their alley. Just keep these rules in mind if you feel like you're doing everything right, but you're still getting shut down.

Style

When it comes to attracting women, looks definitely matter, but not as much as you might think. For those who don't have the chiseled face of a model or the toned body of an athlete, you can rely on style to improve your odds at attracting women. Not just any style mind you, but your own *personal* style that suits you and sends the message that, although you may be overweight, short, skinny, pale, or anything else about you that's less than perfect, you still know how to dress well.

Everyone has seen at least one guy who didn't seem physically appealing, but was in the company of a beautiful woman. He may have been wealthy or maybe he just knew how to make the best of what he had by developing his own personal style. Just as women are able to make themselves look dropdead gorgeous by using make-up, high heels, hair coloring, acrylic nails, push-up bras, and more, men can use similar tactics to make themselves appear more attractive than when they wake up in the morning.

You can't change the looks you were born with unless a knife and thousands of dollars are involved, but you can take what you've been given and dress it up as best as you can. Style is more than just dropping some cash and picking up some expensive, trendy clothes. In fact, trendy clothes may be the exact opposite of what you need, depending on the types of places you like to hang out. Style means wearing the right clothes in the right situations as well as keeping a high standard when it comes to personal grooming. The look you want to achieve should allow you to talk to women you find attractive without being dismissed out-of-hand before you even open your mouth because you don't look "cool."

Choosing the Right Clothes

Whatever the social situation is, when you dress the part and you know you look good, you *feel* good too. Feeling comfortable in social situations increases your confidence and helps you feel more relaxed when you're talking to people. However, most guys don't like to shop and when they do, have no idea what they're doing and want to get it over with as soon as possible. Before you start buying clothes, get some input from people who know what they're talking about. Any guy can tap into the following resources for help on improving their style:

Men's fashion magazines

GQ, *Men's Vogue*, or any of the countless "laddie" magazines like *Maxim* and *FHM* offer dozens of pages filled with fashion shoots of the hottest trends in menswear. Take note of fashions that appeal to you or rip the pages out and keep them with you when you go shopping. Typically, the designer brands shown in the magazines are out of the price range of most men, but if you show the clerks at large department stores what you're interested in, they can usually find something similar or direct you to another store.

Store clerks

If you have the time to develop relationships with the salespeople at the stores you like, you should. If someone helped you out and found clothes that look good and work well for you, consider offering them something from Starbucks or a dessert shop. Most customers are indifferent, while some are just rude, but a small gesture of goodwill and a business card could result in a phone call when the next big sale happens. Not only that, the next time you visit, they'll direct you to fashions they think you'll like, saving you a lot of time.

Review your closet

Not every guy needs to find a new style that works for him; he may have already found it. If you feel you've already got the right threads for the right occasions, just make sure your clothes are in good shape. Women are notorious for their attention to detail and might read the tiny ink stain on your shirt as a sign that you're a slob. Review all of the clothes, socks, and accessories in your wardrobe to make sure none of them have food stains, wrinkles, holes, or pit stains. If you find any of these blemishes, either get rid of them or visit a drycleaner to find out whether they can be salvaged.

Trendy men

If you know a friend, relative, or colleague who seems to know exactly how to dress at all times, compliment them, and ask them where they shop for clothes. Fashionable men are rarely embarrassed when you ask them about what they're wearing. In fact, since most guys aren't particularly fashionable, they rarely get compliments from other guys and sometimes they're eager to finally talk about one of their interests with another guy without feeling embarrassed about it.

Fashionable women

It's no secret that women love to shop, so if you know someone who loves nothing better than a day at the mall, tell her you need to go shopping and want some help. Women are invaluable at helping you choose styles that work for you, but make sure you're not interested in her romantically, so you can stay focused and walk away with the clothes you need.

Finding your style

Luckily, there isn't just a single style to which everyone in the world slavishly adheres. The[re are] a lot of different "looks" that can be considered stylish, but not every one of those is going t[o] for you. The challenge is finding something that's stylish, that fits, that you can wear comfo[rtably] and looks appropriate for your social scenes.

Some guys who wouldn't be confused for male models and haven't had much luck with w[omen] tend to overcompensate for their shortcomings by buying expensive designer clothes and accessories that go along with them. They might start with a suit and not get the results they [want] so they buy snakeskin shoes, then diamond cufflinks, then a Rolex, and still they aren't end[ing up] with women that make them happy.

I knew a guy like this. The more he spent on clothes and jewelry, the more miserable [he] came. He knew he was near the end of this approach because he had the best of everythin[g and] never had the type of woman to whom he was attracted. He came to visit me in Los Angel[es and] when he arrived, his bags somehow never made it on the plane, so he had to live in the clot[hes he] was wearing: designer jeans, an old wrinkled button-down shirt, and some brown mocs.

His entire reason for visiting me was so I could impart some tips, so he could rely on som[ething] other than high-end fashion for confidence. He wasn't completely onboard with the idea an[d this] became more apparent when I told him he couldn't borrow any of my clothes, mainly because [we are] completely different body types. He begged to go to Melrose or Rodeo; I refused and told h[im I] needed to get ready to go out that night. He refused, but some vodka shots and a few insult[s later] and he was out the door in his wrinkled, disheveled clothes.

Since I always keep a pen handy, I pulled him aside on the way to a nice restaurant/b[ar and] wrote on the palm of one hand "I don't even live in LA" and in the other palm "so I don't [give a] shit." I told him that if I wasn't around to pepper him with advice, he could look at his han[ds] affirm how nothing that happened that night really mattered.

Surprisingly, he seemed to turn a corner the instant we walked into the bar and he really didn't give a shit because he didn't have the crutch on which he had always relied. He basically gave up on the idea of meeting any cute girls that night. Fortunately, fate had a much different idea because between his carefree attitude and his just-off-the-plane look, women wanted to know what his story was. My friend was dressed down compared to the rest of the bar and it didn't faze him one bit. He told me he had one of the most relaxing, engaging, fun nights he could remember. He got some phone numbers and even made out with the girl I had been talking to!

His bags arrived the next day and he opened them up and pulled out some underwear and toiletries, but left everything else in the bag. We ended up going to Melrose, but he only shopped in vintage stores and tried to get variations on the one style that worked for him in his entire life. I've never seen him in a suit since and now he uses his cash to fly around the world, hardly caring about the clothes on his back.

The point of the story is that it doesn't matter what brand or type of clothing you wear as long as you're comfortable wearing it. My friend wasn't comfortable in suits because he knew he was wearing "the best" and it wasn't working for him and he had nothing to fall back on. Some guys look their best in suits, some in leather pants, and others in jeans and a t-shirt. If you think you can wear what Brad Pitt wears and have Brad's success with women, you'll find out the hard way that the clothes don't make the man— the man makes his clothes work for him.

Don't be embarrassed to visit a large mall and move from one type of store to the next, trying out completely different outfits from punk rocker to investment banker. Try anything and everything until you find something that really suits you. Before you rip the tags off, invite some trustworthy friends over to assess your new look and don't be afraid to tell them why you're doing this and why it's important to you. Just like all of the different types of hats in the world, only a few look good on your particular head and the same holds true for your personal style.

The Basics

Styles are always changing from region to region, season to season, and through the decades. What defined hip and cutting-edge last year is now available for ten bucks at Wal-Mart and everybody has it. Not everyone desires or can afford to keep up with all the latest trends, but if you don't hang out in expensive clubs and bars, you don't need to. However, even if you're more of a dive bar and bowling alley kind of guy, or you just don't want to look like your mom dressed you, you need to keep a few fashion basics ready to go.

For the most part fashion basics have been, and probably will forever be, accepted as good-looking, as long as they're clean and they fit you. You probably already own a lot of items on the following list, but if you don't, before you start dropping money on the designer threads, get one or two of each fashion staple and make sure they look good on you. Either bring a fashionable friend or make sure the stores have a generous exchange policy. Also, if you really don't think you will be buying jeans that cost a week's salary, consider buying the best of these basics. Believe it or not, they usually last longer and have more sizes than their generic versions.

Black, White, and Grey T-shirts

White t-shirts are particularly attractive with a pair of jeans; especially if you can fill it out with a bit of muscle. For those who don't prefer the James Dean look, black t-shirts go well with some black sneakers, but not garish tennis and basketball shoes, think Converse. Grey t-shirts are the happy medium that can take a little more wear compared to white t-shirts and go with almost any pair of jeans and shoes. Avoid logos or slogans and if you need a little something so you don't feel generic, wear a subtle necklace that looks like it came from India or Thailand that you can find in most "head" shops.

Jeans

Every man in the Western world owns a pair of jeans, if not five, so you should try yours on and examine how well they fit. If you have long legs, avoid extremely tight jeans. If you have a belly, make sure there is room for it in the waist of the jeans, not hanging out over them. If your jeans don't look or feel right on you, it's probably time to retire them and buy a few new pairs.

Jeans come in many styles, from completely destroyed to stiff as cardboard and in as many colors. Every few years the trend veers from dark blue to light blue, which make color one of the few considerations you need to make when buying a new pair. Jeans are extremely versatile so don't assume that just because you're wearing them, you're dressed down. With the right shoes, cool t-shirt, and a blazer, you're club-ready in most cities.

White Button-Down

At the trendiest of clubs in some of the larger cities, a white button-down shirt is considered a bit passé. For the rest of the world, it still looks classy and if you wear it right, casual. Some guys think that wherever there are buttons on a shirt, they must be buttoned, which might work for a job interview, but not for attracting women. Dress shirts should be worn casually when your goal is to meet and attract women, so don't be afraid to show a little chest hair or let the sleeves hang open.

If you wear a really nice button-down shirt that fits, women will sense a bit of class. If you don't tuck the shirt into your jeans, unbutton a button or two around the collar, and roll the sleeves up a little, she'll sense casualness. If you can pull off both classy and casual, she'll be paying attention to you and what you're saying, not stuck on what you're wearing, which is exactly what your goal is.

Blazer

Some situations, like weddings and barmitzvahs, require you to dress up more than usual, especially if you're usually stylish in casual settings. A nice blazer, thrown over a button-down shirt, plus jeans and dress shoes can usually carry the day. In fact, you'll probably look more stylish than guys wearing suits and ties unless the event specifically calls for them. At the very least, you will stand out because all of the other guys will look near identical.

Before you sport a blazer, make sure you find one that fits you well. When it's time to buy one, bring your favorite dress shirt with you and make sure a quarter-inch of sleeve shows beyond the blazer cuff when you're trying it on. Don't buy anything unless you look and feel good in it, because if you can't feel good in a store with no one around, you won't feel any better at a reception or dinner party.

Sunglasses

Even if it rains eight months out of the year where you live, you need to have a pair of stylish, but not necessarily expensive, sunglasses. With the right shades perched on top of your head you can pull off a classy, casual look despite whatever else you might be wearing. Plus, when the sun shines in your eyes, you can actually use the sunglasses so you don't have to squint and cover your eyes when talking to people.

Don't be embarrassed to wear sunglasses in the early evening because most people will assume you've been enjoying yourself in the sun all day, whether you have or not. Ray-Ban makes a lot of different styles, but a solid black pair and/or an aviator pair are fairly timeless. You can buy a name brand if you want something that will last a long time or a ten-dollar pair from a street vendor—it depends on your budget and your tendency to lose sunglasses.

Two-piece suit

Some companies throw elaborate Christmas parties and require you to wear a suit. Or, you may have a rich uncle getting married and you want to look the part. Or maybe you just enjoy looking like a million bucks when you go to the martini bar. Whatever the reason, most guys need at least one fasionable suit. Suits wear out and some styles go out of fashion, so if your current suit you would work better at a disco-themed party, it's time to upgrade. Also, for upscale events, wearing a threadbare, outdated suit is worse than wearing ripped jeans and a t-shirt because at least then you give the impression that you're not really trying.

Since it's preferred to have a tailored suit over an off-the-rack version, you should plan on buying a suit before you actually need one. Purchasing a tailored suit requires you to get measured and it can take a week or longer to have it altered, so it's better to have a pressed suit waiting in your closet just in case you need it. You should probably own at least two suits, one light in color and the other dark so you're covered for all four seasons. If you don't want to drop hundreds of dollars every year, make sure you take care of your suits by dry-cleaning them and storing them properly.

Simple Leather Wallet

Your wallet is your life, so regardless of whether you're buying a pack of gum or an expensive dinner, your wallet should be classy and stylish, just like you. If you stick with a simple, black, bi-fold leather wallet, without too many pockets, you're set. Avoid anything with Velcro or snaps and stay away from anything that has slogans, cartoons, or designer names on it.

Also, don't overstuff your wallet with random junk that you probably don't need to carry with you every day. Remove punch cards, grocery cards, old receipts, condoms, etc., and stick with a few bills, a credit card or two, your ID and medical card, and a picture of you and your niece, or you wearing a Santa hat. Make sure these cute photo is visible every time you open your wallet and women will be sure to ask you about it.

Black belt

Every guy should have at least one black leather belt. Belts shouldn't be too wide, nor too skinny and definitely not worn out due to overuse. Add a nice silver buckle that's also not too large and not too small and you're set. Although in most situations I recommend not tucking your shirt in, you should still wear a belt if you're wearing nice shoes.

Your belt should be sized one level above your pant size so you have some breathing room. You should be able to fasten your belt somewhere in the middle of the available loops and once it's on, you shouldn't notice it once you're out. Belts are used to tie a wardrobe together and keep your pant's waistline in place, not keep your pants up and your gut strapped down.

The Finer Details

As you acquire the essentials as well as the unique and stylish clothes that set you apart from the pack, never forget the one extra ingredient that helps attract women—your attention to detail. Most women think highly of men who appreciate the finer elements of style, so try not to disappoint. The following tips will help you fine-tune your look so you can catch the eyes of fashionable, discerning women everywhere.

★ Whether you decide to wear suits or distressed jeans and t-shirts, your clothes should be clean, wrinkle-free, and fit well.

★ Your pockets should carry the bare minimums so they don't look lumpy and overfilled.

★ When you wear belts, make sure they match your shoes. They should also match the type of pants you're wearing.

★ White socks should never be worn with dress shoes. If you don't have nice black socks or you've run out, do not improvise—buy some.

★ Dress shoes should always be shiny, scuff-free, and in decent shape. If the heels are worn down, the leather cracked, or the laces frayed, either have the shoes reconditioned or buy a new pair.

★ If you wear glasses, make sure the frames look appropriate for your face and head shape. If you can't find something that works for you, consider contacts or corrective surgery.

Women seem to always notice the little details, so take the time to look your best, from top to bottom. It may seem superficial, but that's the reality. Women initially judge men on how they look, talk and carry themselves. Whether you're wealthy or poor, if you dress like a bum, you'll be perceived as a bum. If you dress stylishly and look confident doing so, you'll be perceived as stylish and confident. So no matter where you go, if you think you might see women you're attracted to and want to approach, look your best.

Creating a Girl-Friendly Environment

Imagine that you've mastered all of the possible grooming techniques and you're dressed head-to-toe in the most stylish gear. You can throw Openers around like nobody's business and can hold a witty, intelligent conversation with just about anybody. You tell a woman that your crew is headed to another club and that she should come along and because you've got everything working for you, she eagerly agrees. As you grin at each other and hold hands, you stride toward the parking lot where you open the door of the oldest, ugliest rust-bucket in the parking lot. At this point she happens to remember why she couldn't possibly leave her friends at the bar and politely declines your invitation.

Physical Sex Appeal—In the Gym

As you already know, confidence and charm plus good grooming and style are great qualities to have to attract women. However, you can really enhance your attractiveness by eating healthily and working on your physique. Build and maintain all of these elements and you've got a lethal combination when it comes to sexual attraction. You might even find that you don't have to approach as much, since women will be hovering around you like moths to a light bulb.

Most guys are not genetically blessed to be born with a great body; it's something they have to focus on and work hard at. The benefits greatly outweigh the effort because you'll feel better, look better, and your confidence will shoot through the roof. After you've been working out for six months you can look in the mirror and see a guy that looks great and has a lot of sex appeal. When you start to believe it, everyone around you will believe it too, especially because it's true.

No matter how great the results of your workout regimen, never forget that a rock-hard body cannot replace humor, charm, wit, or any of the other qualities women look for. Only a small percentage of women look past a horrible personality and want a guy just for his looks. Often these women have flawed personalities themselves and can be superficial, jealous, and self-destructive. For the most part, you don't want to attract these types of women.

Since there are only about a thousand books devoted to health, fitness, and weightlifting, I'll only briefly gloss over the parts of the body that women find most attractive. You're encouraged to develop a balanced workout that hits all the major parts of your body, but if you want to focus on a few of the more "sexy" areas, these are the four that women seem to like the most:

If you plan to take a woman that you've just met somewhere in your car or to your house, both should be a reflection of the style and grooming you maintain when you go out on the town. You want to avoid situations like the above where everything was clicking until she saw your car or she had to

Glutes: Glutes are also known as your butt muscles and women undeniably love a man who has a nice ass. If you can fill a tight pair of jeans with a sculpted ass, you can push a woman's sexual imagination into overdrive. Squats are the classic exercise for glutes, but they also work out many of the other not-so-sexy areas of the body, which makes them an all-around good exercise.

Abs: Healthy, fitness-minded women like to see a six-pack on the guys they date. Walk along a beach with your shirt off and your abs tightening with every step and you'll see women look you up and down wondering what the rest of you looks like unclothed. Not every guy can attain visible abdominal muscles, so even if you're rock solid everywhere else, you might be genetically inclined to hold a little fat over your abs. If you get to this point, most women will still think you're hot as hell. For the rest of the guys with guts, the only six-pack you should be thinking about is the one you're *not going to drink so you can eventually see your toes.*

Shoulders: Muscular, powerful shoulders, as well as a strong back, help your entire body out, but the shoulders are also a muscle group that you can show off through a t-shirt. What's the point in just focusing on your abs when, by the time most women see them, they're moments away from sleeping with you? Strong shoulders and biceps are usually easier to attain than the other muscle groups since they're smaller and don't have as much fat to work through.

Biceps: Biceps are the easiest group to work out and given their size, show improvement faster than almost any other area. Hug a woman from behind as you watch the sun set and those tight biceps nudging her from both sides will not go unnoticed. Like your shoulders, biceps can get attention even when your shirt is on. Just don't be lame and force flex every time someone asks you for directions or you need to scratch your chin.

On Being Short

There is no getting around the fact that women like tall men, especially if they're tall as well. Unfortunately there is only so much you can do to add a little height to your frame, so you can either let your size prevent you from meeting a majority of women, or you can look at yourself in a different light and see someone who has lots of other great qualities. For many women, as long as you have a great personality, your height isn't a big deal.

What does it mean to be short, anyway? Next to an NBA player or a leggy supermodel, most people are considered short. In most parts of the Western world, the average height of a man is between 5'8" and 5'11, but that never stopped guys like Tom Cruise, Prince, or Jack Welch from ruling the world and it shouldn't hold you back either. Just because you don't reach the average height doesn't mean you should feel insecure or less of a man.

If you feel sorry for yourself and blame your lack of success with women on your height, women will pick up on this and believe it as well. Women are turned off by men who are insecure and unhappy, but if you're confident about who you are and where you're going, she won't be bothered by your height either. You can also increase your success rate by aiming for women closer to your own height who are still gorgeous, but petite.

If you don't have height going for you, focus on demonstrating your other attractive qualities like confidence, intelligence, a sense of humor, your good looks, or hundreds of others. As long as you have confidence and don't view yourself as short and therefore inadequate, women won't see your height as a flaw either and will be open to getting to know you. And remember, you don't need height in order to look good—that's where style and good grooming come into play.

use your disgusting bathroom. It's so crucial because if you've got your game together and you're in the final stretch of a pick-up, you don't want to break the mood because you weren't prepared for female company.

The experience a woman has in your car and your home can have the effect of either sealing the deal or ruining the possibility that you will ever hook up. Alcohol and darkness can definitely help mitigate a messy room or a rundown car, but in the morning she'll look to both of these to either affirm or counter her decision to sleep with you. If you planned on seeing her again and she sees condom wrappers in your bathroom, she'll probably lose your number.

Read the suggestions below and then take a look at both your car and your home and decide whether you need to make a few changes so that they're both appropriately "girl-friendly" before you leave the house.

Your Car

You know the difference between a clean car and a dirty one, so if there is any chance that a new lady-friend is going to travel with you, clean it or get it cleaned. You may also view your car as an essential part of your game, in which case it needs to be stocked with anything you might need to make the night go smoothly. Some of the usual items include blankets, pillows, gum, cologne, deodorant, underwear, condoms, mood music, air fresheners, wine, and anything else you might need. Just remember to keep these items in a box in your trunk, not laying all over the backseat or floorboards.

Your House or Apartment

As you already know, a traditional date at a restaurant or a movie isn't likely to result in much action. Instead, invest that time and energy into preparing your place for a night on the couch watching DVDs and drinking wine, which is much more conducive to nakedness. A respectable pad and a funny DVD help alleviate you from having to be "on" as much as you were when you first met, which can relieve a lot of stress.

In order to have a respectable pad, your place, just like your car, should be clean, at least the parts of it in which you might be entertaining. Unfortunately that doesn't mean "guy" clean, but "girl" clean, so just tidying up isn't going to cut it. Of course, picking up your random guy junk is essential, including the *Maxims,* the porn DVDs, the beer bottles, ashtrays, dirty dishes, clothes piled up around the bed, and anything else that might stink.

After you get your place somewhat organized, break out the vacuum, the mop, the dust rag, and everything else you watched your mom use when she cleaned the house. Pay special attention to the kitchen if you plan to be in there, since food crust on the counters is a turnoff. Even more important is the bathroom, which your lady will be guaranteed to check out even if she doesn't need to use it. Be prepared to get on your hands and knees and scrub, including all of the errant pubes on and around the toilet. A girl's bathroom is her sanctuary and even though yours will never live up to that standard, she needs to be comfortable doing her business and adjusting her makeup and clothes.

Next, break out the air fresheners, the incense, and the candles. Use a few of them as you clean and save a few for when you end up back at your place, showing her pictures of when you were riding the family dog at age two. I recommend finding some musky, male-oriented candles and incense instead of anything flowery. If you can't find anything, spray a few squirts of cologne around to cover up any remaining odors.

If all goes according to plan, you should end up in the bedroom, or if you're both in a hurry, the couch. In case you *do* make it to your bed, make sure you have clean sheets with a decent thread count so she doesn't get scratched up. She may be spending the night with you, so make sure she has her own pillows and a comforter in case she gets cold. Also, little details can really endear her to you, if that's what you want, so think about some getting some extra toothbrushes.

Style and Grooming Checklist

If the style you were originally sporting wasn't very up-to-date or required a significant overhaul, this chapter was probably a lot to take in. You certainly can't expect to read this entire chapter every time you need to leave the house. To make your life a little easier, the following checklist encapsulates some of the best practice tips on how to groom and style yourself before you go out. Consider photocopying it and adding your own checkboxes as needed, then consult the list every time you're getting ready until you eventually internalize all that you need to do to look your best.

★ **Shower:** There is no excuse for leaving the house without taking a shower. It takes five minutes involving water, soap, and a towel. Don't forget to wash and condition your hair as well.

★ **Hands:** Clip your nails if there is too much white showing on the tips. Scrape any dirt from underneath using the clearing tool on a set of nail clippers. Wash your hands when you're done and use some lotion to keep them smooth, if that's your thing.

★ **Face:** You don't have to shave if that's your look, but eyeball your entire face in the mirror to make sure it's clean and free of any lint, hair, or other "debris." Also check your eyes for crusties and your ears for any soap buildup.

★ **Hair:** Your hair grows regularly, so you should trim it regularly. Keep facial hair trim and remove any visible ear and nose hair. Style or comb your hair to your liking after it dries.

★ **Lips:** You don't want dry or chapped lips and no one will want to kiss them if you do. Keep lip balm in your bathroom and in your pocket and apply whenever they feel dry. Don't apply too much or you'll look like you're wearing lip gloss.

★ **Clothes:** After you put on your clothes and shoes, check yourself in a full-length mirror to make sure everything is in place and fits properly. If you have any hair or lint on your clothes, use a roller to remove it or change clothes.

★ **Shoes:** Women typically look at a man's shoes within a minute or two of meeting him, if not during his approach. If you're wearing dress shoes, make sure they've been shined and aren't scuffed up. If you're wearing casual shoes, make sure they're clean and don't stink.

★ **Scent:** Use scented body soap, scented lotion, aftershave, and/or cologne as long as it's done in moderation and the scents don't conflict or over-power one another. If you have a collection, go for a cologne that fits the mood or venue you're going to, like a sporty scent for the beach or a woodsy fragrance for a classy, old-school restaurant.

Chapter 5

Understanding Women

In this Chapter

★ Examining why women act and react emotionally and how to work with it, not against it

★ Getting to know different female character traits and how to choose a type that's right for you

★ Revealing what female sexual confidence is and how to find out if a woman has it

Understanding Women

While it's impossible for a man to ever truly understand a woman and vice versa, it *is* possible to understand how men and women think and act differently. If you never bother to learn these differences and incorporate them into the way you communicate with women, you'll always be at a disadvantage. While women never learn, or want to learn, how men think and operate, they do a much better job of navigating our differences. In other words, when it comes to relationships women have been working from a position of strength for decades and in some cases, men pay the price for their ignorance.

Men are often frustrated by women's behavior and are quick to blame hormones, penis envy, or a host of other excuses that are both wrong and unhelpful in learning how to work with the fairer sex so you both can get what you want. In this chapter, you'll begin by learning not only how men and women think and act differently, but also how to treat women if you hope to stay in the game beyond one or two relationships. Women talk to one another and karma is a bitch, so you want to learn how to enjoy yourself with women without hurting or humiliating them. It's both possible and desirable to have many sexual relationships one after another, or even concurrently, *and* hold your head up high.

Most men don't spend much time considering what type of women they like to spend time with, usually because they haven't been with enough women to be able to pick and choose what works for them and what doesn't. This can lead to a host of problems that never seem to resolve themselves, even after multiple relationships and/or several marriages. If you truly want to be the kind of guy who chooses the women he spends time with, you have to set standards of who you find acceptable and who you find appalling. The second half of this chapter details many positive and negative female character traits that will help you make better decisions on who to reel in and who to cut loose.

What Women Say Versus What They Do

For centuries and beyond women have had the unique ability to say one thing, while their actions directly contradicted what they said they would do. Men and women may lie to each other in equal amounts, but the prize for being able to deceive oneself belongs solely to women. Understanding this will help you communicate with women as well as influence their behavior to your benefit.

Men have been trying to figure out why a woman's mind works the way it does for thousands of years. For men, understanding the inner workings of the female gender might allow them to avoid the frustrations that arise when interacting with women, such as rejection, guilt, intimidation, and self-exploitation. The media portrays women as if the way they think and act are incomprehensible to men, either because women are too complex, men are too dense, or both. Pushing that idea helps sell self-help books and "battle of the sexes" sitcoms, but men and women are actually quite similar in the way they act.

While sociologists focus on the differences between men and women, it's in the vast similarities and *one* major difference where you can make leaps in understanding how women think. While men are slaves to the testosterone coursing through them, women are equally victim to their dominant hormone, estrogen, which, among other things, makes them far more emotional than logical. So the secret to understanding how women interpret the world, including the men in their lives, is to realize that they think, act, and react based on their emotions.

Women and Emotions

Because women act through their emotions, you can't always take what they say at face value, especially when it comes to their relationships with men. For the most part, men and women respond similarly to matters of loyalty, sexual desire, infidelity, and fantasies. However, since women filter what they say through their emotions, they can camouflage their true intentions in a way that makes them seem more acceptable to their social circles and society as a whole.

For example, a woman will never say that she's attracted to controlling men who make her suffer through emotional roller coaster rides. Instead, she'll say she's looking for a nice, romantic, intelligent man. Why? Because her emotions tell her that it sounds right and it's the romantic ideal. Or, a woman may love getting on all fours and having her ass spanked, but it takes a lot of mental contortions for her to verbalize it. In fact, as a guy, you will probably miss it, but her friends will pick up on it.

Most women end up doing what their heart tells them, not what their mind and mouth are spouting. Fortunately, no matter what seems socially appropriate to her, it's millions of years of evolution and the profound events of her childhood that drive her actions, not the good intentions and social rules burned into her brain by her family, school, and church. Believe it or not, it's to your benefit that women don't always deliver on their words, so long as you know it.

You will only waste your time and energy trying to understand *why* a woman's behavior is driven by her emotions instead of logic. What you really need to understand is that it's a woman's actions and not her words that mean much of anything. If you ever find yourself confused by what a woman says to you, or if you're going crazy because she says one thing and does another, consider the following:

★ Ultimately, a woman's actions are very similar to a man's actions when physically possible.

★ Ask yourself what you would do in her situation and the chances are high that she will do exactly what you would have done, even if it contradicts what she said.

★ You can rarely analyze or argue with a woman's emotional arguments and don't try to convince her using logic.

★ A woman's words regarding love and relationships are of little value given the "cover" she must create for her true thoughts and feelings, so place value on her actions instead.

As with any advice given about women in this book, consider it a generalization that applies more often than not. Everyone is unique, including their words and their actions, so use the above as a guiding principle instead of an inflexible rule.

Treating Women as Women

Most guys, especially those who didn't grow up with women in their lives, believe that women are inherently better than men. This belief is derived from the notion that all forms of sex, except marital, missionary sex, are morally wrong and that men want other types of sex (pre-marital, oral, anal, etc.) and women do not. Most men are ashamed to have these feelings when they're around someone to whom they are attracted. However, as discussed in the previous section, women act very similarly to men, especially when it comes to sex, but their words have to betray those thoughts and actions.

The media tends to portray women as virtuous saviors and in the instances where they portray women as lustful, they usually get punished for their promiscuity. Plus, the deepest relationship a man usually has is with a woman, his mother, so most men believe that all women are similarly good and well-intentioned. As men, we are extremely lucky that this is not the case.

Once you realize that women aren't inherently "good" or "virtuous," at least compared to men, you begin to understand that there is no reason to give women special attention. That's not to say you should treat women like garbage, but you can't allow yourself to put women you don't know on a pedestal. If you treat a woman as if she's better than you, she will treat you accordingly and you'll quickly be relegated to the "nice guy" bin.

Unfortunately, few men understand that women think and act a lot like men. The nice guys of the world continue to betray their confidence, letting their egos get crushed because women have become so used to being treated as superior to men. Once you realize that women have the capacity for self-interest and ruthlessness as men, you'll become a stronger person without fear of approaching or being rejected, because you understand that they're *just* women, no more or less—just people with whom you're interacting.

Once you understand how women think and how they can be just as manipulative as men, you should refrain from putting them on a pedestal without them first proving that they're worth that sort of treatment. Women who expect special treatment just because they were born female are brats and you need to treat them accordingly.

You might be surprised when you call women on their shitty behavior and they realize that you see right through them. They usually stop being bratty because they know what they're doing and it's embarrassing to be caught acting like a child. They also recognize you as someone to be reckoned with, someone who deserves and demands respect. If they don't get it, you'll have to make things clearer by simply turning your back to them, finding someone else to talk to, and slowly moving your back toward them. After that, it shouldn't be difficult for her to understand the point you're making.

Jealousy and Competition

Many women like having more than one guy fawn over them and compete for their attention as it gives them options. They understand how much power it gives them and for that reason, they hate to be on the other side of the competitive equation. Women love to be competed for, but despise the feeling that they're competing with other women for the affections of one guy. Competing for a man doesn't feel right to women, so they try as quickly as possible to head off any competition, secure the "prize," and become the alpha female.

In many cases, a woman gains true passion for a man when she starts to feel that she could lose him at any moment. By demonstrating to a woman that your affection is not a "given" and is actively being sought by other women, you convey that you have options and your relationship can never be taken for granted. However, if you put up with abuse, head games, and disrespect, she never experiences the stress that she might lose someone she's attracted to and any passion she had quickly fades away.

Sometimes, in order to present yourself as a "catch" and ensure you won't be taken for granted, you have to create a little bit of perceived competition. A small amount of jealousy can make you seem more attractive in a woman's eyes, causing her to believe she has to put effort into getting and keeping you. You can create some innocent competition just by entering bars and clubs with female friends. It's even more effective if you invite a woman to hang out with you and your friends and when she shows up, she sees that most of your friends are women, not men. This may not make every woman jealous, but it would keep most on their toes.

If you feel like this is tough talk and somewhat insulting to women, then you still don't understand why your own response to a woman's behavior causes her to lose respect for you. This isn't about treating a woman poorly; it's about treating yourself with respect and not allowing a woman to view you as anything less than equal. Read and reread this chapter until you understand that a woman is just another person, someone you wouldn't be the least bit intimidated to walk up and talk to. If you're scared to talk to a woman, even the most beautiful woman in the world, then you view yourself as inferior. If that's your own opinion of yourself, you can never expect women to treat you with respect.

Respecting Women

Most guys, if not all, wish they had the good looks and effortless charm to attract any woman they want without putting forth much effort. Unfortunately, very few men have this ability, so they resort to more reprehensible methods, specifically manipulating women into following their deceived hearts and surrendering to a night of passion. There is no doubt that lying and manipulating women can be an effective way to get what you want, but it doesn't take long for even the worst players to realize there is no thrill or excitement involved in tricking women into having sex.

To better your ability to meet and attract women, you have to be willing to give them more credit in terms of intelligence and sexual confidence—in other words, respect. Women love and enjoy sex, so there is absolutely no need to deceive them into doing something they know they want to do. In turn, women will give you a lot more credit when you let them know where you stand, and allow them to decide for themselves whether they like what they hear.

Just because you treat women with respect, however, doesn't mean you let them walk all over you. You shouldn't consider yourself a jerk just because you treat women as equals, and women shouldn't think of you as a jerk either. You just have to subtly let women know they don't get special treatment just because they're women; they have to prove themselves in your eyes if they expect such treatment.

Finally, avoid being a used car salesmen who always wants to make the sale without ever thinking about repeat business. In the long run, once you have solid game, you'll feel better about yourself when you know a woman is with you because she's attracted to you, not because you lied to her. Plus, women *do* pay attention when they see flirtatious guys with women that keep coming back to them and who have nothing but good things to say about them. Despite being such incorrigible flirts, women want to know what's so great about these types of guys and you can be one of them.

Some guys need explicit pointers on how to treat women with whom they're romantically involved, so the following are a few of the big rules on acting like a man and treating women with respect:

Don't Kiss and Tell

Women hate finding out about their sexual exploits through their network of friends or, even worse, casual acquaintances. Look at the big picture and don't tell people explicit details about your love life. It's impossible to refrain from telling your close friends who you're having sex with, but try to avoid the details. Think of it this way: If you can manage to keep your mouth shut, women are more likely to keep playing naughty games with you without having to worry about hearing about it at work, at the gym, in class, or anywhere else.

Don't Lie

No one enjoys being lied to and women especially detest being lied to just so someone can have sex with them. Making empty promises to a woman just to satisfy your own short-term needs is disrespectful. If word gets out that you're a liar, your reputation suffers long-term repercussions and if you live in a small town, word gets around fast. One of the major points of this book is that you don't have to be rich or famous to attract women, so why would you need to lie about it?

Don't Cheat

As with lying, there is no honor in cheating. This holds true for poker, for golf, and for sex and relationships. If you've really been working on your game and you're good at what you do, you should be able to confidently end relationships when it's time to move on. Cheating is for men who are weak, who can't be honest about who they are and what they want, so they have to make up stories, avoid certain places, get their stories straight, and other behavior that you can't describe as anything other than cowardly. If you're unhappy with the woman you're with, end it and move on. Plus, every time a guy cheats on a woman, he makes it that much harder for the rest of us.

Types of Women

Even though the primary aim of this book is to help you meet women, you should give some consideration to what happens after you meet them for the first time. Whether you're just looking for a hook-up or a long-term relationship, you're going to have to spend some time, maybe a *lot* of time, getting to know them as they're getting to know you. With all of the broken, twisted people out there, both men and women, you need to get some sense of the types of women you actually want to hang out with past the initial flirting phase.

If your end goal is to find one, or maybe three, great women to spend your time with, you need to really scan the terrain of personality traits and find a few that you like. Are you looking for a free spirit who is always up for an adventure? Or maybe you like the sweet girl-next-door type who, once you really get to know her, is extremely devoted to you. Perhaps you just want an independent sex kitten who loves her own life, but who reliably makes time to get her freak on with you. As you can tell, different types of guys can dig completely different, but very cool, types of girls.

Almost as important as knowing the types of women you like is knowing the types of women you should stay away from. The ultra-feminist, the man hater, the diva, the drama queen; you've probably met them all in your lifetime and you may have even dated them. The difference now is that you're in the driver's seat. You don't passively latch on to any relationship that comes your way just because you don't know when the next will fall in your lap. From now on, you'll charge into social situations, chat up women, and feel them out for who they are and then decide whether you think you might hit it off. With that in mind you should have some criteria for who is a keeper and who to throw back into the sea. If your sole aim is to hook up with women left and right and drop them the next day, you can probably skip this section, since personality doesn't play much of a factor.

While reading through this section, remember that these are traits, not people. Only stock characters in movies are solely "sweet" or "angry." Use this list to help you come up with a list of qualities you do and do not want in a woman you want to hang out with. It's always easier to get what you want out of life if you know what you want; otherwise you just end up with whatever breezes your way.

Sweetheart

Sweethearts are positive, content with life, always upbeat and a blast to be around. They're usually genuine, don't have much to complain about and are always happy to see you. You'll know a sweetheart when you always find yourself looking forward to spending time with them. True sweethearts are usually snapped up out of the dating pool right away, so they're pretty rare. But if you can find one, you've got something special on your hands.

Generous

Generous women are extremely giving in both their time and money, not only with the men in their lives, but their friends, family, even complete strangers. Some men are intimidated by women with money, but if you can get over yourself, you will find generous women to be a pleasant alternative to self-centered, gold-diggers. If a generous woman likes you, you shouldn't care if she wants to take you to Vegas or Hawaii. If

Bitchy

Bitchy women are malicious, spiteful, overbearing harpies notable for their intense ill-will and spitefulness to most other human beings. Women who are bitchy usually possess a majority of the other negative personality traits, especially being controlling and self-centered. Unfortunately, some of the best-looking women are bitchy, but they can be easily identified and dismissed by their perma-scowl and imperial strut.

Gold-digger

Gold-diggers are high maintenance because they expect a man to pay for their entire life simply because they were born female. Gold-diggers fully expect men to pay for drinks, dinner, trips, clothes, jewelry, and more without the slightest bit of guilt or compulsion to reciprocate, ever. Another word for gold-digger is prostitute, although sometimes without the sex. Gold-diggers are greedy and have no

she's going to splash her money around on somebody, it might as well be you. Generous women usually love being generous, so it's best never to make an issue out of it.

concept of "enough"—their only interest is in getting what they want without working for it. Luckily, gold-diggers are easy to spot, so you can avoid them.

Fair

A fair women is a true feminist—not a radical man-hater who thinks that equality means "I demand equal rights and an equal salary, but a man still has to take care of me." Women who are fair genuinely like men and understand that equality means equality across the board, from holding the door open to fighting on the frontlines. They believe that a relationship should be a 50/50 partnership and are more than willing to shoulder their half of the responsibilities and dating expenses—just because it's the right thing to do.

Feminist

Feminists believe that all of society's ills have been orchestrated by men and that the world would be utopia if only the male "patriarchy" would allow women to rule exclusively. In their heart of hearts, they believe that men are the root of all evil. Women who believe these absurdities live in a fantasy world and have no problem treating men in a way they would never allow themselves to be treated. You can easily identify feminists by their incessant mantra—"All men think with their penises."

Sex Kitten

Sex kittens love men and sex and make no apologies about it. They don't sell sex or use it as a tool to

Tease

Teases flirt with any decent-looking guy within sight and flaunt their sexuality at every opportunity. Teas-

manipulate men; they just naturally crave it. Sex kittens should not be confused with nymphomaniacs, because they don't absolutely need sex with just anybody, but they somehow bypassed the social conditioning that demands that women save themselves for the "right" guy. Unfortunately, other women hate sex kittens because of their liberated attitude and because they think they're just "giving it away." Men love sex kittens for their free spirit and because they're actually honest about their sex drive.

es love to bask in their sexual power by attracting many men and eventually shutting them all down. Most teases sexually matured earlier than their peers and realized the power it can give a young girl. From the men to the boys, they were able to flirt to get their way. It worked then and it usually works now. The bottom line is you can't trust a tease—they crave attention and if someone better comes along, they'll quickly disappear. Teases can be fun to play with for a few minutes, but avoid wasting too much time on them.

Buddy

Similar to sweethearts, buddies are also a joy to be around. Buddies are the kind of women you're totally in sync with—you like the same things, watch the same TV shows, enjoy going to the same places. You can spend five minutes with them and feel like you've known them for years. They're always on your side, laugh at all your jokes, and call you just to say "hi"

Self-Centered

Self-centered women think only of themselves, usually at the expense of everyone around them. In social situations, they need to be the center of attention or they're unhappy. They are selfish, self-indulgent, self-serving narcissists who usually grew up as "Daddy's little girl." Now that they've grown up, they're looking for a replacement, someone that allows them to indulge because they genuinely miss you. A word of warning, though—with female "buddies" you have to make your romantic interest known from the outset because if they get it into their mind that you are "just friends," it's almost impossible to undo.

in their self-centered behavior. It's one thing to treat a woman like a brat—it's a great way to flirt—but it's something altogether different when they act like a brat. Unless you enjoy being with someone who acts like a child, stay away and let her be someone else's problem.

Straight-shooter

Straight-shooters are women who know how to communicate well with men. With straight-shooters, there aren't any head games, flaky behavior, or expectations of men to be mind readers. Straight-shooters are confident and have no trouble picking up the phone and asking a guy out if they want to. Straight-shooters also do what they say they will do—not say one thing and do the opposite. Although a straight-shooter may be blunt at times, you will always know where you stand and you never have to spend hours trying to decode contradictory or emotion-based behavior.

Dreamer

Women who grew up on a steady diet of Lifetime movies and romance novels sometimes grow into women who expect Prince Charming to sweep her off her feet and ride off to an English castle. That may be a slight exaggeration, but there are definitely single women out there reading bridal magazines, just waiting for a guy to "save" them. You don't want to be the guy who's responsible for someone who was coddled by her parents and constantly referred to as "princess." Some women's hopes and dreams tread heavily on a fantasy life that just doesn't exist.

Independent

Independent women are great women to find if you don't have a lot of time to invest in a full-blown relationship or you're the type of guy who needs a lot of space. Independent women have full, rich lives of their own and are happy to pursue their own interests with or without you. Independent women usually want a man in their life, but never *need* a man in their life. Since they own their attitude and handle their own responsibilities, they're never looking for men to solve their problems or blame men when things don't go their way.

Loyal

Loyal women never cheat on you or stay on the lookout for a "better deal." When you go out, loyal women don't scan the room for other guys, but keep their attention focused on you, the man in their life. They're also more apt to stick around if times get tough. Depending on where you live, loyal women

Needy

Women who agree with everything you say, who suddenly like the same music you do, and who don't understand the concept of "me" time are needy. They literally need you to be in their presence or on the phone or they're unhappy. Needy women have deep psychological problems, so avoid getting involved with them. Problems arise when you end things—annoying phone calls turn into broken tail lights, which turn into calls to your boss or break-ins at your home. If you think the woman you're talking to might be needy, walk away.

Elusive

Elusive women initially come across as flirty and romantic, but you eventually find out they're one of the "walking wounded," women who were hurt in a past relationship, sometimes several. Elusive women sabotage their relationships so they never get hurt again. Dealing with elusive women is an exer-

can be difficult to find, especially in larger cities where their own experiences have taught them to be ever-suspiscious of men. However, most women have the capacity for loyalty; you just have to demonstrate that you're worthy of it.

Carefree

While many women are chomping at the bit to get married, carefree women haven't fallen prey to any such agenda. They're happy with their life and happy just to be with you. With carefree women you don't get any "Where is our relationship going?" questions or window-shopping for rings at the jewelry store. They may want to get married at some point, but they are in no hurry—they think that if it happens, it will happen naturally. Their carefree attitude usually extends to everything they do in life, which can make carefree women very easy and enjoyable to be with.

cise in frustration as they initially show great interest in you and then quickly end any possibility of taking things further. They may repeat this cycle many times, so once you start getting any pushback from an elusive woman, end it.

Controlling

Typically, controlling women have little control over their own lives and that powerlessness gets redirected into dictating every phase of their boyfriend's life. From what to wear, who they can talk to, and what they can eat, controlling women's tentacles slowly pervade every facet of their boyfriend's existence. If you don't play along, they withhold sex, cry fake tears, scream, and finally pout until they get kicked to the curb. Controlling women will try just about anything to force you to succumb to their demands. If you feel like a woman might be trying to change you, she probably is.

Self-Confident

Self-confident women accept themselves for who they are and are comfortable with their good features as well as the bad, plus they usually feel the same about you and your features. Self-confident women are secure with themselves and don't need constant attention to shore up a sagging ego. Self-confident women actually have plenty of self-esteem and are always going in their own positive direction.

Interesting

The standard "personality" jokes aside, women who are interesting and have a great personality can be a wonderful find. True, they might not be the best-looking women in the room, but they might be. Beyond looks, their intelligence, wit, and sparkling presence light up a room and they draw people to them like a magnet. Interesting women have a great personality and are so charming it easily overcomes any

Insecure

Insecure women are really nice at first, until you realize that their pleasantness is rooted in their insecurities in themselves and their ability to find a man. Insecure women are always stressed that they aren't good enough for you and need constant affirmation that they're attractive and loved. One way to spot an insecure woman is through her mannerisms such as incessantly worrying about her makeup and hair.

Dumb

Most guys like to hang out with women who get their jokes and don't need instructions to open a door. Dumb women certainly have their place in the world, but problems arise when they want to hang out or meet your friends or visit you at work. Dumb women also don't handle their emotions very well, so while you can easily dump them, some of them flip a switch from dumb to angry. You want to

deficiencies in the looks depart-ment, just because they're so great to be around.

avoid having to explain to an angry woman why she's too dumb to see "seriously."

Low Maintenance

Unfortunately in short supply these days, low maintenance women don't care about how much money you have—they just like you for you and not for what they can get from you. Low maintenance women are also likely to be fair-minded and will gladly pay their share of any dating expenses. If you can find a low maintenance woman, hang on to her.

Diva

Divas are in love with themselves and no one else. Granted, most are beautiful creatures, sometimes with actual talents such as dancing, sing-ing, and acting, but they use their talents as an excuse to treat everyone else like shit. In their mind, they're superstars and everyone around them are just "regular" people. If you find yourself holding her purse, picking up her dry-cleaning, or any of the thousands of tasks she can't handle, then you're with a diva.

Conclusion

It's sad to say, but finding women with an abundance of positive qualities is becoming scarcer in today's world, so if you find someone that has any combination of the good traits previously discussed, act fast. Just remember to keep your checklist in mind when you meet women—keep your eyes open and you just might get lucky and find your ideal woman.

Sexual Self-Esteem

We've covered in detail most of the desirable and less-than-desirable qualities to look for in a woman. For those guys who aren't in the game for the long haul, the ones who date many women at a time or enjoy very brief encounters, personality traits aren't much of a deciding factor. A guy looking for fun doesn't mind so much if a women is controlling or insecure or a hopeless dreamer because he is, as every woman will tell you, interested in only one thing.

If your motive is one-night, one-week, or one-month stands, you need to be able to identify women who have enough self-confidence to get involved with a guy without getting emotionally attached. Contrary to what your mom may have told you, not all women are looking for a relationship at all times in their lives. However, some women also pretend not to be looking for a relationship and will "go along" with your lifestyle with the hopes of hooking you into something long-term. Although it might not be your fault, it becomes your problem, so it pays to find women with your frame of mind.

Hopefully, after reading this book, you no longer feel ashamed for wanting and pursuing sex. If you're confident, you should be able to talk freely about where you're at in life, and explain that you're just looking to enjoy yourself at the moment. If you can be open about who you are and what you're looking for, you're much more likely to find women who open up to you and express the same desire. There are millions of women out there who are just looking for fun and experience and they've built up enough self-esteem that they don't believe in the double-standard applied to sexually experienced women.

Beyond just being open about your own state of mind and what you're looking for in life right now, there are also some signs to look out for and some

Confidence in Valuing Your Time

Have you ever hung out with a woman you didn't know very well, but once you got home you started thinking about how you could avoid seeing or speaking to her ever again? Did you ask yourself why you didn't see it coming and how you could have avoided it? A lot of guys, especially in their early twenties, never look past a woman's good looks to see the whole package, including the emotional baggage she might be carrying. Perhaps if they did, they would have noticed that some of the women they talk to, date, and have relationships with were trouble just waiting to happen.

Next time you find yourself attracted to someone, run through a mental checklist of all the negative female personality traits listed in this section. No matter how attractive she might seem, if she comes across as a gold-digger, a diva, or any of the other disastrous personality types, find a way to end things as quickly as possible. It's hard for some guys to turn down the prospect of sex, even when they know she's a freak show, but eventually, you will learn to avoid getting sucked into relationships with psychos, stalkers, and drama queens, no matter how hot they are.

tests you can use to make sure the women you talk to are capable of enjoying what you have to offer—sex with no strings attached. It shouldn't take more than five or ten minutes to find out whether you're talking to a free spirit or a relationship-seeker. As you would assume, it's better to do your investigating upfront before you wake up with someone who says you're her new boyfriend.

You might think you're writing off good-looking women too quickly, but if you're just looking for fun, you have to make sure she has all of the right qualities so you can avoid guilt and harassment. She needs to have the right mindset to know what she's looking for and enough self-confidence not to feel guilty about it. She also has to have some interest in you and preferably no baggage in the form of a husband or boyfriend. As you practice steering your conversation through a few of the following tests, you'll find it increasingly easier to find desirable women who don't want to leave their blow-dryer at your house:

Indicators

Indicators aren't tests, but rather clues to keep your eyes and ears open for. You're looking specifically for body language and traits that let you know she has sexual self- confidence. If you pick up on more than two or three of these, you should probably move on:

★ She doesn't look you in the eye when she talks.

★ She slouches and her posture slumps inward.

★ She fidgets a lot and looks distracted.

★ She puts herself down as a way for you to disagree with her and affirm that she's pretty, interesting, etc.

★ She fishes for compliments for similar affirmation.

★ She seems unsure of what she's saying to you but upticks the end of her sentences, i.e. ending statements in the form of questions.

★ She is obviously interested in you, but seems embarrassed when you get close or casually touch her.

All of the above are signals to watch out for, but since every person and every conversation is different, you may not be able to pick up on any overt mannerisms. If you really want to find out whether she is an insecure relationship-seeker, you might need to force the issue by employing a few little tests.

Ask her opinion

Don't ask her opinion as you would for an opinion Opener. Instead, ask about more subjective experiences like movies, music, food, etc. She might not have an opinion on the things you're asking about and that's perfectly fine as long as she admits it. However, many women with low self-esteem act as though they should have an opinion on something if you do. If that's the case, she will make up an opinion, usually paraphrasing your own answers. If you get the feeling she is just agreeing with you, she probably is and it's a sign of low self-esteem.

Joke about sex

If you're trying to find out whether a woman is open to casual sex without the usual commitments, you obviously need to be able to talk about sex freely without her getting embarrassed. Not only does sex talk help steer her mind in the right direction, it also helps you find out whether she's confident about her sexual performance and whether she judges you for bringing up sex so soon in the conversation. She doesn't necessarily have to fully engage you in what you're talking about, but she should be able to listen without being offended. If the entire concept of sex makes her uncomfortable, you should move on.

Tease her

Casual teasing is a great way to get some playful, casual touching started. When you tease her, she should know you're kidding without you having to tell her and should have no problem teasing you back. It's a good sign when a woman can both dish it out and take it without getting her feelings hurt, or needs to get nasty with comebacks and put-downs. If you can't tease her without her getting upset, she's taking you too seriously as if something is truly at stake between you two other than "fun." As long as you aren't teasing her about personal things that really touch people's nerves, she should be able to play along. Someone who takes flirting seriously doesn't have the right mindset for casual sex.

Compliment her

As you already know, you should only use compliments when a woman least expects them. However, when you eventually give her one, you should carefully observe her reaction to get a sense of her sexual self-esteem. The chart below is a guideline in determining a woman's level of self-esteem based on her reaction to a compliment. Her reaction shouldn't be your sole consideration; it should be used in conjunction with her overall demeanor and the other indicators and tests described in this section.

Reaction	Self-Esteem Level
Denies it	Low
Blushes, smiles, and looks away	Slightly low
Returns a compliment right away	Good
Blushes, looks at you, and smiles	Better
Simply thanks you	High
Agrees	Too high

If you can recognize a woman with high sexual self-esteem and the proper state of mind to engage a guy for casual sex, you will save yourself a lot of time trying to sweet talk the wrong women.

Conclusion

While understanding women might seem impossible, it's worth some amount of effort to be aware of how they think about the men to whom they're attracted. The most important lesson to take away from this chapter is that women and men aren't that different in the way they act when it comes to sex and relationships, but usually light years apart in terms of how they talk about it. Instead of focusing a lot of attention on what a woman says about men and relationships, pay close attention to her actions because they tell you so much more about a woman than what her friends, family, and society expect her to say.

It's also a good idea to have a sense of what type of women you're attracted to and, more importantly, willing to spend time with. If you aim for the dumbest women with the fakest body parts, you can easily end up with severely insecure and emotionally disturbed women who challenge your sanity and drain your bank account. Your goal isn't to *pretend* to be choosy because it demonstrates social value, but to actually *be* selective about the women you spend your time with. After reading this chapter you should have a mental checklist of the qualities you're attracted to and those you aren't, so you can loosely follow this list when you meet women.

Finally, after you meet a woman who appears to match your basic requirements, you should try to find out how much sexual self-confidence she has. Knowing whether she's insecure about her body, comfortable with how she looks, or thinks she's "all that and a bag of chips," can help you determine whether she would be a good one-night stand, casual partner, or long-term girlfriend. More often than not, knowing whether a woman is sexually self-confident tells you if you're going home with someone that night. If you're looking to get laid in the near term, look for signs as to whether a woman would be up for it. This can save you a lot of time and energy so you don't spend all night talking to someone who won't have sex until marriage.

Chapter 6

What Women Want

In this Chapter

★ Getting to know the male personality traits that women like and dislike

★ Maximizing the impact of your most desirable qualities and downplaying the rest

★ Identifying the things women notice about a guy when he approaches and how to emphasize them

What Women Want

Asking what women want from men may seem like a loaded question. Most men feel as though it's impossible to ever grasp what women seek in men, since every one of them appears to have a different set of ever-evolving requirements. Not only that, women further complicate men's efforts to meet their expectations by stating what they want, while in practice appearing to be attracted to a completely different set of qualities. At least most women are honest about how fickle they are when it comes to men and relationships, but they seem incapable of ever making it any easier for men to please them.

For most men, the difficulty in pleasing women stems from the very act of *trying* to please them by sacrificing being who they are. A lot of guys are quick to compromise who they are to adapt to the needs and wants of a woman they're attracted to, quite often with rapidly diminishing returns. While it's doubtful a woman would acknowledge it, the more they notice you actively trying to cater to their whims, the more they realize they can do better than you—at least during any courtship process. With that said, there are ways to demonstrate attractive behavior while still remaining true to yourself, which serves to increase your confidence and in turn, your attractiveness.

You've probably met at least a few guys in your lifetime who lived by their own rules, who never compromised who they were just to please a woman, and who had more women chasing after them than they knew what to do with. These guys have a few things going for them that most women find irresistible, namely confidence and knowing that they possess desirable qualities that attract women. You're about to learn about the qualities that almost all women find universally attractive and which ones they find offensive. Regardless of what you look like or how much money you have, if you can master the ability to confidently demonstrate attractive traits and downplay negative ones, women will find you attractive.

By displaying certain attractive qualities, women can feel happy, intrigued, and safe—among other emotions—while in your presence. It's not because you're trying to do specific things to make a particular woman happy, but because you *know* you possess desirable qualities and effortlessly highlight them by being your best self. Not only that, but you recognize your weaknesses and consciously minimize them when you're around attractive women. Finally, since good first impressions are based on the visual as well as the emotional, you know which of your physical features to flaunt and which to conceal.

By combining all of these elements—emphasizing your best qualities and features and down-playing unattractive ones—you no longer have to *try* to please women through specific actions. You can leave the house knowing that you're attractive as-is and without having to worry about whether you have a woman's approval. You know you're a catch because you understand the types of traits women find attractive, and if you happen to not meet a woman's approval, you can assume it's because of her personal issues, not because of who you are or what you look like.

Guy Traits That Women Hate

Hopefully you aren't naïve enough to believe that it's just women who have personality problems. You might even be hesitant to approach women because you already know there is something about you that just turns them off and away. Instead of digging a little deeper as to what the problem is, maybe you've accepted that women just don't seem to like you. That's unfortunate because it might just be one little trouble area that isn't as severe as you think. However, even little negative quirks send the wrong signal and throw up all kinds of red flags in a woman's mind as to why you might be trouble.

Women tend to have finely tuned antennae when it comes to sniffing out a guy's weaknesses, almost to a fault. One of the main reasons why guys need to learn more about what women look for in men is because women are quick to make snap decisions on whether or not a guy is "right" for them. Women do themselves a disservice by holding up a single perceived flaw as a reason why it "just wouldn't work." Consequently many end up spend their weeknights bitching to their girlfriends on the phone while watching *Sex and the City*. Regardless, most women are quick to write off guys for seemingly minor transgressions, so don't give them an excuse to turn you down before they even get a chance to get to know you.

Read through all the negative traits below and really examine yourself and be honest about whether any of them apply to you. I'm not suggesting that you need to completely change who you are to match a woman's idealistic version of a man, but every guy has his positives and his negatives, and if you want to attract a multitude of women, you must emphasize the positive and downplay the negative. Your aim is to create a good first impression, so if you find yourself consistently arguing, complaining, or bragging about yourself, you need to condition yourself to keep it in check.

Needy

Needy guys are overly emotional and share all their feelings with a woman from the first moment they meet. Someone who is emotionally needy also has little confidence and needs constant validation on his relationship, job, and friendships. Most women look for a strong, independent guy they can depend on during good times and bad. If you're constantly relying on a woman to prop up your self-esteem, she probably won't be around for long. Women usually bring their own set of insecurities to a relationship, so they don't want to have to deal with yours too.

If you think you might be classified as a needy guy, you need to learn how to keep your innermost feelings to yourself when you first meet someone. Sharing your doubts and insecurities about yourself before she has a complete picture of who you are and where you're coming from is often a dealbreaker. Once you find yourself in a full-blown relationship, you can start to reveal some, if not all, of the inner you. In fact, she'll actually appreciate knowing what's on your mind and you'll deepen the bond that's developing, but remember that timing is everything when it comes to truly opening up.

Predictable

Nobody likes to be with someone who is completely predictable, especially when they're just getting to know them. Guys who follow strict routines and never throw out any surprises are boring to be with. When women say they want a nice guy, they can mean a lot of different things, but it never means they want someone who's predictable. This is especially true when you meet someone for the first few times you hang out. Most people live boring lives to begin with, so instead of adding to the problem, keep things lively by being unpredictable.

You don't have to be a "bad boy" or completely crazy to come off as unpredictable, but you *do* need to become a free spirit of sorts who can inject something fresh into an otherwise dull moment. These are the moments she'll remember and tell her friends about, and it keeps her guessing what might happen next. After she gets to know you better, you can still keep your routines; just remember to throw in a few surprises along the way to keep things fresh. Plus, she's likely to do the same for you, keeping you interested and on your toes.

Arrogant

If your ego has a hard time making it through the door and you're always condescending toward people around you, such as waitresses and cabbies and anyone else you have to insult to make yourself feel important, then you're an asshole. True, some women like assholes, but those types of people deserve to spend the rest of their miserable lives together. You've probably had moments in your life when someone was rude to you and it probably stuck with you the entire night, maybe even days later. You do not want to be remembered by anyone as the egotistic, condescending, rude asshole.

Women often look at how a man treats other people to assess his personality and better understand how he might act in front of her friends, family, and co-workers. Even if you treat a woman like a princess and everyone else like crap, she'll likely only remember how horribly you acted toward the people around you. Obviously you know not to talk down to women you're trying to impress, but you also need to take your ego down a few pegs and treat everyone you encounter with respect. Not only is it the honorable way to act, it also makes you look like a humble guy, another one of the unsung traits women desire.

Loutish

In this case, loutish means checking out other women while you should be concentrating on the woman right in from of you. You're not creating jealousy by hitting on the waitresses as they pass, nor do you impress her by bringing up your past conquests. If you act like this, the only thing she will see is a guy who doesn't respect women in general and her in particular. If you're loutish, by now you already know it and that's probably why you're reading this book. All you need to do is turn your head around and give a woman some undivided attention when it's required.

If you can't completely correct your loutish behavior, you have to keep it to a minimum if you have any hopes of making a decent first impression. If you've been flirting and it caught the attention of someone you might be into, change gears and stop flirting with everyone around you. When you're talking to a woman, you don't always have to directly engage her with positive body language, but if you're attracted to her, keep your hands off of other women and your wandering eyes focused on her.

Cheap

It's difficult to come off as cheap when you're just chatting to a woman for a few minutes, but it's possible and extremely unflattering. Instead of demonstrating how cheap a guy is, he can infer it when he complains about how much a drink costs or how ridiculous the cover charge is. You probably won't get much disagreement if the drinks and cover charge are pricey, but of all the things you can talk about, why complain? After all, you did pay the cover charge and you are holding a drink, so don't dwell on how much you paid for them and just enjoy yourself.

Women hate paying for drinks and cover charges, so let them bitch about it to their girlfriends. Keep her mind on positive aspects like the music, the crowd, and the energy in the room, so you don't find yourselves in an endless cycle of complaining. You may think you're hitting it off because you both agree on something, but the next day she won't have any positive feelings associated with you. Stay positive and help her break out of her normal, boring life by giving her something exciting and interesting to do or think about.

Argumentative

If you think you're scoring points by getting into an argument with a woman and "winning," you're 180 degrees from where your head needs to be. First of all, you need to avoid any controversial topics that might dredge up her firmly held beliefs. Secondly, lighthearted arguments are definitely encouraged, like who was cooler: young hip shaker Elvis or fat jumpsuit Elvis. It can be fun to have these pseudo-debates because nothing is really at stake and it creates playful tension. Arguments about politics and religion, for example, are forbidden because it can make a woman feel self-conscious and puts her on the defensive. Imagine if you were on the defensive while talking to someone you hardly know—you probably wouldn't find it enjoyable and neither will she.

Your job is to create a little sexual tension and minimize all other forms of stress in your interaction. Help her relax and don't stress her out by arguing over anything that puts her on the defensive. If you find yourself arguing with attractive women, it's probably because you're nervous or you aren't sure what to say. So before you go out to meet new people, brainstorm some playful topics that you feel comfortable talking about without getting into heated arguments. If you have a few things ready to go, you won't likely revert to arguing when the conversation slows down.

Self-Righteous

Whatever a self-righteous guy does in his life is exactly the "right" way to live and if anyone in the world lives differently, they're "wrong." Self-righteous guys usually fall into the extreme liberal or, much more frequently, extreme conservative camps and have no understanding for those who don't believe what they believe. Not only are these types self-righteous, but they're usually judgmental too, meaning they have no problem letting you know that your opinions and lifestyle are wrong. If you find yourself preaching to others, maybe telling them they shouldn't eat meat, smoke, or have pre-marital sex, then you're a self-righteous prick.

Nobody likes to be judged, especially when they're trying to have a good time, because it's rude and annoying. Until you're in a relationship with a woman, her drinking, smoking, sexual orientation, religious beliefs, and much more are none of your concern. Again, keep your initial conversations very lighthearted and ultimately fun and don't tell others how to live their lives.

Misogynistic

Misogynists are bitter toward the entire female gender; they can barely contain their resentment toward women as if it were a manly badge of honor. A misogynist makes his presence known by making rude and insulting comments toward women. Of all the negative personality traits, this is one that earns men the quickest dismissal.

If you've developed a "style" as a woman-hater, you need to re-evaluate why you consciously decided to be that kind of guy. More often, if you're a misogynist, you've slowly developed a hatred of women because your mom didn't hug you enough or you've been badly burned in past relationships, or both. It can be an issue that starts small but over the years really snowballs into a hardened, impenetrable shell. If you can't figure out how to work this trait out of your system, consider professional help because it only gets worse as you get older.

Conclusion

Don't stress out too much if you see elements of yourself on the list you just read. But remember, these are behaviors that women look out for at the beginning of a relationship, both short- and long-term. If you want to put your best foot forward and make a good impression, study the list and make sure to keep these female-unfriendly behaviors to a minimum. Women create enough obstacles to meeting them, so don't encourage them by demonstrating traits that you know will turn them off.

If you find that you possess some of the negative traits previously mentioned, just remember that you're out to make a good impression on the people you meet and being cheap or argumentative, for example, aren't good ways to go about it. You may be great at arguing and deep down you may be "frugal," but these aren't your best features. Keep your negative aspects under wraps and read the next section on positive traits you should demonstrate, so you can make sure you're putting your best foot forward when you meet people.

Traits Women Seek in Men

Unfortunately for guys, women have exceedingly high standards and unless they just got dumped or they're drunk, they usually stick to them, especially when their girlfriends are around. Considering all the choices in men that women have, it's difficult to blame them for being choosy. When a woman has ten guys swirling around her on a given night, she has every right to decide who the "best" guy for her is, if anyone at all.

Guys settle for less than ideal all the time, but women generally stick to their checklist until they get older or have a divorce or two under their belt. A lot of men fail to realize that every woman has her own list of most desired qualities in a partner, but they vary greatly from one to the next. In fact some women may really like needy or argumentative guys, traits most women loathe.

Instead of including a comprehensive list of every possible quality a woman may want in a guy, I've included the top eight personality traits or qualities the majority of women look for when they meet a guy—note that I said "when they meet a guy," so this is not necessarily what they look for in a long-term relationship, but what they are initially attracted to. For instance a woman may be really attracted to spontaneous guys, but she would go crazy if she dated a guy who was *always* unpredictable. Conversely, you won't see "nice" in the following list, although 99% of women say that "nice" is something they want in a mate.

Confident

Women love confident men who are sure of themselves and secure in who they are. Confident men are assertive and give off a natural vibe of power and control, within reason. Because they're confident, they don't get jealous of other men or feel threatened when someone talks to a woman in whom they're interested. Confidence, not arrogance, is one of the key ingredients to being an attractive man; without it your chances for success are diminished to the level of dumb luck. Confident men know what they want and go after it; men without confidence merely accept whatever comes their way, if anything.

Next time you go out, notice that the majority of men seek women's approval by bragging about their job, clothes, cars, or other expensive toys. Confident men don't brag about their possessions or status, because they already know they possess qualities woman desire—they don't have to sell themselves. Confident men follow their own rules and don't feel the need to change who they are to please anyone else—they are who they are without having to explain themselves.

This confidence ultimately comes from being happy with who you are and where you're going—loving your single life. If you don't feel confident, at least look the part by standing straight with your shoulders squared and making your movements deliberate and unhurried. Above all, when talking to someone, look them in their eyes without too much blinking or looking away. If you can't manage that, look between their eyes or focus on the bridge of their nose since they won't know the difference.

Funny

Women are usually quite open about their desire to date men with a sense of humor and in this instance, it's absolutely true. Laughter helps almost anyone feel at ease, but it's especially true of women who may initially feel uncomfortable talking to someone they don't know. When two people can laugh together, no matter what it's about, they're sharing the same emotion at the same time, which builds comfort and rapport—both of which are essential for turning a random conversation into a real connection.

A sense of humor is perfect for keeping a conversation moving—anytime you say something that makes a woman laugh, you can usually jump to a new topic without any awkward pauses. Remember not to use too much self-deprecating humor, especially if that's your style, because while you may get some laughs, ultimately women will assume that you're insecure, especially if you pile one self-deprecating joke on top of another. Also, keep your comedy light by joking about celebrities and the people around you; avoid anything vulgar or offensive like crass sex jokes and jokes about bodily functions.

Since everyone has their own peculiar sense of humor, no list of jokes will help you become funny overnight. If you were not blessed with a funny bone, there are books, movies, and comedy workshops you can look into to try to brush up on what makes people laugh. At the very least, you will meet new people in class and it might even include a few humor-challenged women worth approaching. Much like confidence, a minimal amount of humor is a must when meeting and attracting women, because you want to be seen as a fun-loving guy who doesn't take life too seriously. If you aren't getting women to laugh or at least smile, this is an area on which you need to work.

Spontaneous

Women love men who are spontaneous, at least initially. It may not endure as a desirable long-term quality, but when you first meet a woman, spontaneity counts for a lot in her book. For both men and women, spontaneity equals excitement, and nearly every woman wants and needs some excitement in their frequently boring lives. Spontaneous can mean a lot of things when you're in a relationship, but when you're meeting someone for the first time, the bar is set much lower.

Whatever a woman might be expecting from you and your encounter, you must provide something different, something unexpected. Luckily this book is filled with Openers and routines that are anything but ordinary. You can also try something off-the-wall like bar magic, palm reading, childish games like thumb wrestling…the list goes on and on. The goal is to give her something to remember you by to keep you from blending in with all the other guys she met who talked about their jobs and cars.

The best part of being spontaneous isn't that you always have to be doing crazy things. Instead, you can get away with talking about all the crazy things you do or have done. Whether riding motorcycles down the coast, flying airplanes, skipping work to have a tiki party, or wacky road trips, just talking about the exciting things you do can cover you for the spontaneous quality women seek.

Intelligent

Not all women love a man with intelligence, especially the dumb ones who feel like they're being talked down to. However, most women expect a guy to be able to hold a reasonably intelligent conversation on topics other than cars, women, and sports. Out of all the traits described in this section, intelligence can be difficult to ramp up on in just a matter of weeks. Also, intelligence is extremely tricky to fake unless the woman you're talking to is sufficiently stupid to believe anything someone says as long as it "sounds" intelligent.

You really can't *try* to be intelligent, but you know you're on the right track if you're able to initiate clever, stimulating conversation with just about anyone around you, and you enjoy doing it. You also need to be a good listener so you can pick up on whatever a woman is talking about and build on it. You can make sparks fly if you know about something she's talking about and you can tell her something she didn't already know. Not only are you confident and funny, but you just taught her something she was already interested in, creating intellectual attraction.

Remember that intelligence doesn't mean serious and it doesn't mean arrogance in knowing more than someone else. Your intelligent conversations still require a clever sense of humor and an ability to make something that might normally be considered boring, interesting. Also, being intelligent doesn't give you license to talk any more than you normally would. Make her draw it out of you in a way that makes you almost embarrassed to be talking intelligently when you feel you should be having fun. Not only will she find that intelligent, but also charming.

Charming

Some guys are naturally gifted with charm, but most just lack the skills or never learned how to be charming through regular social interaction. Luckily, you don't need to be born with charm, you can learn by doing. Once you understand what people find charming and you try it out again and again, you eventually internalize it and presto, you've developed a charming personality.

For a lot of people, charm is hard to identify and they believe you either have it or you don't. Charm isn't that complicated; it's simply letting someone know you feel good about them or what they're doing, without asking or expecting anything in return. In other words, charm is an end goal, not a means to another end. As long as you keep that in mind when you compliment someone, you won't give the impression that you are *trying* to flatter someone in the hopes of getting something in return, whether a compliment, a drink, or sex.

The secret to charming someone is to be warm and selfless in your words, not sexual. Don't use a cheesy, deep "charming" voice that signals what you're doing. Instead, your compliments should be lightweight and pleasant, but you must believe in what you're saying to make them powerful and memorable. The meta-message for your compliments is "You are a terrific person, thank you for basking me in your glow." Never say as much, but that's the feeling people should take away after they've met you, so they will seek you out in the future to recapture that wonderful feeling you gave them.

Classy

Most women have three basic categories for men's behavior: rude, average, and classy. Average behavior covers about eighty percent of the male population and both rude and classy cover 10%. Since most women expect an average guy to act average, if you can stand out as a classy guy, you are likely to be remembered as above average and worth following up on.

How do women separate merely average guys from classy ones? Women are usually hard-pressed to give you a definition. Most women say they "know it when they see it," but some say that a classy guy carries himself in a way that commands their attention. Least informative of all, some woman say that classy men just have an aura around them. Since clichés aren't particularly instructive, you should try to demystify "class" so you have something to work toward when you're interacting with women.

A classy guy does everything in life with style, not necessarily in what he wears but the way he walks, talks, and carries himself. His actions are deliberate and unhurried, mostly allowing the world to come to him except for a few key moments of decisive action. Classy guys are just as interested in other people as they are in themselves and are generally humble toward others, with or without merit. Finally, without exception, classy guys treat all women with respect.

Generous

While there are certainly gold-diggers out there who are interested solely in what they can get from you, even the most worldly, selfless women will admit that they aren't attracted to cheap men. However, when it comes to generosity, it isn't always the money you spend that women are interested in, but how you spend it and what it represents. Women view how a man spends, or fails to spend, his money as a reflection on how generous he is, not just with his money, but with all aspects of his character.

Fair or not, women project the way a guy spends his money onto other aspects of his character, such as his feelings and his ability to share himself with a woman. I'm not suggesting that women equate love with money, but they're drawn to men who are generous not only with their money, but their time, energy, words, spirit, and more. If a guy seems cheap when he socializes, she is likely to think he's cheap in other, even more important, ways.

Finally, beyond all the psychology, everyone prefers hanging out with generous people. No one enjoys hanging out with people who put their own bottom line above all else. All things being equal, women will choose a generous man over a stingy one, so be willing to share the wealth with your friends, especially when attractive women are around, but preferably all of the time.

Honest

You can absolutely get away with being a movie producer, a talent scout, or a race car driver, but that's merely factual lying and eventually you will get found out. It's the emotional dishonesty, especially when you first meet, that women quickly notice. If you are emotionally dishonest and she senses it, she will most likely walk away. On the flip side, pure, raw honesty is one of the sexiest, most intriguing traits a guy can have. Honesty, especially with someone you barely know, shows courage and self-confidence.

Women will tell you they want and expect brutal honesty, but for their own good you should refrain from telling them exactly "how it is" when you're talking about them. However, when you talk about yourself, you should be emboldened to speak your mind and open up about who you are and what you want. Brutal emotional honesty means, for example, having the balls to tell a woman that you recently ended a long-term relationship and are looking for no-strings-attached fun. Compare that to someone who lacks the confidence to be honest about what he wants and instead lies to get what he wants from women, usually with disastrous results.

You can actually benefit by being honest about where you're at in your life, so there won't be any surprises down the road about your lack of interest in having a girlfriend. Men who trick women into sleeping with them under the pretenses of getting into a relationship can find themselves tricked into something far worse, like fatherhood. By being honest, you can save yourself these headaches and also attract women who might share your no-strings-attached sensibilities. In the rare case that a woman doesn't appreciate honesty, assume that she's quite comfortable lying to people and stay away from her.

Mysterious

Most guys feel the best way to impress a woman is to tell her everything about themselves within the first few minutes of meeting. Guys seem compelled to tell women what they do for a living, what they drive, where they went to school, and all the other things they think are wonderful about themselves without ever being asked. When men treat friendly initial conversations like job interviews they explain the most boring details about themselves with-

Be Mysterious

If you find yourself talking a lot more than she is, remember a few key pointers:

1. **Drive the conversation toward her**

   As long as you ask questions and steer her questions back toward her, you won't give away too much about yourself. Allow her to talk as much as she wants, so she feels like you're interested in her. If you playfully challenge her on what she says, she feels she has to prove her worthiness to you instead of the other way around.

2. **Forget the past**

   No matter whether you broke up with someone last year or yesterday, keep it to yourself. If you still have your ex on the brain, find something to take your mind off of it, instead of boring a stranger with your bitterness. If she spent ten minutes talking about her ex, you would run for the hills, so don't look for an unfamiliar shoulder to cry on.

3. **Make like you're an orphan**

   Forget about your uncle who committed suicide, your cousin who just came out of the closet, your Dad's drinking problem, or your Mom's gambling addiction. Whoever you're talking to is out to have fun, so leave any big family issues at home and avoid making someone your therapist for the night.

4. **Skip the details**

   It's not inherently wrong to discuss your job because the women you talk to will probably bring it up anyway. But if you have to talk about it, talk about your challenges and personal rewards, not about how much money you make or how powerful you are. Not every woman cares about the money you make, but for those that do, they're smart enough to figure it out based on what you do and how you hold yourself.

out providing any mystique. Without an air of ambiguity, men lose one of the qualities to which women are initially very attracted—their mysteriousness.

Women prefer men who have many layers, like an onion, that can be slowly peeled away to reveal a great guy, someone special that only the right women ever get to see. The secret to developing such "layers" is to hold your tongue and reveal only the essential information needed to keep a woman's interest level high. Instead of forcing details about yourself into a conversation, hold back, listen, and respond as simply as possible to the things she asks about. Once you reveal a little bit about yourself, steer the conversation back toward her.

Being vague about the details of your life can work to your benefit because it gives a woman less information about you and reduces the reasons why she might think it wouldn't "work out." Also, women consider mysterious men to be challenges, someone that they *must* get to know better if for no other reason than to figure out what makes them tick. So, whenever a woman asks you questions about yourself, remember to tell her just enough to momentarily satisfy her curiosity, and then allow her to continue indicating her interest by asking you more questions, hoping to reveal yet another layer.

Conclusion

Don't think that you need to try too hard to display any of these personality traits. Chances are that you already have some of these traits, but maybe you just aren't exhibiting them very well. If you try too hard to be someone you're not, it shows, and whoever you are talking to will take it as a sign of insecurity or insanity. Instead of focusing on specific traits, try to get inside a woman's head and understand *why* they like the traits previously described.

For instance, don't focus on being generous but think about some of the token gestures you can display that help reveal your generosity. Keep them in mind and just drop one out there whenever the mood or moment strikes you. It may seem insincere to think of these things in advance, but consider how much time a woman spends preparing to go out so she can look better than she naturally does. She's merely accentuating her beauty and you're merely accentuating your generosity or intelligence or adventurousness. Plus, with these gestures pre-planned, you can focus on the women you're talking to and listen to what they have to say instead of worrying about doing the wrong thing.

What Women Notice When You Approach

Contrary to popular belief, women are every bit as visual as men when it comes to checking out the opposite sex. Guys don't notice as much about the women they talk to, including whether or not they're wearing a wedding ring. Long legs, perky breasts, and a handful of ass are about all most guys remember on top of whether she was annoying or not. Women notice a lot about guys that casually walk by, and they take note of almost *everything* regarding the guys they meet.

Women aren't nearly as obvious when it comes to checking out guys, which makes them especially good at it. Men might admire a shapely body, but women inspect men for little clues on what their personalities are like and whether it might be compatible with theirs. Women make these quick calculations all the time yet men rarely take notice—at their own peril. A woman may decide she's interested in you before she's even caught your eye or grabbed your attention. Before you even open your mouth she may already feel as though she has a sense about who you are, so you need to act fast to confirm or refute these assumptions.

Where guys are mostly interested in curves, women notice eyes, hands, smiles, posture, and dozens of other little things, all without you ever noticing that you're being checked out. Given just thirty seconds between you walking in her direction and then talking to her, her brain is already working to figure out how classy you are based on what kind of shoes you're wearing. A woman's interpretation of what she noticed about you is very important in terms of how open she'll be to your approach. It's important to know what kind of impression you give so you can incorporate it into your Opener.

In Chapter 4, "Style and Grooming" you learned the basics of how to keep yourself clean, smelling good, and looking great. This follow section provides insight on why you need to do all of these things, plus what women see when you do and do not have proper grooming and effortless style.

Your Eyes

If you're in close proximity to a woman, the first thing she usually notices are your eyes, especially if they're aimed right at her. Knowing this, you want to look directly into her eyes so she can see a sexy gleam as if you were going to hypnotize her, all while giving her a slight "I like what I see" smile and nod. You should always use your eyes to flirt for the first few seconds as you make your approach. There is nothing wrong with looking at someone suggestively, so they get a sense of your intentions before you open your mouth.

Women aren't so much interested in what your eyes look like, but how you use them. While men seem to avoid eye contact with women they're interested in, women use their eyes to communicate their interest. A man who knows how to use his eyes to convey interest is viewed as confident, someone who knows what he wants. A man who continually averts his eyes when he notices he's been "caught" looking at someone is considered shy at best, a stalker at worst. Considering this, eye contact is a critical part of flirting, so don't be afraid to return and hold eye contact.

Most women hate it when men stare their bodies up and down, but you should never be ashamed to look directly into a woman's eyes if you're interested in her. Women melt when a man they find attractive looks deeply into their eyes before and while approaching and Opening. If you dart your eyes away when a women notices you looking at her, she interprets that as a sign that you're not used to being with women as attractive as she is, and that you lack confidence in your actions.

Your Smile

Guys never smile as easily as women do. Look around at any club or bar on a Friday night and you'll see women laughing and chatting amongst themselves, maybe with a few guys joining in the fun. You'll also see groups of guys, clutching their drinks, scanning the room, somewhat frowning. Most of these guys look like they don't want to be there and it can make for an uncomfortable scene, at least until the third round of drinks. What you should take to heart is that even an average-looking guy who can smile and laugh is more appealing than a truly handsome man who never smiles.

A guy with a genuine smile shows that he's friendly and expressive with his feelings, likes what he's doing at the moment and, most importantly, that he's approachable. You know that guy in the club surrounded by ten beautiful women who is smiling from ear to ear? He most likely had that smile well before the first girl showed up. That's the smile and attitude you need to hold on to all night no matter what happens. It's infectious and women who arrive at a club always look for guys smiling and having fun as if they own the place.

Your Shoes

Women love shoes, especially their own, but if you notice a woman peering down as you approach or talk to her, it's not because she's disinterested. Women feel they can learn a lot about a man by the shoes he wears. For instance, most women like stylish men, so if you're in a nice club and you're wearing gym shoes, she'll likely interpret that to mean you're socially incompetent. Women put so much effort into matching the right shoes to the right outfit for the right occasion that they expect men to put in at least a minimal amount of effort in the shoes they wear. You might be surprised at the impression you give a woman by wearing nice Italian leather shoes, even when the rest of your outfit is run-of-the-mill.

Luckily, women in no way expect men to be as fanatical about shoes as they are, but they do expect you to adhere to some basic rules of footwear etiquette. First and foremost, if you're wearing a nice button-down shirt, even with jeans, you should wear upscale shoes and most likely a matching belt. In addition, whatever belt you choose should generally color-compliment the shirt you wear and the color of your shoes. For example, if you wear earth tones, consider a brown belt and shoes. If you wear almost any other color, you should wear a black belt and shoes.

You also need to take care of your shoes because you'll score far fewer points with a woman if your once-pristine black leather dress shoes are dull, scuffed, or marred with other blemishes. If you wear nice shoes that can be polished, by all means make sure they get polished regularly and that the laces aren't frayed or broken. You can do all of the maintenance yourself, but if you can swing it, take your shoes to a professional. Experts can sometimes restore shoes that belong at a garage sale back to their former glory, saving you a trip to the shoe store. If you spent a lot of money on one nice pair of shoes, spend a little bit every month or two to keep them looking their best.

Your Hands/Nails

A man's hands say a lot about what he does for a living and how he takes care of himself. Considering how much effort women put into making their hands soft and their nails stylish, it should come as no surprise that they take notice of men's hands as well. Since women want to know as much about a stranger as possible before they interact, they look to your hands—the way they look and how you use them—to make some preliminary analysis on what kind of guy you might be. Whether you're constantly wringing your well-manicured hands or gesturing wildly with your grease-covered fingers, women think they can learn a lot through a man's hands.

Women naturally look at a man's hands before he approaches or as he Opens if for no other reason than to see whether he's wearing a wedding band. However, while they glance down they take in a few other characteristics for good measure. While there isn't much you can do if you have large meaty paws or delicate little fingers, you can make sure your hands are clean and your nails trim. Some women may want to be with a bike mechanic, but they typically want him to clean up a bit before he goes out. There are many ways to convey your personality to a woman, but it's best not to let your hands do the talking as they may not be an accurate representation of who you are. The best impression your hands can make is that you're clean, you take care of yourself, and you're confident when it's time to shake or hold hands.

Beyond the basics of keeping your hands clean, you should consider some of the various stereotypes that women might employ based on how your hands look. If you wear a lot of rings, they might think you're a gangster or gay. If you have tattoos on your fingers, women are often correct in thinking that you're an ex-felon. If your hands look soft and your nails trim, women often assume that you work in an office. On the other hand, if your hands are marred with scars, bumps, and bruises, she might think you work in construction or other manual labor. While you can't change some of these characteristics, the idea is to keep them in mind so you can prepare yourself for the assumptions a woman makes before she gets to know you.

Your Height, Build, and Posture

Most men don't like to acknowledge their height's affect on how they're perceived when they approach women, but it's true. Most women associate tall men with safety and security, meaning a big guy can protect them from predatory guys and any other threats a woman might confront. Unfortunately, this biologically ingrained belief is held by the majority of the Western female population, but like many obstacles in life, being short is something you have to work with instead of against. Women may associate height with being protected, but that isn't the only factor they subconsciously use to evaluate your ability to keep them safe. There are two other factors that can help mitigate the issues facing vertically challenged men—build and posture.

Unlike height, most men can make immediate improvements on their posture and gradual improvements on their build. If you're smaller than average in stature, examine your posture in the mirror, both when you're seated and when standing. If you notice yourself slouching, with your back hunched over and your shoulders slumped in, you have poor posture and it affects your height as well as your perceived level of confidence. If you slouch, you should make a conscious effort to correct it by acting as though you have a steel rod shot from your ass to the top of your skull. At the same time, pull your shoulders back as if someone were holding on to them and placing their knee in your back. When you do this, recheck your posture in the mirror to make sure you look more like a military man and less like Frankenstein. Good posture makes you look taller, more confident, and classy and it costs absolutely nothing to accomplish.

Another area that you can improve is your build, also known as your physique. There is no way to provide you with the comprehensive information you need to improve your physique in just one paragraph, but the importance of an athletic build is undeniable. Just because you aren't tall doesn't mean you can't be considered big in a woman's eyes. Most women consider a man who is short, stocky, and muscular to be every bit as protective as a tall, lanky guy, and if that's your goal, you have to hit the gym. Everyone has different body types and goals, so you should start by consulting with a physical trainer to assess where you could use improvement and what you could hope to accomplish in three, six, and twelve months. Beyond just the superficial benefits, staying in shape allows you to keep up with women who expect a vigorous workout between the sheets.

Your Scent

Think about how a woman catches a man's attention with the aroma of her seductive perfume. When a man wears good cologne, it grabs a woman's attention in exactly the same way, if not more so since women have a better ability to smell fragrances than men do. Considering the emphasis women put on smelling good, you should have a few colognes and aftershave lotions you can splash on to add another dimension to your profile.

After splashing on some aftershave, have you ever noticed women turning to look in your direction after they walk by? They might even tell you that you smell good, whether they're attracted to you or not. Women can pick up on the slightest bit of aftershave because it grabs their attention. Some women even know the name of certain aftershave lotions and get a kick out of telling you what you're wearing. An interesting scent can even help initiate a conversation with a woman that had no previous interest in you.

Most men don't regularly wear aftershave or cologne, so wearing some can help separate you from the crowd of competitors. Just remember to use quality cologne and apply it in moderation so you don't suffocate yourself or singe anyone's nostrils. A dab on each wrist, on both sides of your neck, and on the insides of your elbows should cover you for a few hours.

Your Drink

Typically, a woman is only able to notice what you're drinking in bars, clubs, restaurants, and social functions like parties and weddings. It may be one of the least important things a woman notices about you, but some women put a lot of stock into divining your personality based on your drink of choice, whether beer, wine, spirits, or exotic cocktails. You wouldn't be alone in thinking it's idiotic to judge a person by what they drink, but on a given night, you might want to take an idiot home with you.

In no way am I suggesting that you change your drinking habits on the off chance that you meet someone who thinks they can figure out your personality based on what you're drinking. However, you might want to keep in mind where you're at, and ensure your drink and your rate of drinking are appropriate for the situation. For instance, if you're at a dive bar and you're the only one drinking Chardonnay, you might get some eye rolls when you approach a girl who's drinking Pabst Blue Ribbon. Similarly, you might be at a classy work function where your co-workers are casually drinking Pinot Noir while you're throwing back shots of whiskey like the world is coming to an end.

Sometimes you go out just to have fun and get drunk, but other times you want to charm the pants off the woman sitting next to you to who's sucking on a maraschino cherry. If that's the case, keep drinking, but consider mirroring what she's drinking if it's acceptably "manly" enough. It can also be a great conversation starter to look down at your boring beer and then at her colorful cocktail and tell her it looks good and ask whether she thinks a guy would like it. You can keep things going by toasting to "trying new things" and asking her what was the last new thing she tried.

Conclusion

Knowing which characteristics women are attracted to and which they find repulsive is undoubtedly the most important part of the "A" game. It does you absolutely no good to learn the five-stage progression from meeting women to sleeping with them if your behavior and attitude instantly turn women off. Before you develop Openers or sharpen your interesting or hilarious stories, you have to make sure that you're able to effectively demonstrate your attractive personality during simple interactions.

If you find yourself constantly stuck Opening women and never progressing past the Hook stage, there's a good chance that you aren't demonstrating the kinds of qualities to which women are attracted. If that's the case, you should spend some time examining your behavior after each interaction and try to isolate the exact point when things seemed to fall apart. Was it something you said, something you did, or maybe your negative body language betrayed your confident frame of mind? If you get the feeling that you're coming across as arrogant, needy, or self-righteous, work on downplaying those unattractive traits.

If you catch yourself making social mistakes, start by making small adjustments to your attitude or your behavior and note whether your success rate improves or diminishes. It doesn't take much self-awareness to realize when women are attracted to you. So, while you're learning how you demonstrate your attractive qualities, pay attention to women's reactions as you try out a new attitude or different body language, for example. Continue making adjustments until you break through the Hook barrier until you are successfully attracting women with your winning personality.

Chapter 7

Where to Meet Women

In this Chapter

★ Getting to know the three basic ways men and women meet each other

★ Discovering why non-traditional locations are some of the easiest places to meet women

★ Exploring many of the best places in your area to meet attractive, single women

Where to Meet Women

Think back to when you were in school and you'll probably remember a place swarming with an endless supply of girls. From classes, rallies, concerts, football games, road trips, and just about everywhere else you went, there were girls everywhere. Back then you may or may not have had any success with the crush of women you saw day in and day out, but they were always there. Unfortunately, you probably got a job without a lot of access to single women, so now you have to take the initiative to find them yourself.

If you're still in school or work around one, you already know where women are— everywhere you look. However, if you're no longer in school, you quickly realize how shallow the dating pool gets when you don't have homecoming games or house parties to attend. Since you no longer have access to the bustling social scene of a college campus, you're going to have to survey your everyday life and seek out locations that attract single women. If you live in a small town or you just don't get out that much, you're going to have to a commit yourself to leaving your comfort zone to find places that offer dozens, if not hundreds, of women to meet.

Meeting women can be difficult, but if you're never around any women to approach, it's nearly impossible. This chapter details the most common locations to meet women, from the usual bars and cafés to places most guys overlook like hardware stores and extension classes. It's impossible to include a definitive list of places to meet women, but if you find it difficult to find anyone worth approaching, start by visiting any or all of the places in this chapter. Once you're comfortable approaching women in these "known" locations, you can start approaching women wherever you go.

Types of Encounters

Before detailing all the great places to meet women, we'll start by examining the types of encounters you can have at different types of places, like a random encounter or a friendly encounter. Later on, as you read about the specific places to meet women, keep these classifications in mind so you can start thinking about the types of Openers you can use.

Most women shed their dreams of precisely whom they'll marry, where they'll live, and how many kids they'll have, but many still hold on to a general notion of how and where they'd like to meet the man of their dreams. For the most part, women want to meet their Prince Charming casually, not through blind dates, bar hookups, or speed dating, even though most will dabble in all of these at some point. Women are strong believers in fate, so they have to believe their soul mate will find them accidentally, by chance, so it's best to try to work with the scenarios they have in mind.

'Casually' means different things to different women, but it typically includes meeting someone at a private party, like a wedding or birthday party, or being introduced by mutual friends over dinner, drinks, or other social functions. Women especially love to meet men through their activities and personal interests, like school, work, hobbies, sports, and more. Women want to meet a guy that they know little about, but whatever he says or does, it makes them want to find out more. This is important to keep in mind because it helps to have an understanding about which locations and events will bring you the most success and which will not, based in part on where women are most agreeable to meeting guys.

Understanding what women expect when it comes to meeting men can also help you accept far more rejections when approaching women randomly, such as on a sidewalk, in the mall, or on a subway train. As your power to Open and Attract increases, it won't matter *where* you are as much as *what* you do and say, but in the beginning you may find it discouraging when women you've never seen before seem apprehensive to talk to you, especially if they're alone. Randomly meeting a woman is completely different from what they're dreaming of, and you have the added difficulty of putting your attractive personality out there without the benefit of mutual friends, relatives, and others vouching for your good nature.

Waiting in line

We are a nation who waits. We wait at the bank, at the DMV, at the airport, at the grocery store, at the beer tent—we wait everywhere for everything. For most guys, this is the time to look at a cell phone and act as though they're busy and important. What you should be doing is finding the line with the cute girl you want to talk to and then Open her. If you're going to be stuck somewhere for a few minutes, you might as well put it to good use by striking up conversations with the people around you, not staring into a piece of plastic.

In general, lines are great places to meet women because you're both stuck there and probably bored out of your minds. Lines also have a built-in time constraint, so women know that no matter how the conversation goes it will end, if she wants it to, in just a few minutes. If you can charm and humor a woman while she's in line in front of you, you'll know she's into you if she waits for you after you get through the line. If you were in front of her, don't be afraid to hang back and wait until she's out of line and pick up where you left off.

You shouldn't be discouraged from approaching someone you're interested in because of where you are or what you're doing. However, you should understand why a stranger on a subway train might seem cold and distant, while a friend-of-a-friend at a wedding reception warms to you instantly, although you essentially said and did the same things. You can adjust your techniques to include more Open and Hook sizzle when you meet women randomly, or dive straight into Attract and Close material when she already thinks you're a good guy. You can also adjust your expectations according to the circumstances—even the most polished gentleman or outrageous bad boy will have significantly lower success rates when meeting women Randomly as opposed to Casual and Friendly encounters.

★ A **Random** encounter is exactly what it sounds like, a chance meeting between two people who just happened to cross paths. Bars and clubs are built for random encounters, as opposed to weddings where everyone is presumably connected to the bride or groom in some way.

★ A **Casual** encounter is between two people who may frequent the same places or the same events, but until that point have never met. Gyms and classes (dancing, cooking, and writing) usually include many of the same people who see each other somewhat regularly, but don't always talk to each other.

★ A **Friendly** encounter is between two people who already know each other or have mutual friends, but aren't friends themselves. Weddings and parties include disparate groups of people who may have never met, but a connection of some sort is implied, making it easier for people to meet.

Random

A random encounter is when an attractive woman catches your eye and you make the effort to approach and talk to her, although you don't know each other. Anytime you walk up to a woman at a store, bar, or mall, for example, and you've never seen each other before, it's a random encounter. It's random because it would have never happened had life's circumstances not brought the two of you into the same vicinity.

A lot of guys have a problem with random encounters because they have no context, no reason, for talking to someone they don't know, or at least they can't think of any. Their worst fear is that a woman will freak out and scream as if he were attacking her, or she'll be outraged that a man interrupted her day just to talk to her. Fears like this are completely unfounded and are simply excuses that guys use to avoid rejection.

Random encounters are likely to be the most frequent, but also the least successful, simply because they're random and you never know what you're walking into until you're in the middle of it. She may be attractive, but she might also have a boyfriend or she just lost her job or she has five kids with three different guys—you just don't know what her status is until you find out, which is exactly what you have to do. If she's *that* attractive, she's worth risking rejection to find out whether she's interesting enough to ask out.

Example Locations: Parks, sidewalks, cafés, bars, bookstores, malls, and beaches.

Casual

A casual encounter is more than just meeting someone you've never met before, but they aren't a friend or acquaintance either. A casual encounter involves women that you've seen before, who have also likely seen you, but neither of you have struck up a conversation yet. If you go to the same café every day or you frequent the same gym, you probably recognize some of the same people and they recognize you. With a casual encounter, you approach a woman that you've seen around before and now want to find out more about.

Guys feel much more comfortable approaching familiar faces than they do random women because it gives them time, sometimes weeks or months, to figure out how they're going to approach. Men also feel more comfortable working on their own turf and not feeling the "now or never" pressure they feel when they don't think they'll see someone again. Plus, since they're approaching someone at a location they visit regularly, they have some context to work with when coming up with an Opener.

Casual encounters are preferred by most women because in that context a guy can seem both familiar and mysterious at the same time. If a woman goes to the same gym every day and frequently sees you on the treadmill, she already knows that she has something in common with you—keeping fit. However, since you aren't a friend-of-a-friend, she doesn't have to worry about dating someone's ex-boyfriend or think about the long-term implications if it ends badly. Since both men and women prefer casual encounters, it's in your best interest to follow up on any flirtatious signals you might get at your usual hangouts and it never hurts to put out your own signals as well.

Example Locations: Gyms, classes, cafés, and co-ed sports leagues.

Friendly

Approaching the friend-of-a-friend or an acquaintance is usually the easiest way to meet someone. In both cases, you are a known entity or you can become known quite easily, another way of saying she assumes you're not a creep or a killer, which is more than she can say about a random stranger. This is a distinct advantage that you can't easily get with random and casual encounters, but just because it's the easiest way to meet someone doesn't mean it's the best or most successful way.

As you would expect, guys don't have much problem meeting friends-of-friends, especially if they're at a party and everyone is drinking and having a good time. Guys don't have to spend a second thinking about what they're going to say because there is a lot of common ground including your mutual friends and the event you're at, which can both be mined for Opener material. It also helps when you're at a wedding or party, the alcohol is flowing, and over half the people in the room are already coupled, creating the perfect storm for women who are tired of waking up to an empty bed.

Attracting friends-of-friends has some built-in advantages the other two types of encounters don't have. The biggest benefit is that women already believe you're friendly and non-threatening, simply because you're friends with someone they already know. You usually don't need to Open or Hook her and her friends because it's implied that you have a reason to talk to them (mutual friends), and that you're accepted as part of the group (because you're at the same party), which means you can move directly into the Attract, Connect, and Close stages.

Example Locations: Parties, reunions, weddings, and barmitzvahs.

Conclusion

Different types of locations offer you multiple ways to meet women, including randomly, casually, or friendly. It's helpful to keep in mind what types of encounters are generally possible at a particular location so you can calibrate your techniques to the situation. Understanding the difference in how to Open a complete stranger and how to Open a friend-of-a-friend can dramatically affect your success rate. However, don't restrict yourself to just one type of encounter just because it seems easier or because you think a location dictates it.

Where Women Are

If you think about it, you can meet women just about anywhere you go as long as you don't live in a monastery or an off-shore oil rig. Every time you walk out the door to work, to school, to eat, to shop, and more, there are women around who are interested in meeting you, as long as you take the initiative. Eventually, knowing *where* to meet women isn't nearly as important as *how* you meet them, but if you're just getting started you should try to use every advantage at your disposal, including going to places that are well stocked with attractive women.

Since you're still learning how to Open and Attract women, you want to find environments that will offer you as much opportunity and practice as possible, so that eventually your skills—not your location—drive your success. Attracting women takes time, but it also takes a great deal of exposure. If you pick the right locations at the right times, you can save a considerable amount of effort, because instead of searching for women to talk to, you're at locations that appeal to many attractive women.

When most guys think about meeting women, or "hooking up" as is usually the case, they only consider a few places like bars and clubs. Bars and clubs are always a good place to meet people, but then again, everyone knows this, making competition particularly fierce. Not only that, some women are intimidated by bars, so they go with a group of friends who you have to contend with before you can ever make much progress.

By broadening the scope of potential places where you feel comfortable meeting women, you'll find they aren't nearly as defensive as they seem in bars. Women aren't always with their friends, so they don't look for their group's approval on whether or not they should talk to you. It's essential to learn how to approach and Open groups of people, but it can make life easier and increase your success rate when women can deal with you one-on-one without interference from their friends.

After a few visits to some non-traditional locations, you'll find that you can make far more progress when you initially meet them in cafés, malls, and bookstores over bars and clubs. Eventually you won't go to a particular type of venue because you want to find women to approach, but instead you'll learn how to create attraction wherever you go. In fact, as your confidence grows, you'll start testing your abilities to see whether you can create attraction no matter who the woman is or what the circumstances are.

Malls

If you find yourself missing your old college or high school days when you were surrounded by women, look no further than your local mall to recapture that "fish in a barrel" feeling. While bars can offer you a lot of women with their guard up and a park can offer you a few women with their guard down, a mall gives you the best of both worlds. Malls are filled with women doing what they love to do and since they aren't used to being approached by men in malls, they're much more open to casual conversation without thinking you have an ulterior motive.

Most guys out of their teens look past malls as a great place to meet women, mainly because they hate to shop and think malls are boring. It's a mistake to look at malls solely as a place to eat and shop because they're a Mecca for young, single women who would never expect a guy to tease and charm them while they're shopping. Since most guys disregard malls, it's an especially potent location for a guy who's looking for women and knows how to attract them. Just because women aren't used to being approached by guys at the mall doesn't mean it wouldn't work, in fact malls offer some of the best success rates compared to any other type of location.

From the cookware store to the stationery store, your presence is usually enough to get some looks and since you're just a "dumb" guy who doesn't know how to shop, you'll definitely need to ask the prettiest women what the best roasting pan is, or which birthday card you should buy for your mom. Beyond the stores, the food court on a Saturday afternoon has more attractive, single women than just about anywhere else in your area. All you need to do at a food court is find a woman eating by herself, sit down at her table, then ask her what she's eating and whether it's any good. You have a lot of different directions you can go from there and if it doesn't work out, move to another table and another until you find some interesting company.

Grocery Stores

Almost everyone has to go to the grocery store once in a while, including single women. Most guys spend as little time as possible trolling the aisle of a supermarket, mainly because they feel out of their element. Guys usually get their food by reciting a number into a speaker at a drive-thru, from Mom, or the occasional barbeque cookout. If you view going to the grocery store as a chore, something to do as quickly and as infrequently as possible, you're really missing out on one of the world's best places to meet women.

The grocery store is a great place to meet women for several reasons. First, there are usually twice as many single women shopping at a grocery store in the early evening than single men, who shop at 7-11 or just eat fast food. Second, the grocery store is a low-pressure atmosphere, so women are far less guarded when it comes to talking to men. Finally, grocery stores offer an almost unlimited number of ways to strike up a conversation from asking where something is to getting an opinion on a good bottle of white wine. Grocery stores, like malls, provide you with the context you need for meeting someone you don't know.

One of the most important factors in meeting single women in a grocery store is to make sure you're there during the times that woman are likely to be there—weekdays, in the early evening, after work. You should also aim for the larger supermarkets or the trendy natural food stores to find available women. Above all, actually shop at the grocery store and don't wander around looking for women without having any groceries in your cart. Shop for yourself and use the contents of your cart as the basis for your Openers and then proceed as you normally would.

Fitness Clubs

Fitness clubs used to be the singles bars of the early eighties, when the entire country seemingly caught the fitness bug. Back then, a lot of people went to the gym to meet other singles, not get into shape, which gave gyms a bad reputation. Because of this sordid history, there is still a negative stigma associated with approaching women while working out. Luckily, a lot of those stereotypes have faded away and gyms are back to being a great place to meet women—especially fit women who take care of themselves from the inside out.

The best part of meeting women in gyms is that you know exactly what shape a woman is in before you ever approach, just like at a beach. If you're fitness-minded, you have something in common with every woman in the gym, so you already have a point of interest before you approach someone. With that in mind, there are hundreds of things you can ask about while you're working out like whether she usually does ab workouts before or after she runs. Or, if she looks like she's new to the gym, you can offer some pointers of your own as long as you don't act like a know-it-all meathead.

The key to approaching someone in the gym is to keep your eyes focused on her eyes and nowhere else. She knows she's not wearing much and you should have had ample opportunity to check out her curves before you approached, so once you do, stay focused on her and what she's saying and not on that bead of sweat moving down her chest. If you feel like complimenting her, and it's not a bad time to do so since she's actively working on her physique, compliment her on her energy or how determined she looks. A lot of people work out by themselves, so a little positive encouragement can go a long way.

Co-Ed Sports Leagues

If you are athletic and competitive, you should try to get involved with one or two co-ed sports leagues in your area. As with gyms, when you meet someone you're playing with or against, you already have commonality built in and you don't need to think of reasons to talk to someone. Most guys don't play sports as a means of meeting women, but a lot of women do and many of them are more interested in meeting men than playing the game. While other guys obsess about winning or complaining about bad calls by the ref, take the opportunity to find someone you're interested in and talk to her.

The biggest problem guys have with meeting women when they play sports is that they devote all of their energy to winning the game, not winning the girl. Men are competitive creatures who don't play to have a good time—they play to win, even when sweaty girls in gym shorts are around. You don't want to be a drag on the team, so try your best, but always keep your eyes open for women on the opposing team and women on the sidelines who might need some convincing to get involved. It's always good to win the game, but it's even better if you have someone to celebrate with when you win or commiserate with if you lose.

Some of the best co-ed sports leagues to meet women in are softball, volleyball, golf, bowling, and dodge ball. Since women can get the competitive spirit when they're around highly competitive guys, it's a good opportunity to tease and try to deflate some tension. For instance, you can jokingly tease a hottie on the other team that she runs or hits like a girl. Or you can take a different tack by coaching a woman on your team and telling her that she has good form, but if she adjusted her hips a little bit, she would have great form. Above all, don't get upset by the game and keep your priorities in check by focusing on the women first and the game second.

Hardware Stores

Have you ever had that bewildered feeling as you walked up and down the aisles of a supermarket trying to piece together everything you need to cook dinner? Wouldn't it be nice if an attractive woman asked if you needed help finding everything you needed? Most women have the same bewildered feeling when they walk up and down the aisles of a hardware mega-store. A lot of women in those circumstances would love for an attractive guy to approach them and help them with everything they need.

Hardware stores may seem like an unlikely place to meet women, but more and more women are becoming do-it-yourself types when they need to spruce up a bathroom or kitchen. Even though hardware stores are hardly teeming with women, attractive or otherwise, the women who do shop there are usually *very* open to conversation. This is especially true when they look up and down the aisles with wide, beaming eyes, confused at what they're looking at. If you can be the guy who successfully guides her through the store and checkout line, there's a good chance she'll be open to future encounters.

Before you start approaching women and telling them they look like they could use some help, make sure you have a basic idea of what you're talking about. You're likely to lose her attention if you have to grab a clerk to answer her questions for her. If you truly don't have any hardware knowledge, play along and then mention how hard it is to find anything since they've reorganized the store. Also joke around about your shopping services being free, but say you charge for house calls—she just might ask you over to help her with her project.

Bars and Clubs

Guys already know that bars are a good place to meet women; the problem is that most think it's the *only* place to meet them. Bars can definitely be a great place to find attractive women, but not as much long-term success can be found there compared to cafés, malls, parks, and just about everywhere else. Women know that guys are on the prowl when they're at a bar, so they keep their defenses up, making your job much more difficult. However, bars do have their place in the world and present you with some of the best opportunities for indiscreet grinding, random make-outs, and one-night stands.

Whenever guys want to meet women, a popular bar is usually the first place that comes to mind. Packs of men routinely go out on the prowl together to try and hook up with whoever they can get, however they can get it.

It's for this reason that so many women are skipping the bar scene or putting up a defensive "shield" when they go out. You can use this to your advantage because while all the other guys will be delivering lame pick-up lines and cheesy compliments, you'll take a different approach. The techniques in this book are designed for the bar and club scene. As long as you follow the basic principles, you can work around those shields as if they don't exist to you.

The key to meeting women in bars is to have fun above everything else, and to give women just a taste of who you are and what you're about before moving on to another group. Unless you really get a sense that you're going to hook up that night, you can put a damper on any sparks you create if you try to accomplish too much at a bar. Most women go to bars in groups and they're out to have a good time with their friends, not go on a date with someone they've never met before, although this is sometimes possible. With this in mind, aim to spend just five to ten minutes charming, humoring, and attracting a woman before exchanging numbers and moving on. If you do a good job Opening, Hooking, and Attracting, you'll be able to pick up where you left off at a more suitable location, maybe even your house.

Beaches and Parks

Unless you live near the coast or a great lake, decent beaches are hard to find, but just about everyone has a park nearby. For whatever reason, parks have become the best location for women to meet their dream guy, which is why you need to find your way to a park as often as possible. Women like parks because they can walk their dogs, jog, people-watch, and just maybe run into a guy worth bragging about to their friends. You should learn to love parks because most single women want to be approached by attractive guys there, above just about anywhere else in the world.

Although most guys understand that parks are a great place to meet women, they seldom go there unless there's a soccer or basketball game to play. If it takes a game to get you to the park, so be it, but if you really want to meet women, you should walk around and talk to women you're interested in before and after the game. Beyond the soccer field or basketball court you can find a lot of women strolling around seemingly preoccupied by their iPod, but many are scouting for guys. When they see a cute guy, they'll usually put themselves somewhere in his trajectory so he can notice them and hopefully chat them up.

If you have a dog, child, niece, or nephew, you have no reason not to take them to the park every once in a while. If you have none of the above, you can earn points with a friend by babysitting his or her kid for an afternoon at the park. Once you're there, make a point of having some difficulty with the child or dog, and then ask an attractive woman for help. Most women feel comfortable talking to a guy with a cute dog or a cute kid, especially if they have one as well. For whatever reason, beaches and parks spark a lot of romances, so get yourself to the biggest, most popular one around you and get to work.

Cafés

Cafés might just be the most well-known place to meet women except for bars, however your chances of actually meeting and connecting with someone at a café is far greater than at a bar. Cafés are well lit, warm, comfortable atmospheres where people go to talk, read, and listen to music, so you're far less likely to get resistance to a simple Opener than you would at a bar or club. Also, it's not at all uncommon to see women sitting by themselves at cafés. So not only are women less apprehensive about talking to guys they don't know, they also don't look to their friends for approval, because they aren't around. These are just a few of the reasons why cafés have become the ideal place to meet women.

Guys are starting to pick up on the fact that cafés have become one of the best places to meet women. Even if you're not into the idea of spending five dollars on coffee that you don't really want, consider that it's *a lot* less expensive than going to a bar and potentially more rewarding. Just one cup of coffee can buy you an hour or two in a well-trafficked café, which can offer you dozens of prospects. Instead of circling a bar as if you're a tiger on the prowl, you can read a book or listen to music and if someone interesting shows up, casually approach and Open them with far less game-playing than you find in a bar or a club.

Whenever someone sits down at a café, they're there to do more than just drink coffee, such as read a book or magazine, write in a journal, or listen to music. Whatever it is they're doing, they're probably displaying a sentiment or two, like looking relaxed, intrigued, or amused. What they're doing and how they are responding to it gives you the material you need to approach someone. If she's listening to music and seems really happy, ask her what she's listening to and why it puts her into a good mood. If she's reading a book and seems captivated, ask her what she's reading and whether she thinks a guy would be into it. As you can tell, cafés give you a lot of opportunities to meet women who give you all the information you need for great Openers that can spawn lengthy conversations that allow you to show off your attractive personality.

Restaurants

Everyone has to eat and people are dining out more than ever, giving guys even more opportunities to meet women. When people dine out, not including drive-through windows, they go out not just to eat, but to relax and socialize. This is especially true for women who dine in pairs or as part of a group. While many women are forgoing the bar scene entirely, they never give up on going out for a great meal with good friends at a fine restaurant. Given their age and disposable income, fine dining can range from a huge chain restaurant that serves deep-fried onion blossoms and fishbowl-sized mixed drinks to the trendiest fusion bistros with executive chefs and impossible-to-get reservations.

Men have a lot of difficulty meeting women in restaurants for one main reason: everyone is sitting down. Most guys feel awkward hovering over a group of women and they never seem to get over the feeling that they're performing, like a court jester, in front of a bunch of judgmental women who they're positive will laugh in their face. In Chapter 9, "Open," you will learn more about how to Open a group of seated women. Alternatively, approach women in bars connected to restaurants where they aren't nearly as defensive as in a traditional bar.

Stand-alone restaurants aren't the only dining establishments you should frequent— restaurants connected to upscale hotels are one of the best locations for meeting single women on the make. Try to locate some nice hotels near the largest airport around you and then find out which ones are known for their restaurants. If you're looking for a no-strings-attached good time, you can always go to an expensive resort on a faraway beach, or you can go to a hotel's restaurant and find the stewardesses, the business travelers, and the ignored and mistreated wives of businessmen who are almost always up for a good time.

Public Transportation

If you really want to put the three-second rule to the test, nothing will provide you with more opportunities than public transportation. Even in bars and clubs, if you don't act in three seconds, odds are good that you'll get another chance to make a move later in the night. When it comes to buses, subways, airports, and terminals, you might only have a few minutes to approach, Open, and get a phone number, so getting over yourself and approaching without hesitation becomes paramount. The upside to public transportation is that you have to push yourself to act quickly, and the fact that you probably won't see that person or anyone around you ever again means you can act without worrying about your reputation. The downside is how awful your success rate can be solely because your time is limited and women are apprehensive of strangers on public transportation.

In some areas of the world, public transportation is the main way people get around, so if you're spending your travel time texting friends and looking out the window, take a minute and look around to see whether there are any attractive women who look like they could use your company. Airplanes and terminals are generally a good place to meet women because you usually have more time to spend talking and attracting as opposed to a subway train or bus, where you or the woman you're talking to might have to leave at any moment. Regardless, wherever you might be traveling to and whatever you might be traveling in, public transportation frees you from the aggravation of driving so you can enjoy yourself and the company of women who might be as bored as you are.

Think of the vehicle that you're riding in as a moving café and apply all of the same techniques that you normally would. Public transportation can resemble cafés in the sense that she's probably not traveling with a group of friends, she doesn't have anyone to talk to, and she's usually focused on a book or music. Women in these circumstances are usually up for taking a break from whatever they were doing to meet a charming guy who is headed in the same direction they are. Whatever she's currently doing, whatever you're doing, and questions about the mode of transport are always good topics with which to start. If you're lucky enough to be heading to the same destination for a vacation, a plane ride can be the beginnings of a very fruitful "when in Rome" romance.

Weddings

Weddings aren't necessarily *the* best place to meet women, but they present you with the best opportunity to hook up with someone for an evening of no-strings-attached sex. Women who are in any kind of emotional state are particularly vulnerable to a guy who can make them feel sexy or secure, if only for one evening. Weddings can be a particularly emotional event for single women, especially as they get older. Most single women, but in particular bridesmaids, seem hell-bent on finding an attractive guy to make them feel special on their friend's big day. If that's what you're interested in, do *anything* you can do to get invited to as many of these social debaucheries as possible.

It's unfortunate, but most guys seem to focus on the open bar first and the available women second when they're at a wedding reception. Sometimes it can take a lot of alcohol to start dancing and flirting with the women around you, but if you don't keep your priorities in check, you'll end up puking and she'll end up sleeping in an empty hotel bed. Better to secure a "date" for the evening before hitting the sauce too hard. Once you've locked in and socialized a bit, don't be afraid to grab a bottle of champagne and tell her you'd like to celebrate with a little more privacy. If she declines, drop her and find someone who can get into the spirit of things.

Unless you crashed the wedding, you already have plenty of built-in Openers, so you shouldn't spend a second considering if and how you should ask someone to dance or go get drinks. One thing you want to keep in mind is to demonstrate your Hook skills by getting the attention and approval of the wedding party, family, friends, and anyone else seen having a good time with a woman you find attractive. Until she's on her fifth glass of champagne, she might have some reservations about leaving the party to spend some naked time with someone she just met. However, if you get involved in the festivities, then you're not some random guy; you're part of the wedding party and leaving with you is just an extension of the party. When it comes to weddings, make a scene, get involved, show off your dancing skills, and have a no-regrets good time.

Churches

If you don't consider yourself religious or you do but don't go to church very often, if ever, churches should remain low on your list of places to meet women. However, if you regularly attend services or a church group, you shouldn't discount them as places to meet women who share similar values and spirituality. A lot of religious couples meet and eventually get married through their church and some churchgoing women look to their house of worship as a great place to meet someone with whom they're compatible. Not only that, churches can offer you access to an entire community of people who want to set up a nice upstanding churchgoer like yourself with their friends and relatives.

Some guys who go to church are conflicted about taking a romantic interest in female parishioners because they feel it's unethical. Whether they think they shouldn't be lusting after someone in a place of worship, or they don't think religious women are interested in dating men they go to church with, many guys consider church to be off-limits. If you're of this mindset, you should reconsider your outlook because women are much more comfortable being approached by men who share their spirituality than men who don't. Plus, when you're already in a woman's "club," you come pre-approved, allowing you to skip a lot of Open and Hook material that you might normally have to use to get her attention.

An important aspect of meeting attractive women your age is to get involved with activities available through the church beyond just Sunday services. Ask people in the congregation about activities and groups organized by your church. The activities you get involved in provide natural opportunities to start conversations. If you're new to town or your church doesn't have many singles, consider looking for a congregation that suits your lifestyle and relationship goals. The more you like the people at your church, the more you will want to get involved and as a result you'll start getting attention from the single women there.

Bookstores and Libraries

The reading habits of most guys tend to taper off quickly after they leave school, if they ever read that much to begin with. Because guys don't like to shop and many have stopped reading for enjoyment, bookstores have remained an untapped resource for meeting women. Bookstores and libraries are great places to meet intelligent, educated women who usually take care of both their minds *and* their bodies. Because bookstores and libraries are even more underutilized than malls and classes, they can provide you with a great male-to-female ratio and you both get the benefit of some pre-qualification, because you're both presumably intelligent people shopping for books.

Some guys feel intimidated in a bookstore or a library because they don't frequent these places unless they have a very critical reason for needing some information. However, there's a fine distinction between just *being* confused and *knowing* that you're confused, because if you know you're confused, you can ask someone—the cuter the better—for help. A bookstore should give you the context you need to approach and Open women in whom you're interested. If she's in a section of the store you're interested in, you have a perfect opportunity to ask her whether she's into the same things you are. You can also ask her for recommendations or provide them.

The best part of being in a library or bookstore is that it's one of the most conducive places for meeting and having a conversation with someone. People are quiet, the atmosphere is well lit, women are shopping, they have their guard down and they're in an intellectual mode, so they're usually open to talking about mutual interests. Another great thing about bookstores and libraries is that they are always within close proximity to at least one café, sometimes located right in the building. If you have a great conversation while shopping for books, it's only natural to tell her that you're going to get some coffee and you think such an interesting person should keep you company.

Classes

Classes, like gyms, are a great place to meet women because you automatically know that you both have something in common. Not only that, women are at least twice as likely as men to register for self-improvement classes like cooking, dancing, screenwriting, photography, and hundreds more, which greatly improves the odds of meeting someone. Even if there aren't any single or attractive women in the classes you participate in, you can still make friends with other students who would love to introduce a guy who wants to better himself to one of their cute friends.

Much like with libraries and bookstores, most guys aren't interested in any more school or extracurricular learning than they've already endured. Luckily for guys who want to learn a new skill, they find they also clean up nicely when it comes to meeting intelligent women also trying to improve themselves. Just like in high school, you can easily find yourself involved in a group project or having a study partner and now that you're both adults, you're free to have a little wine while you work in cafés, libraries, and most often, each others' homes. Classes allow for so many opportunities to show off your attractive traits and features that women will be asking you to come over to exchange notes, test each other, and possibly more.

The best part of extending yourself and attending classes is that they are valuable far beyond the time you spend in class trying to attract other students. Dancing and cooking, for example, are just two of the great skills you can learn to better attract women outside of the classroom. Some other classes you might want to consider include yoga, painting, language, pottery, massage, and even self-defense. Almost all of these classes will have an overabundance of single female students and for the few hours a week you attend class, you have them almost all to yourself to demonstrate what a great guy you are.

Workplace

A lot of people meet and eventually get married through workplace romances and it's a no-brainer since people spend the majority of their adult lives working five days a week in the same place, year after year. If you have to spend eight hours a day working, it makes perfect sense that you would want to find a diversion in the form of an office romance or co-worker tryst. The circumstances and the desire are mostly unavoidable, so I'll save you the warnings about gossip, sexual harassment, and shitting where you eat because if you're stuck somewhere and you're hot for that bookish girl in accounting, you're going to go for it anyway, right?

Women know the workplace is a good environment to meet someone because they can study and assess a guy over weeks, or even months, before ever making their feelings known. Before a woman even thinks of pursuing a relationship at work, she knows you're employed, what your relationship status is, where you are in the male hierarchical food chain, and whether you're nice, an asshole, or a player. Women can only get this kind of advantage at work and maybe through their church, but church is only one day a week as opposed to five, giving a woman a lot more time to find out whether you're what she's looking for. You need to know these things because your role in a workplace romance is to either confirm or deny any feelings you might have for someone, not make any unwanted advances or drop any sexual innuendos.

Unless you want to get fired, you have to play it safe in the workplace by *not* taking the initiative until you are as sure as you can reasonably be that any advances you make are not only welcome, but expected and desired. Luckily, women on the make have no problem giving you the green light; you just have to keep your senses alert to pick up on anything she says or does that a normal co-worker wouldn't. Some examples include telling you that you look stressed and could use a back rub, bringing food or gifts for no one but you, asking you why you don't have a girlfriend, asking you to go on smoke breaks with her, and countless others. If she isn't currently involved with anyone, spends her free office time with you, wants to get together during non-work hours, and never mentions that you're a "great friend," you're probably in good standing to pursue her romantically.

Conclusion

Unless you live in a very remote area, attractive women are all around you—from the grocery store checkout line to the food court at the mall to the dog park across town. Never look to a particular place as your savior for meeting women, because if you can't walk up to someone in a low-pressure situation like a park or café, going to the city's hottest clubs and bars will rarely increase your success rate.

The locations listed in this chapter aren't magical places stocked with attractive women who haven't seen a man in five years. The places you probably already frequent—from sporting events to the hardware store—may not have as many available women walking around as a club, but since you're already where you want to be, take advantage of being comfortable and in your element. You don't need to go to a café with your "pick-up hat" on—wear it all the time and try to find opportunities wherever you are.

If you only think about meeting women at one or two specific locations, you're cheating yourself out of many opportunities to meet hundreds of great women. The right place is that spot you're standing in when you see a woman that captures your attention. The fact is you can be in a bar where women are easy to meet and still not succeed because you didn't make a move. On the other hand, you can be at church and successfully meet a woman because you had the courage to approach. You can approach any woman in just about any place, as long as your timing is right and you do it with confidence and respect.

Chapter 8

Introduction to The "A" Game

In this Chapter

★ Exploring the stages of The "A" Game and why each is crital to building attraction

★ Revealing how each stage naturally builds from one to the next towards a successful Close

★ Discovering how to put the stages together so you can effortlessly flow through each one

Introduction to The "A" Game

Finally, after learning the myths and rules, how to adjust your attitude, finding your personal style, not to mention learning what women are attracted to and where to find them, now comes the real heart of *The "A" Game.* You're about to learn what took me years of trial and error and countless successes and failures to learn how to do: meet and attract women anywhere, anyplace, anytime.

As you read, always keep in mind that *The "A" Game* isn't about memorizing lines and procedures, but getting a general idea of what works and what doesn't in a variety of situations. As I mentioned in the Introduction, the next five chapters should be considered your toolbox to navigating the singles scene no matter where you might be, not a strict step-by-step approach that must be followed. Try to read just a few pages at a time so you can slowly incorporate each new skill or concept. If you can do that, you'll be well on your way to mastering *The "A" Game.*

The next five chapters can be a lot of information to take in, so read the following sections to get a brief overview of how *The "A" Game* works and how all five stages fit together. From Opening a women or her group all the way through the Close, you're about to learn the true secrets of *The "A" Game.*

Open

How do you walk up to a woman or even a group of women and interrupt what they're doing and grab their attention? It's one of the most difficult things you have to do when you've run out of friends-of-friends and casual acquaintances to date. In this chapter you'll learn that meeting women isn't difficult as long as you have a few killer Openers. "Opening" means creating a window of opportunity and quickly demonstrating how interesting, humorous, and charming you are all within a few minutes. After you Open a group, you can stick around for awhile so you can tell stories, crack jokes, and find out if any of the women are attractive or interesting enough to warrant further attention.

The Open chapter shows you how it's done, step-by-step, so that even the shyest guy can confidently walk up to a stranger and strike up a conversation. No more waiting, pacing around the bar, desperately thinking of something to say or looking for an easy "in". The Open chapter cuts through the bullshit and gets you talking within seconds of seeing an attractive woman you want to meet. Once you've created an Opening and you've got women at your attention, it's time to Hook them in and bring them into your world.

In the Open chapter, you'll learn how to:

★ Pick a good location to meet women

★ Work the room

★ Use indirect openers

★ Playfully tease women

★ Take control of the interaction

Hook

OK, so you have their attention, but now what? If you're talking to just one woman, you rarely need to "Hook" her, but if she's with a group, it's essential. By Hooking her group, you gain their approval and for the time being, they accept you as someone who has social value—a guy who brings something interesting or entertaining to their evening. Women almost always go out in groups and they typically look to their friends for cues on who they should and shouldn't talk to. By Hooking a group, you entertain, charm, and prove your worth to these gatekeepers, because if you don't, they'll never allow you to pull away with one of their friends and into the Attract stage.

The Hook chapter provides all of the essential techniques necessary to demonstrate your social value through interesting and humorous stories that show off your playful personality and attractiveness. You only have a few minute to work with, so you have to make every one of them count by being different than any other guy around. Whatever most guys do when they meet women—brag about their car, offer to buy them a drink, or worse—you'll learn how to do the exact opposite with the utmost confidence. After you Hook the group and you're walking away with one of them, you can be sure that they won't soon forget how interesting and hilarious you are.

In the Hook chapter, you'll learn how to:

★ Demonstrate social value

★ Emotionally stimulate everyone around you

★ Maintain your frame of mind

★ Hold interesting, playful, and flirtatious conversations

★ Stir the conversational pot

Attract

While you were Hooking her group, you virtually ignored the woman you were attracted to just so you could gain her friends' approval, but near the end you gave her a little attention, just enough to let her know that she caught your eye. Because her friends are now your friends, you can easily pull her to the side where you can continue flirting, building attraction, and gauging how interested you are in her.

The Attract stage can and should be a lot of fun; because while you're breaking through her natural defenses and finding out if she's your kind of girl, you're also teasing her, playing games, laughing, and having a great time. If you can show a girl a good time, even for just a few minutes, you're well ahead of the competition, which is what *The "A" Game* is all about.

Without a doubt, as you apply the techniques in this chapter, you *will* build attraction with just about any woman you talk to. The Attract chapter shows you how easy it is to flirt like a natural, break the touch barrier with ease, and further demonstrate your attractive personality. Now that you know she's into you, you're in the driver's seat. It's up to you to decide where things go from here—get her phone number, send her back to her friends, or even bring her along with you to the next club—you're the man with the plan.

In the Attract chapter, you'll learn how to:

★ Initiate basic touching

★ Flirt with confidence

★ Test her interest in you

★ Plan for the Close

★ Transition to the Connect stage

Connect

You know she's into you and she knows you're into her, so now it's time to lead the way from casual conversation into something much more intimate. A woman who is attracted to you, who feels comfortable and safe in your presence and feels the two of you share a connection beyond the physical will follow your lead when you're ready to Close. Whether you quickly work through the first three stages and move directly into the Connect stage or exchange numbers and pick up where you left off, the Connect chapter shows you how to transition initially random encounters into something hot and heavy.

True be told, not every woman requires a real Connection with the men she becomes intimate with, but like a good little boy scout, it always helps to be prepared. In this chapter you'll learn how to shift from the flirty, playful man-about-town into the introspective man of mystery who captures her imagination and prepares her for an erotic journey into your world. From asking her open-ended questions and learning her buy strategy to accelerating her attraction so she can't keep her hands off of you, the Connect chapter takes you through the final stage before you say the four most beautiful words in the English language: Your place or mine?

In the Connect chapter, you'll learn how to:

★ Build rapport

★ Learn her buy strategy

★ Capture her imagination

★ Link yourself to her desired emotional state

★ Accelerate her attraction

Close

In a perfect world, there would only be the Close stage, but because you know how to Open a group and make fast friends, you actually enjoy the chase. Before *The "A" Game*, Closing was largely chance, but now it's a skill and after reading this chapter, you'll be well on your way to mastering it. Closing isn't so much about technique, but about taking a woman's passion for you and helping guide it towards a night of ecstasy. While some enlightened women know just what to do, most are looking for a little guidance and look to you to lead the way. The Close chapter provides everything you need to navigate the logistics of finding a hotel room, a bathroom stall, or something in-between.

The Close chapter covers every conceivable outcome to an intimate interaction from getting a phone number, taking her to another club, or taking her home so you can sweat up the sheets. You'll learn how to read situations and determine if a girl is up for a no-strings attached good time or if she needs a lot of courting and long walks on the beach. Whatever you're in the mood for, it helps to know what it's going to take before you dive down the rabbit hole. Finally, because most women are subconsciously seeking permission to go wild, but still feel respected, you'll learn how to deal with any last minute resistance so a woman can embrace her sexuality and feel good about it... aren't you the gentleman!

In the Close chapter, you'll learn how to:

★ Handle rejection

★ Get her number

★ Initiate the first kiss

★ Take her with you

★ Pick a place to get naked

Chapter 9

Open

In this Chapter

★ Learning how to pick a good venue and working the room to demonstrate your attractive personality

★ Understanding why indirect Openers greatly increases your rate of success

★ Mastering how to playfully tease and engage women so you can put them at ease

Open

Most guys don't have a clue about what approach to use when they want to meet a women. When they see a woman they're attracted to, they often just stare at her while they think of a way to strike up a conversation. When they finally gather the courage to talk, sometimes thirty minutes and a few beers later, another guy has beaten them to it.

Sound familiar? You shouldn't feel alone, because the same scenario plays out millions of times a day and it happens to even the best-looking guys. However, as harsh at it may sound, if you can't immediately approach women you're attracted to, you can't complain that you never get laid or never have a girlfriend. Even if you aren't guaranteed success and you aren't sure what to do, you *have* to try. Fortunately, you are about to learn what to do and how to increase your success rate using some of the best techniques for approaching, meeting, and attracting women wherever you go.

Remember, your learning doesn't end with this book—it's only the beginning. To get what you want out of life and relationships, you must take the initiative and talk to as many women as possible. The more women you talk to, the better your odds are of attracting one or more of them. If you don't make the attempt, how do you expect to ever meet and attract the women you desire? But before you start "talking" and building attraction, you need to create some initial interest through attention-grabbing Openers.

What's an Opener?

The term "Opener" is shorthand for a conversational routine that allows you to interrupt whatever a woman—or group of women—is doing and, in just a minute or two, demonstrate that you're funny, charming, and socially adept. If your Opener is more entertaining or interesting than whatever she was previously doing, your unwelcome interruption turns into a pleasant and enjoyable interaction. You can say anything really, as long as it's playful and conveys that you're more interested in having fun than hitting on women.

An Opener is just enough interaction to *open* a window of opportunity for additional conversations—some funny, some interesting, some flirtatious. These conversations should create enough approval from the group to enable you to break away with one of the women without getting shut down. As you develop more comfort and rapport with her, she'll signal her interest in you and vice versa. From there, you can decide whether you want to see her again, either later that night or sometime in the future. This chapter explains how to easily create a window of opportunity with a woman or a group of women, so you can then quickly transition to the Hook stage where you gain their approval before isolating one of the women in the group.

Getting Started with Openers

Before you ever set foot into a venue, walk up to a woman or group of women, and deliver an Opener, there are steps you should take to ensure the highest success rate possible. It's not just a killer Opener that allows you to take control of a group—from picking locations with lots of single women to demonstrating your social value— everything you can do to attract positive attention *before* you use an Opener will dramatically impact how well they work. Always keep in mind that an Opener isn't just a line you spit out whenever you meet someone new, but a series of tactics you use to ensure that your Opener, and by extension your personality, are well received so you can quickly move from the Open to the Hook stage.

Pick a Good Location

It's possible to meet beautiful women just about anywhere, but you'll definitely increase your odds of finding and attracting women if you go to the places where they tend to gather. Choosing the right locations to meet women is one of the most important initial aspects of your game, because no matter how great your pick-up skills are, it won't matter if there's no one attractive or interesting enough to meet. You've probably heard that attracting women is a numbers game, which is true, so make sure you increase your odds of attracting someone by going to places that provide you with many options and opportunities.

Chapter 7, "Where to Meet Women," fully explores different places, like malls and cafés, where you're likely to meet attractive women. For now, you just need to understand that you want to be where people gather to relax and enjoy themselves. The more single, attractive women there are, the more opportunities you have to practice Opening. The more chances you have, the faster you will learn and improve your ability to attract women. Your goal is to be able to attract women anywhere, anytime, but before you can reach that goal, you need to put thought into the where and what time.

Before you get dressed to go out, you should think about whether the places you plan on going will be stocked with single women, and if they'll be there at the same time as you. A dive bar at 8:00 PM might be a great place to go to meet women before they head to better bars or clubs, but by midnight, the most desirable women are nowhere to be found. A college library could be an excellent place to meet women, but far more women will need a humorous break from studying during midterms than during the middle of the summer. Beautiful women never disappear, they're always *somewhere*, so put yourself in a woman's shoes and figure out where they are and when.

Whether you choose a place that's meant specifically for meeting new people, like a party, or somewhere that's not traditionally associated with socializing, like a library, women are generally open to meeting interesting guys wherever they might be. Even when you see women swatting away all of the "nice" guys they seem so annoyed by, they are still out in public, socializing. With that said, take every opportunity to meet women you're attracted to whether you're in a "singles-friendly" environment or not.

Demonstrate Social Value

From the moment you enter the venue, don't scan the bar or walk around looking for friends or women you might want to talk to later. Instead, zero in on a group that looks friendly and start talking to them within five seconds of entering the door. Initially, it might seem awkward to ignore a crowd of people and just start talking to a group without really thinking about it. However, your goal at this stage isn't to make new friends or in any way settle on one of the first women you meet. What you're actually trying to do is quickly establish yourself as someone who knows people. Of course you don't really know them, but no one else can really tell.

What you say to the first group of people you talk to doesn't really matter, but it should fit within the context of the location. If you're at a bar, you can ask them who the better bartender is, where the bathrooms are, or whether they serve food there. These are normal questions that people ask strangers, so as long as you're sincere and at least appear interested in the answer, no one will think anything of it. You can easily transition into questions about whether the bar is a good drinking spot, what they're drinking, or if there are other cool bars nearby.

At a café, you follow the same basic approach by entering, finding a group of seemingly friendly people, and asking them if the café serves free trade coffee, if they know the time, or if they've seen your friend around. After they answer your questions, order coffee and then go back to thank the group and ask a few follow-up questions. While doing this, you should subtly scan for a woman you want to talk to, so that after you thank the group for their help, you can sit near her. When you approach her, she'll already have accepted you as someone who is friendly and known at the café, so some of her natural fears about "strange men" will be disarmed.

Building and displaying social value applies everywhere you go to meet women. The point of these conversations is to immediately demonstrate to everyone that you're friendly, that you're there to have a good time, and that you have an "in" because you seem to already know people. These conversations also help loosen you up by forcing you to talk to people you don't know.

Work the Room

Since you've picked a location with plenty of attractive women and you've started off on the right foot by being friendly with the first group you saw, you're ready to work the room. The next step is to pull another group into your conversation with the first group, or break from the first group and move to another so you can continue building and displaying social value. Your goal is to have fun, meet more people, and casually explore the room until you see a woman you want to approach.

Why is Social Value Important?

Most women look for men who have more exciting and enjoyable lives than their own. By pairing herself with a guy who is better known and regarded than she is, her social status gets a lift purely by association. Granted this isn't necessarily an important factor for women looking for a relationship, but it's a subconscious element that helps create initial attraction. Women are drawn to men who appear to know a lot of people and seem to always be having a good time, so it benefits you to be one of those types of guys.

When most men enter a bar or club, they start scoping out the room to find someone they know, so they can head straight to them to avoid feeling uncomfortable. Or, they search for women they might want to talk to after they've circled the place a few times and had a few drinks to bolster their courage. Women notice this behavior and interpret it as creepy and predatory, so when the guy finally approaches, she's already wary of his intentions and skeptical of what he says. You want to refrain from overtly scanning and eyeballing people like a caged tiger, because it lowers your perceived social value.

Even when guys arrive in groups, they sometimes maintain the same behavior—looking around, not talking to anyone, not smiling or laughing—in other words, not having a great time. When guys don't work toward being part of, if not the center of, the mix, they lose social value and consequently, they don't seem that important to talk to. Considering there are probably groups of guys already mixing it up and creating a scene, women will be drawn away from the wallflowers and toward the funny, interesting guys with apparent social value.

It's still relatively unimportant who you talk to, as long as you don't make a great effort to talk to them, especially if they're attractive women. For example, you don't want to be seen placing great importance on beautiful women by going out of your way to talk to them. Allow them to notice you talking and laughing with everyone else and they'll usually make sure to give you an opportunity to charm them as well.

Once you start displaying social value by having fun with whoever is around you, you'll soon find more attractive women nearby. Because women are attracted to a man's social value, they make themselves more available to men who seem socially adept. This includes physically moving closer to a guy, directly facing him, holding an open body posture, and other little tics like hair flipping and lip licking. Since women are socially conditioned not to approach men, they focus on making themselves as attractive as possible, and then place themselves close enough to men they're attracted to so they get noticed and approached.

Also, women notice when men are hesitant and unsure of what they want to say before they approach. If you don't make a move within seconds of her noticing you, she'll think you lack confidence, which lowers your value in her eyes. However, if you bounce from one group to another and another, laughing it up and having fun while you do it, you can ride on that energy as you move toward groups of more attractive and/or interesting women. Since you've been pre-occupied with having a good time instead of targeting just one group of women, you'll be able to easily transition out of one group and into another without hesitation.

When you work a room with ease, groups of attractive women perceive you as someone who is funny and interesting just by watching you. When you finally notice them and casually enter their orbit, most women will drop their shields because everyone else seems to already know and like you. From the moment you engage them, you only have a few minutes to demonstrate your value as a social creature and get them invested in interacting with you. You don't want to disappoint women who have these expectations, so when you finally make it toward a group with a woman you're attracted to, you'll need to have an indirect Opener ready to go.

Use Indirect Openers

The point of an indirect Opener is to have something to say that engages a group without them suspecting that, surprise, you have an interest in them beyond just having a good time. An indirect Opener is usually an interesting question, humorous story, or unique viewpoint that provides an entertaining break from what the group was talking about. Whatever your Opener is, it should be exciting enough that the group welcomes your interruption just long enough for you to demonstrate social value to the group, and your attractive qualities to a particular woman in the group.

Examples of "Simple" Indirect Openers:

★ "Hey, guys, help me out, I've got to get female opinion on this..."

★ "I just had to come over and say that you guys have really good energy together, you must be sisters—how do you know each other?"

★ "Holy shit, did you guys see those two girls fighting out there? It was the craziest..."

Examples of "Involved" Indirect Openers:

★ **Childhood Teddy Bear Opener**

I only have a minute, but I could really use a female opinion on something. It's a matter of a life and death! OK, get this, one of my friends over there - I'm not going to point him out - but, well, he's good looking, has a great job, dates around, but apparently he's having a problem with getting dumped after just a month or two after going out with someone. He asked us what we though the problem was, but we really didn't know what to tell him until something happened last night. See, he was staying over at our place and we set up the couch with a pillow and blanket and all that and when it came time to go to sleep, he opens a suitcase and pulls out his old teddy bear from when he was three years old. Apparenlty he still sleeps with it and now we think that when women see this ratty old thing, they go running for the hills. So, here's where we need a female opinion: is it a dealbreaker to still sleep with your old teddy bear or is it kind of sweet and endearing? Personally, I think it's creepy, but what do you guys think?"

★ **Where did you get that... Opener**

"Ohmygod! Where did you get that necklace/earrings/scarf?! My sister/ niece described something just like it when she came to visit. She made me run all over town for two hours to find one, but we never did. Oh man! Her birthday is coming up, so if I can get it for her, I'll be her favorite uncle. Actually, I already am... But seriously, you have to tell me where you got it and please don't tell me it came from some place in Africa!"

★ **Jealous Boyfriend Opener**

"Hey, let me ask you something: do you think it's cheating when someone's girlfriend kisses someone else without telling the boyfriend? OK, so what if it ends up that the person she was kissing was another girl in a club when she was on vacation and nothing else happened? See, this is what's going on with one of my best friends and personally I think it's kind of hot and it could make her a "keeper," but he's all freaked out about it and thinks it could lead to other things, including a breakup. So do you still think that's cheating and what should I tell this guy? I'm into it, he's not, but I don't want to give him bad advice. Is it really cheating when a girl kisses another girl?"

By contrast, a Direct Opener is something that explicitly communicates that a guy is interested in one or more women based purely on their sex appeal. For most guys, a Direct Opener is traditionally the only thing they know to say when confronted with an attractive woman. Women are used to hearing over-used, obvious pick-up lines, so they shut down almost any guy who's dumb enough to use them. When a woman hears a compliment that could be said to any other woman, she can't help but think the guy delivering it is a player who wants to use her for sex. To avoid using a Direct Opener, make sure that what you say can in no way be construed as a compliment, especially one regarding their beauty.

Examples of Direct Openers:

★ "Hey, can I buy you a drink?"

★ "You have the most beautiful smile in this entire bar."

★ "Are your legs tired? Cause you've been running through my mind all night."

Openers and circumstances are not necessarily interchangeable, so there isn't a single Opener you can always use to demonstrate higher value and attain social approval from a group. You can use some of the examples you've just read to get started. Whenever the time comes to use one, don't hesitate, just lob it out there and if it falls flat, keep working the room until you get another opportunity. Also, just because you have a memorized Opener ready to go, doesn't mean you have to use it. Consider the examples as training wheels that you want to get off of your bike as soon as possible, so if you try something new and it works, stick with it and soon you'll have your own collection of reliable Openers.

Women almost always go out with friends when they want to have fun, but banding together also helps them provide each other with support and security when they're meeting new people. Because women usually travel in pairs and groups, you have to become comfortable approaching groups of women as well as mixed groups of women and their male friends. An indirect Opener should engage and entertain the entire group until you can transition to more interesting stories and conversation topics in the Hook stage. During the Hook stage your goal is to gain the approval of a woman's peers, which is critical before taking control of the interaction and aiming more attractive behavior at a specific woman.

Time Constraints

For a moment, put yourself into the shoes of a very attractive woman. Imagine you are alone at a bar, waiting for your friends to show up, and in those fifteen minutes ten guys stare you up and down, four walk by, three compliment you on your looks, and one sat down and spent ten minutes explaining how important he was at his job and how much money he made. Regardless of how many hints you dropped, he still stuck around until you finally lied and told him you were waiting for your boyfriend. Now, multiply that scenario over the past ten years.

The previous hypothetical situation is what most attractive women have to deal with, to a varying degree, every day of their beautiful lives. You don't have to feel sorry for the beautiful women of the world, but it's always helpful to try and get inside their heads so you can better understand how to approach them. By imagining how much time and energy a woman has to waste fending off unwanted advances, you realize how important it is to break through her initial perception of you as just another time-waster, long enough for her to observe your attractive qualities.

By now you understand that you have to display attractive qualities and you have a limited time to do so. For most guys the limitation is set by the woman they're talking to who has developed her own strategies for ridding herself of all the time-wasters that approach her. You want to prevent her from imposing those limitations by verbally imposing them on yourself, also known as a time constraint. The following are some examples of reasons you can mix-and-match when you want to tell a group of women why you "only have a minute."

Constraint	Context
I only have a minute…	…my friends get rowdy if I don't look after them.
I can only stay a second…	…I need to get back to my friends.
You know, I really gotta get out of here…	…I'm buying the next round for my friends.
I want to ask you guys something real quick because…	…I'm taking my niece/sister/mom shopping.
I don't have much time…	…I'm on my way to get a drink/pick up my Mom/play dodge ball.

Knowing that women get hit on and leered at all the time means that even though you have something interesting or outrageously funny to say, you have to create a conceptual boundary around the interaction. By letting her know that your time is valuable and in demand and despite that you still have something to say or ask, she won't balk, since your presence in her life is presumably short-lived. Once she understands this, you won't automatically get lumped with the letches and losers who mistake her politeness for attraction. Knowing upfront that no matter what becomes of the interaction, it won't drag on and waste her time, allows her to relax and actually listen to what you have to say.

Teasing

Playfully teasing attractive women is another way to put them at ease while you continue to demonstrate your attractive qualities. As you've just been reminded, beautiful women attract a lot of unwanted attention and you have to provide a few hints that the interaction with you is going to be pleasantly different. Some guys offer to buy drinks as a way to secure an exclusive conversation with a woman. Other guys brag about their status, money, or possessions. In other words, they're trying to impress and please her in some way so she'll find them attractive.

Your frame of mind should always be that of a picky guy who values his time and doesn't waste it on drama queens and divas. You're casually looking for a woman who can impress you, not the other way around. One of the first steps in establishing your role as a "selector" of women is to playfully tease them as if they were your kid sister. Rarely is a guy ever worried about hurting his sibling's feelings when he mocks and teases, so if you have a younger relative, lock into that state of mind. If not, it shouldn't be that difficult to imagine.

An important distinction to make is that you aren't trying to hurt a woman's feelings or belittle her in any way. Instead, you're conveying that you're not the least bit intimidated by her looks or attitude by teasing her and using backhanded compliments. At first she may seem offended, but she'll quickly realize that while every other guy kisses her ass, you're not and she'll wonder why. Since she's not used to such treatment from a stranger, she'll usually be intrigued enough to continue interacting with you. However, during this initial phase, her goal is still the same—to blow you off and reaffirm her ability to attract and reject any guy who approaches her.

As long as you can hold your frame of mind—that you're a choosy guy and she has done nothing to impress you yet—she'll come to the conclusion that you're not interested in her solely for her beauty. Not only have you teased her, but you've limited the interaction to just a few minutes, and you've interacted with her more like a big brother than a typical player. As long as you're sufficiently interesting, funny, and demonstrate additional attractive qualities, she'll welcome your company. Her other option is to stop talking to this non-superficial, interesting guy and start dealing with the ass-kissing losers again. You've now successfully lowered her shield and opened the door to a conversation and perhaps much more.

Backhanded Compliments

An example of a backhanded compliment might involve acting as though you suddenly smelled something very good and very familiar.

You: [sniffing, looking around] Something smells really nice...can you smell that?

Her: ...

You: [lean toward her] I think it's your hair. What kind of shampoo do you use?

Her: It's xxx.

You: Oh yeah! I remember that...I know I've seen it somewhere...I think I saw it in the shower at my Grandma's house. [sly grin]

Notice that you've complimented her on smelling "really nice" which leads her to believe that you're complimenting her as most other guys would so you can gain her approval. However, you quickly follow up by telling her that your grandmother uses the same shampoo, which isn't an insult, but completely deflates what would have been a typical compliment. It's a push/pull dynamic that obscures your intentions and keeps her on her toes.

Teasing

Teasing is more reactive to something she said; possibly to a question you ask if for no other reason than to tease her about her answer.

You: Okay, help me settle a bet with my best friend…who's better: The Rolling Stones or the Beatles? Biggie or Tupac? Angelina or Jennifer?

Her: …

You: [grinning] No way! Are you crazy?!

Her: *Defends her answer…*

You: You know what? You and I are never gonna get along because we'll fight all the time…and I'll *always* win. [sly grin]

Call her on her "bitch shield"

A lot of women default to bitchy behavior if they aren't around their friends from whom they take cues on whether they should be talking to a particular stranger. If she seems to be giving you a hard time or putting effort into being standoffish, don't accept someone being rude to you for no reason—it simply isn't an acceptable way for an adult to act. Instead, frankly ask, "Why are you so cold?" or "How's the bad attitude working out for you?" When you ask, don't be rude, but confident and matter-of-fact, as if she is truly acting inappropriately.

Often, if you try to cut through her shields with a straightforward question, she will snap out of her childish behavior and open up just to prove that you're wrong about her. She might continue to test your patience every few minutes to see what she can get away with, but for the time being, you can now proceed with your Opener. In some instances, she'll completely reverse her attitude because she doesn't want to be perceived as rude, even by a stranger, so you might find her to be extremely interested in your Opener.

You begin with the context of settling a debate and then ask for her opinion. Regardless of her answer, you defend the opposite choice and mock her for picking the "wrong" answer. Then, you add more disinterest by telling her that you two would never get along. As a bonus, if she tries to change her answer to yours, she's sending you an indication of her interest in you by adopting your point of view.

Teasing is an integral part of attracting beautiful women and defusing their defense mechanisms. Not only that, playful teasing is what keeps interactions at any stage of a relationship fresh and infused with sexual tension. However, just because you've got her attention now, doesn't mean you'll keep it. Whenever a woman does or says something dumb, or you just feel like disagreeing about something of little importance, don't be afraid to grin and call her on it.

Approaching Singles and Groups

Attractive women are almost everywhere and in every configuration possible—single, in a group, in a mixed group, seated, walking—so you have to prepare yourself for all these situations. If you only feel comfortable talking to women who are by themselves, you drastically limit the opportunities you have to meet new people. You may want to start by talking to women who aren't in groups, but eventually you have to work your way up to engaging groups of both men and women. If you can walk into a large group of people and hold their attention, you'll be on your way to getting their approval, which you need in order to talk to someone in the group one-on-one.

Singles

Women who are alone can sometimes feel uncomfortable and vulnerable. Using time constraints is important so she understands that you're just passing by and have something you wanted to say or ask. While you can wait for eye contact before initiating an approach, it's preferable to approach the moment you see a woman who could use your company.

Hesitation creates unwanted tension because she might not have anything to occupy her time other than noticing that you're staring at her. Since she's alone, she might think the worst about your intentions. A woman's "shields" are that much more difficult to break through when she feels you've been calculating how to approach her. If possible, let your words be the first thing she notices about you.

If she notices you *before* you have a chance to approach, you must instantly approach her as if you were already doing so. As soon as your eyes lock, smile, move in her direction, and deliver your Opener. Since it's just you and her, your Opener is likely to be a little more direct since you can't play off of any of her friends using their opinions or attitudes. Just remember that your frame of mind should be that of a choosy guy who sees a pretty face and is wondering whether there is anything of interest behind those good looks.

If a woman is alone in a social setting, chances are she has friends around, so you must be prepared for an interruption by one or more people while you're talking to her. Subsequent sections explain how to deal with her group, whether other women or both men and women. However, for the time being you can relieve yourself of having to entertain and gain approval of her friends just so you can have a one-on-one conversation. In this instance, you've saved yourself some time and effort because you're already talking to her one-on-one.

Groups

If you aim high, the woman you're most interested in is probably the most attractive of her group. If this is the case, you should strive especially hard to "win over" her friends before attempting to isolate her from them. In fact, no matter how counter-intuitive it may seem, you should try your best to ignore her while getting her friends laughing and more involved in the interaction. By hijacking her friends and ignoring her, she'll most likely try to reassert herself by trying to get your attention and approval.

Attractive women know they're attractive and expect men to hit on them and focus their attention toward them rather than their less beautiful friends. Attractive women are accustomed to this sort of treatment and many are confused when they don't get it. These women will put effort into gaining your attention, if only to blow you off just to reassert their status amongst their friends and affirm their attractiveness. If she interrupts you or positions herself in front of her friends, playfully tease her for it. For instance, ask her friends "Is she always like this?" or "How do you guys hang out with her?" The more attractive she is, the more likely she will need to prove to herself and her friends that she should be the focus of your attention.

Once you've established that looks alone are not enough for you to be attracted to her, and that you're only out to have a good time, you can start to take notice of her. By that point, her friends should be sufficiently entertained and you should be able to tell whether your company is welcome and appreciated. It can take between five and ten minutes to effectively win over a group, but once you do, it's time to subtly indicate who you're interested in getting to know better. The precise time to do this varies with each group, but it must be done early enough so that a woman doesn't believe you're attracted to one of her friends.

Transitioning from talking to a group of women to talking one-on-one with the woman you're interested in is covered in Chapter 11, "Attract." However, at this point start to think about who you might eventually want to hook up with, but don't make any obvious attempts to attract that person. As you work through the Hook stage, you will eventually acknowledge to the group that the woman you've been ignoring hasn't been getting much attention, and that you'd like to take the opportunity to correct that. By that point you will have gained the approval of her friends, who should have no problem as you wrap up your interaction with them and talk to their friend one-on-one. Had you not engaged the entire group, it would have been far more difficult to isolate their friend without creating drama and animosity.

Moving Groups

Women on the move are notoriously difficult to approach because they've already got it in their minds that they're headed somewhere else. Whether they're leaving the venue or moving to the other side of the room, your Opener has to be compelling enough to stop them in their tracks so they can listen to what you've got to say. Given these circumstances, your rate of success with moving groups will be significantly lower than usual. However, if a woman is too attractive to let slip away, don't let the odds prevent you from approaching.

Unless you're already in the process of walking around, you shouldn't go out of your way to approach women on the move. You don't want to appear, to the group or anyone around you, as though you need to chase women from across the room. Sometimes it's more productive to work with what's around you and hope that the group will makes its way back to you. If you noticed her five minutes prior to her leaving, you should have had enough time to leisurely make your way toward her and her group. Trampling over crowds of people to talk to a woman demolishes any social value you've created in the room, so try to keep the bigger picture in mind.

Given that you must avoid the perception that you're chasing after a girl, you have to position yourself so that when you have a chance to Open, you're not moving toward her or trying to play catch-up. It may be impossible depending on the environment or the distance of the group you want to approach. However, if you can place yourself somewhere along their path, you won't be seen as the guy who hunted them down, but as the guy who's enjoying himself in his own space. As they pass by, act as though you just noticed them and then Open them with high energy as you normally would.

Sometimes you'll already be walking around when you see women you want to approach who are also on the move. In this case, try to align yourself so that you and the group are moving in the same direction and then try to advance a few paces past them and continue walking. From there, you can turn your head to look behind you and then Open her or her group. As you begin talking, you should slow down a bit so that you're next to whomever you're talking to and then keep the same pace as you deliver your Opener.

Mixed Groups

As if Opening a group of women staring you down and judging you isn't challenging enough, you have to be prepared to Open mixed sets of men and women, sometimes even just one guy and one girl. No matter, if you're attracted and interested, you can't let any number or combination of people prevent you from finding out more about an attractive woman. There is, however, one distinct advantage when guys are in her group, namely that you're a guy and you have guy friends, so you should already be comfortable talking to them.

Just as with a group of women, your goal is the same even when guys are present—you have to Open the group by befriending them before you can focus on a particular woman. The difference in a mixed group is that you need to make an effort to befriend the guy or guys and get them to realize that you're not a creep or gay, not that there's anything wrong with that. Not only do you need to be friendly to the other guys, but you also have to convey humor and respect.

Even if none of the guys in the group are involved with the woman you're interested in, most guys take on a protective role with their group, so they need to be paid a small amount of respect so they'll allow you to gain an audience with their female friends. The quickest way to do this is to sincerely compliment them on something specific that they're wearing. Most guys simply do not compliment men they don't know, but it works as long as you follow up with a story or a comment that lets them know you're not hitting on them.

If the apparent alpha male of the group is wearing a decent shirt walk up to him and tell him that it's a cool shirt and that you used to have one just like it. Then, follow up by telling him that a girl slept in it at your place and wore it out the door the next day. You can button the story by telling them that you think it's a good idea to get two of every cool shirt because the women you meet always end up taking them. These few short lines convey a lot about you—you have good taste, you're friendly, and you're accomplished enough with women that they often spend the night. If they're not bothered by your presence, continue with one of your standard Openers.

Once you've delivered your Opener, you should find out whether any of the guys are boyfriends of any of the girls. This is especially true if you're talking to one guy and one girl who might actually be a couple. All you have to do is ask how everyone knows each other and if the woman you're interested in is with her boyfriend, one of them will let you know. Before you've even begun talking to her, you'll have found out her status and saved yourself a lot of time. If she's unattached, you can proceed as you normally would with a group.

Seated Groups

Guys who approach a group of seated women while they're standing can feel intimidated, since they quickly begin to feel they're performing and that they could get the veritable hook off the stage at any moment. It can be such an uncomfortable feeling that the mere fact that the group is sitting prevents them from ever making an approach. It's not acceptable to eliminate the possibility of meeting attractive women just because they're sitting down. Whether you're at a bar or a café or even a library, the odds are that most of the women will be sitting down, sometimes involved in their own conversation or immersed in a book.

The best way to power through the feeling that you're a court jester trying to please the Queen's court is to join the group you're speaking to within a few minutes of approaching. If you're confident and equipped to quickly calibrate yourself to the mood of the table, you can be so bold as to take a seat, without asking, then sit down and launch into your Opener as if you own the place. Before most guys can do this, they have to work their way up to becoming comfortable approaching and eventually joining a group of people they've never met before.

The key to creating a minimal amount of comfort with the group—enough to embolden you to sit with them—is to use time constraints. As long as they're made aware that, for instance, you have friends around or an appointment to make, they won't be alarmed that a possible psycho has just latched onto their group. Just remember to always include a time constraint before or during your Opener, and not a minute later. Your goal is to relieve the group of having to contemplate how they're going to get rid of you. Once that's done, you can sit down and become more comfortable now that you're literally on their "level."

It's important that you don't wait to be invited to sit down, ask if you can sit down, or continue talking in the hopes that everyone will stand up and listen to you. Before there are any uncomfortable silences and while you continue to Open the group, casually grab a chair and sit down without bringing any attention to the fact. As long as you're interesting enough and in the middle of a good story or opinion Opener, the group should be looking at your face and paying little attention as you make yourself comfortable.

Once you're seated and your Opener has generated enough interest with the group to continue the interaction, reiterate the time constraint. The group needs to know that no matter what happens in the next few minutes, you're not sticking around, even if you never end up leaving. Without being a jerk, convey that this interaction is costing you valuable time with your friends or something you were in the middle of doing. If you're fun and interesting and your time is in demand, they won't get suspicious of your motives and they'll allow you to proceed as you normally would with a group.

Take Control of the Interaction

A good Opener is important, but not enough to keep women interested in you. One of the problems many men have is that after they successfully Open a group, they aren't sure what to do next. Most men make the mistake of talking about themselves too much, including how many kids they want, why they're still single, or how cool their car is. Instead, you want to keep them talking about the jokes, ideas, and stories that you introduce into the interaction.

Whenever a group is bored, disinterested, walks away, rejects, or ignores you, it means you haven't demonstrated enough value to them. If your Opener had more energy, excitement, and humor than what they were previously doing, they will enjoy the interaction without thinking, *Why is this guy here?* If you don't provide any additional value to their evening, people typically return to whatever they're doing before you arrived. By adding value, through interesting, humorous, or outrageous stories and routines, a group is more likely to appreciate and welcome your company.

Demonstrating the right kind of value and personality, the kind that entertains and attracts, can be difficult in a short conversation. However, you have absolutely nothing to expect from women to whom you do not demonstrate value. No matter how successful your Opener seems, you have to continue demonstrating that you're not solely interested in sleeping with them, and that your momentary presence in their group will make their evening more enjoyable.

If the woman you're interested in smiles during your Opener and generally seems interested in your company for the time being, she hasn't taken a disliking to you so you should continue talking with her and her friends. It's important that you pay attention to her attitude and body language toward you while you're still Opening and once you interpret signs of interest, you transition into multiple conversations with her group to "win them over" and gain their approval so you can talk to her one-on-one.

Conclusion

Now that you've approached and Opened her or her group, you have to move away from all of the Opener material and start "stacking" conversations like you would with your friends or family. The Opener is meant to get your foot in the door, generate a little bit of interest, and create an opportunity to further the interaction. You'll find very quickly that if you linger on the Opener for more than a minute or two, the interaction will run out of steam and you'll feel the need to walk away during an uncomfortable silence.

After a few of these uncomfortable silences, you'll start to get a feeling for when to jump to a new topic immediately after the Opener has done its job. It won't take long before you stop thinking about how to transition from the Open stage to Hook stage, because if you don't, the interaction dies. Eventually, your instincts tell you that the Opener has done its job, so you instantly move on to asking her and her friends open-ended questions, or use any of the other conversational techniques described in the next chapter, "Hook."

Chapter 10

Hook

In this Chapter

★   Demonstrating social value and why women find it so important - even when they don't know it

★   Learning how to emotionally stimulate everyone around you to increase your attractiveness

★   Mastering how to hold interesting, playful, and flirtatious conversations

Hook

While a good Opener is important, it's not enough to keep an attractive woman and her friends interested in you. Once you realize the Opener has in fact "Opened" the group, you're faced with starting new conversational threads that are as interesting, if not more so, as your Opener. You have to keep their interest level high by demonstrating value through interesting and humorous stories that show off your personality and attractiveness.

Some men make the mistake of talking about themselves as much as possible, hoping to impress a woman or her group. Others over-share by talking about how many kids they want, why they're still single, why their ex is a bitch, or other topics that fall under the category of "too much, too soon." Instead of trying to impress or please a group, the goal of the Hook stage is to create enough interest and rapport in order to gain their approval when you want to break away with someone in their group. As you will learn, creating rapport has little to do with impressing people.

Women often look to their girlfriends for approval in their choice of men, which is one of the primary reasons why women stick with their groups, besides just having "fun." If you're sufficiently attracted to a woman and you want to bring her along to the next place, get her number, or bring her home for the night, it's important that you demonstrate value and personality not just to her, but to her group of friends as well.

Along the path to winning over her friends, you also need to plant seeds and begin to take some ambiguity out of the interaction. If you properly Opened the group, you did so indirectly by not telegraphing your intentions, which included playful teasing, time constraints, not complimenting them on their looks, not discussing anything overtly sexual, and not using obvious pick-up lines. This is done to quickly overcome the natural objections that women have when being approached by "strange" men. Now that they've lowered their defenses a bit and they're beginning to enjoy the interaction, you can feel safer in dropping a few flirty comments and letting one of the women know that you *might* be attracted to her.

Demonstrate Social Value

When men look for sexual partners, the values they're most interested in are usually of the physical variety. Is she fat, anorexic, or just right? Does she have a nice rack or is she built like a surfboard? Does she have a "but her" face or is she cute as a button? These are the very basic, very subjective, very easy to determine physical characteristics that initially influence how attractive a woman is to a man. Other traits that women have, like intelligence, humor, independence, wealth, and more are rarely considered "valuable" by men when it comes to initial attraction.

Women, on the other hand, consider a wide variety of traits and characteristics that subconsciously determine how attracted they are to a guy. Naturally a man's physical appearance is the first and easiest trait to consider, but most women evaluate additional traits before they allow attraction to progress to sex. In Chapter 6, "What Women Want," you learned about the traits that women like and dislike in men they find most attractive. This section builds on the positive traits detailed in that chapter by further explaining how to demonstrate them to women you're attracted to, as well as to their friends, who serve to approve or disapprove of their girlfriends' potential partners.

Why do I have to talk to her friends?

The purpose of the Hook is to work with her friends, not around or against them, by demonstrating enough social value that they view you as a possible match for the woman to whom you're attracted. When women go out to have a good time, they almost always go out in groups. When women get together, they often think and act as a group, not as individuals. In a woman's world, harmony amongst her friends is more important than her own individual thoughts or opinions, unless they're talking strictly between themselves. This unconscious desire to think and act as one is why you see women looking to each other to validate what they say and do as well as touching each other, holding hands, whispering, going to the bathroom together, cock-blocking, and any other way they can take care of each other.

Some guys like to approach a woman while she's away from her group so they can avoid dealing with a bunch of women who seemingly want to prevent guys from talking to them. This is a short-sighted approach because you rarely get very far before her friends interrupt you to find out whether "everything is okay." Or, the woman you're talking to will interrupt you because she needs validation from her friends to talk to you. It's a strange concept for most guys, but it's an observable social phenomenon that you should work with, not against.

If you can charm a woman's friends by demonstrating social value, you can disarm them and even get them to work with you to encourage the attraction between you and your target. Women like to play matchmaker if they think a guy shows a lot of promise, which is your goal during the Hook stage—to demonstrate to her friends that you're fun, interesting, charming, and that you'd make a good match for their single friend. Her friends should quickly become your friends, so at the very least they are disarmed and have no qualms about the two of you breaking away from the group later on.

You should already be familiar with the Myths and Rules of meeting and attracting women. Myth #7, *Guys can "convince" women into liking them*, explains that you can't convince a woman to be attracted to you; instead you must display attractive qualities to lots of women and from there they'll indicate whether or not they're interested in you. So, consider the following methods to demonstrate your value to the women you're attracted to using your actions and not male logic:

Arrive with female friends

When you arrive somewhere and hang out with attractive female friends, many nearby single women automatically assume that you're comfortable with women and that you're "safe," meaning you're not a rapist or psychopath. Some women might even view you as the pseudo-protector of the group of women you're with, which is always a positive. Whether you're viewed as a protector or merely safe to be around, you've already gained enough points or "pre-approval" to approach just about any woman knowing that she'll hear what you've got to say. After all, a bunch of women obviously enjoy your company, so other women will want to find out why.

One of the first things women try to assess is whether they're safe in the presence of a man they've just met. A guy who makes sudden movements, whose eyes shift around the room, or is unusually cryptic with personal questions, is considered creepy and unsafe to be around. Men who are nervous, yet perfectly upstanding gentlemen, unknowingly come across as weird or psychotic just because of their nervous mannerisms around women. A guy who arrives with a group of women who, for example, don't think twice when he playfully knocks into them or tickles them, are pre-approved for conversation. Watching you make other women smile and laugh can sometimes allow you to skip the Opener, because they're already interested in understanding why you're with a bunch of women, none of whom are your girlfriend.

Lead your group

When your friends look to you for what's good to drink, where to go next, and how to navigate the social scene, you're the leader of the pack. Women naturally prefer to be with guys who know what they're doing, so much so that they also help to direct their friends with what they're doing. Most women like "take charge" men who always seem to know what they're doing and where they're going because it demonstrates a lot of confidence. Men in control also seem to offer security and comfort because not only are they able to take care of themselves, but also those around them, including the women in their lives.

Leaders are an increasingly rare breed because our school and university systems are far more inclined to produce office workers than entrepreneurs. However, just because you find yourself working in a cubicle doesn't mean you can't be a leader on the basketball court, the paintball arena, or the college study group. If you can be a leader in your personal activities, there's no reason why those same leadership skills can't be put to use when you're out with your friends at bars and clubs.

There are hundreds, perhaps thousands, of books and audio programs on building your leadership skills, and the knowledge they impart can be applied to your pick-up skills as much as they can to your career advancement. Take the initiative to become the leader among men; even if it's just picking the bars you go to, when you leave, where you bounce to next, and beyond. If you can arrive at the bar with friends who view you as the man-with-the-plan, women will naturally want to find out whether your leadership abilities extend to your dating life as well.

Emotionally stimulate everyone around you

Imagine if you made it your life's mission to release pent-up emotions from the people you encounter, especially people you casually brush by in life, never to see again. If you can meet a stranger and make him laugh out loud or get him to angrily take a stand on an issue, you've probably made an impression on that person that will last throughout the day and beyond. Think back to the last time a stranger made an emotional impact on you. The fact that you can even remember a brief encounter from the blur of life demonstrates how powerful and rare it has become.

If you want to emotionally stimulate people, you have to be willing to be emotional so people understand that you're a real person and that it's okay for them to be open with their own thoughts and feelings. If you disagree with someone and you think they're an idiot for saying something, don't be afraid to say so. If someone harmlessly trips up when they walk across the room, playfully laugh at them. If something really shook you up that day, share it with someone. Whatever you're feeling, don't be afraid to mix it up with people and "make a scene." The guys who make a scene and get people involved are memorable and stand out in a crowd, unlike the hipster who stares into the distance and waits to be noticed.

Start talking to people in the grocery line, the old lady at the crosswalk, the secretaries in the elevator, or wherever you find yourself. Practice engaging strangers and see whether you can get a good laugh out of them or a strong opinion on an issue of the day. When you stroll into a bar or club, use the same principles to get groups talking to each other and creating involving experiences that people remember. I know it sounds weird, but that's only because it's so rare. Just remember that a guy who gets fired up, laughs from his belly, or gets a lump in his throat when he's moved is a real person who is in touch with his emotions, something women truly value. It demonstrates exponentially more value if you can get people to open up and do the same.

Tease attractive women

When you playfully tease women without the need to apologize or tell them that you're "just kidding," it communicates that you're comfortable around attractive women. Compare that to the typical male behavior of staring, stuttering, using tired pick-up lines, and giving clichéd compliments that a guy could say to any woman. Teasing subtly conveys that you don't view beautiful

Don't ask for her name, give her one

It only seems natural and polite to ask a woman for her name, but that's what every guy does. Asking for her name before she asks for yours subconsciously communicates that you're more interested in her than she is in you, which you want to avoid at this point. Plus, what if you don't remember her name five minutes later? What if you exchange names and she doesn't remember yours? Luckily, there's an easy way to avoid feeling rude and build attraction at the same time without even asking her name.

As you already know, you should treat women you meet as if they were your bratty sister, and given that siblings rarely call each other by their proper names, you shouldn't either. Instead, make up little nicknames as just another way to tease one another. Whether it's "short-stuff" or "gimpy" or simply "brat," they never call each other by their actual names. The same can also be said for couples, even though it's usually "baby" or "honey" or "lover," because they imply a deep familiarity with one another. Use these two facts to your advantage by coming up with a clever little nickname that you can use when you tease her and give her backhanded compliments.

It sounds far more complicated than it actually is and it doesn't require you to learn anything about her to conjure up a nickname. For example, redheads are "big red" or "pipi." Tall women are "stretch" or "bean pole." If she's wearing huge hoop earrings, she's "hooper" or "hoops." However, if the woman you're talking to is plain and not striking in any particular way, well, why are you even talking to her?

women as superior. In fact, you're so oblivious to their beauty that you don't think twice about making fun of how much she blinks, how her nose wiggles when she talks, or how her nails look good, even though they're fake.

Holding the frame of mind that she's just a bratty girl can really shake the confidence of beautiful women who aren't used to such treatment. Most will actively work to convince you that they are, in fact, something special. Every other guy treats them like a queen and kisses their ass, so if they're sufficiently attracted to you, they'll do whatever it takes to find out why you carry yourself differently than most of the other men they encounter.

Disqualify attractive women as potential partners

Disqualifying is a playful way of telling a woman why the two of you have absolutely no chance of ending up together. You can Open and playfully flirt during the Hook stage, but just as a woman starts to show interest in you, you might say, "I'm not really boyfriend material, but my single friends…they would love you!" Saying something like this before a woman has a chance to turn you down is contrary to typical male behavior. It can sometimes be so jarring to hear that the woman's jaw simply hangs open while she tries to grasp what you said.

Single women, especially in their twenties, are quick to dismiss men who don't meet their standards of an "ideal" man. Whether you're too short, too skinny, too muscular, too fat, or thousands of other superficial reasons, women can decide in less than five minutes why you aren't their perfect match. Because women are predisposed to doing the "choosing," they're caught off-guard when you "choose" for them. As with teasing, they'll quickly try to reassert that they're beautiful and picky and that you're lucky to be around them. You've essentially taken away one of their tools, so they're left scrambling to prove that you aren't too good for them. Unfortunately, once you initially asserted that it is *you* who choose romantic partners, not the other way around, they'll find it difficult to reject your frame of mind.

Some other great ways to playfully disqualify a woman include:

★ It would never work out between us.

★ I'm too high maintenance for you.

★ You're too much of a "good girl" for me.

★ You're trouble—I shouldn't even be talking to you!

★ You and I are not going to get along…you need a nice guy you can walk all over.

★ Take out an imaginary pencil and "write" on your hand as you say "Note to self…do not date this woman."

★ You're from [insert college, town, state, or country]?!? Oh man, my friend warned me about girls from *x*…

Maintain your frame of mind

Most men have a fairly elevated view of themselves, their abilities, and their station in life, *except* when an attractive woman challenges those views. Women deny it, but they challenge guys they meet for the first time by trying to expose cracks in their persona. For example, if a guy comes across as a man of wealth, a woman will find something he says, does, or wears that appears "cheap" and she'll call him on it. For instance, she might make fun of his un-manicured nails or his scuffed shoes. If the guy gets rattled by apologizing or lashing out, she'll perceive him to be phony or at least lacking in confidence.

Always expect these types of "bitch tests" when you meet exceptionally attractive women, for while they may not actually be bitches, they'll test some bitchiness out on you to see how you'll respond. What women are really try-ing to accomplish with these tests is to weed out guys who are insecure or self-conscious by testing their nerve. Most women would never admit it, but they're not just looking for guys who are confident, but also dominant. Her tests are meant to see how you'll respond when your confidence is rattled or your authority challenged. This miniature power play is a quick way for a woman to determine whether she's dealing with a dominant male or a sub-servient wuss.

Since the stakes are fairly high, you have to be prepared to quickly reassert yourself in a way that lets her know that if you two were romantically involved, you would be the dominant one in the relationship. Since women are psycho-logically and biologically inclined to be more submissive than their partner, most will appreciate that you met their challenge and didn't get offended as most guys tend to. As long as you can respond to her tests without insulting her or appearing agitated, she'll become more comfortable being around a guy she knows is strong willed with his beliefs and secure with who he is.

You usually want to acknowledge a woman's challenge by agreeing with her, and then rationally explaining why you're actually proud or indifferent about what she's challenged you about. This serves to put you back on equal footing and reasserts your dominant personality.

1. Stay relaxed, make solid eye contact, and smile genuinely.

2. While speaking clearly and confidently, agree with her.

3. Matter-of-factly explain why you're indifferent or proud of whatever she's mentioned.

4. Turn the challenge around by playfully qualifying her—grammar, at-titude, clothing, etc.

Enjoy yourself no matter the circumstances

It's a fact that men enjoy being in control and sometimes guys have a hard time dealing with a situation if it isn't going their way. Enjoying yourself no matter what the circumstances suggests that you're generally happy, but more importantly that you're emotionally mature and in control of yourself. Women live by their emotions much more than through reason and logic, so they sometimes need an unflappable guy who can help them navigate the traumas and disasters life throws at them. In a social setting, there really shouldn't be any real traumas or disasters, but if you can maintain your cool, even when the night isn't going as planned, you'll convey that you can enjoy yourself no matter what happens.

Consider the guy who gets the wrong type of beer from his waitress. Some guys will make a scene and chase down the waitress to berate her or complain about the beer until he gets another one. Clearly this type of guy doesn't enjoy himself unless he gets his way. However, a guy can demonstrate value to a woman by asking her to try his beer because it doesn't taste right, then declaring that it's "all good" and drinking it anyway, even complimenting the waitress for expanding his "drinking" horizons. This trivial episode can make an impact on a woman because something little didn't go your way, but you made the best out of it. In a way, she'll view you as someone who she can rely on to make the best out of a situation when things don't go *her* way.

Holding Interesting, Playful, and Flirtatious Conversations

You should try to keep the Opener and Hook stages to about five minutes total, although you can reconnect just a few minutes later. Stick to the time constraint you mentioned unless one of them makes it clear that she doesn't

If you can't be with the one you want...

Before you start to make any efforts to charm someone in the group and eventually pull her away from them, make sure you assess the situation to see whether someone else in the group has eyes for you. As you Open and work through all of the steps in the Hook stage you might find that you aren't getting any apparent interest in the woman who initially attracted you to her group. However, since you Opened the entire group, everyone had a chance to observe your attractive qualities, which means any one of them could signal some interest in you.

Women are almost always faithful to their social circle, at least when they're together. Even just a few minutes after you Opened the group, if one of the women moves a little closer, talks a little bit more, or pays a little bit more attention than the others, the rest will back off, even if they were attracted to you. Do not swim against these currents because you will almost always lose. Women may not be faithful to their friends behind their backs, but they always put up a good front when they're together, so you have little choice but to work with it.

Occasionally you'll see women competing for your attention, which can be flattering and extremely amusing. Again, you should work with this dynamic because once a "winner" is determined, she'll likely want to mark her territory as quickly as possible and you'll find yourself making out in no time. If you notice women competing for your attention, consider leaving on a high note for a few minutes and let them work it out. The victor will usually approach you in a few minutes and you can jump right into the Attract stage or even go for the Close if she seems especially aggressive. As always, stay outcome- independent and allow women's jealous tendencies to work in your favor.

want you to leave. Sometimes a woman will corner you or she'll physically pull you in to keep you around. If a woman makes such clear signals in the Hook stage, consider sticking around because you might progress to a favorable Close without much effort.

However, even if things seem to be going well, you most likely want to stick to giving them a taste of who you are and then leaving them wanting more. Just because the conversation is going well, doesn't mean you've been invited to stick around for a half hour. Women are used to being the ones who have to end their conversations with men, so they'll be intrigued by the interesting guy who took off right when things were getting interesting.

With that said, you have just a small window of opportunity to show to the group, especially the woman you're interested in, your attractive personality. While in the later stages it's best to allow a woman to do most of the talking, but during the Opener and Hook stages, you have to bombard a group with lots of fun, interesting topics that demonstrate your humor, wit, intelligence, and other desirable traits. It sounds easy to accomplish, but in practice you may find it difficult to sustain their interest for up to five minutes, at least initially.

Things you know you shouldn't do

Women aren't necessarily looking for the most handsome man in the room; many women simply want a classy guy that can carry himself with confidence and who uses proper etiquette in mixed company. The key word is "mixed" company, as in not a bunch of guys in a locker room. With that in mind, there are some things you should be mindful of when you're talking to a group of women so they aren't distracted from hearing your interesting and exciting stories.

★ Yawning, burping, spitting

★ Fidgeting

★ Incessantly clearing your throat

★ Picking in/around your nose

★ Blowing your nose

★ Scratching your balls or your ass

Unless you're a natural storyteller it can take some time to build a repertoire of stories and interesting conversational topics. Ideally, you need to have far more than five minutes of good material, because not every story or topic will resonate well with a particular group. As with a good DJ, you can't just put on a CD and press play. DJs usually start with the same one or two warm-up songs and then gauge the mood of the audience based on how many people are nodding their head, dancing, or leaving to get drinks. If a particular song is too high energy for the crowd, they quickly cut to a downbeat track. The process of calibrating songs to an audience is similar to calibrating stories and conversation topics to a group of women.

Ultimately, guys who talk the most also get the most action, sometimes in spite of what they talk about. You have to be in a high-energy, talkative mood if you hope to gain the attention of a group of women. The following few sections will help you mine your brain for material that you can talk about passionately. Whenever you approach a group of women, be prepared to talk for over five minutes without much of any help. Be the guy who keeps things lively through crazy stories, provocative topics, and a healthy dose of humor, instead of the guy who walks by and says, "Hey, ladies, what's up?"

Storytelling

Storytelling is an integral part of gaining the trust and approval of a group of women. Merely bringing up topics to gain their opinion may demonstrate that you're interesting and you've got something more on your mind than just getting laid. However, it usually isn't enough for them to allow you to take one of their friends away to another bar, for instance. Beyond demonstrating value, you can create trust and rapport by conveying character traits and qualities that you simply can't demonstrate.

For instance, if a group of women knew that the guy they were talking to was really good with kids, it might just be enough for them to go dancing while you sit alone with one of their friends. Even if there were children around, it would seem beyond creepy if you tried to interact with them just to impress a group of women. However, you can tell a story about how your little niece fell asleep in a pit of plastic balls that day and how you went into the pit and got her out without waking her up. You haven't told them you're good with kids and you haven't demonstrated it either, but you've told a cute story that *conveyed* a desired personality trait.

Women typically label these types of stories "lies," but if the character trait rings true, even if the particular story does not, there isn't much harm in telling them to people. Consider breast implants, which are technically fake, but still enlarge a woman's chest in order to attract male attention. Just because women use a "self-esteem" argument to justify fake body parts doesn't mean you have to buy into it. They bought those fake breasts and you told a fake story and there you both are, totally into each other.

Now that I've rationalized the need to embed your best traits into stories with varying degrees of truth, it's time to construct a few that you can recite whenever the need arises.

1. Start by thinking about which of the desirable male traits (see page 148) you want to convey by telling the story. Just to remind you of the top qualities women are attracted to: confidence, humor, spontaneity, intelligence, charm, class, generosity, honesty, and mystery. Pick one or two traits you truly believe are an important part of what makes you who you are. It sounds girlie, but that's the point.

2. Take a ride in the "way back" machine and mine your brain for memories of when you exhibited those qualities. For instance, if you see

yourself as confident and spontaneous, maybe you remember skydiving for the first time with a girl you met just the day before and you almost died in the process.

3. Consider how to convey the qualities you've chosen without directly stating them. You want to allude to your confidence and spontaneity, not flatly state them. If you don't feel like your story is compelling enough, exaggerate within reason. Then, write out the entire story and edit it down to the bare essentials by removing pointless details. If you have to include boring details, edit them to the core. Remove as much fluff as possible down to the most exciting and revealing parts.

4. Think about the circumstances that allow you to easily launch into your story so it seems like a natural part of the conversation. If your story involves another woman, you can tell one of the women in the group that she looks exactly like this person you went skydiving with, for instance. Always include some context before you tell a story to avoid the impression that you're performing.

5. Create an interesting verbal hook that gets people interested in what you're talking about. You should be able to emphasize certain words that you know will cause people to turn around or lean in. It helps to include the most exciting part of the story in the verbal hook. In this case, you might say, "**OH MY GOD!** You look just like this girl I dated last year named Sara. Actually, I had the **CRAZIEST** first date I've **EVER HAD** in my life with her. In fact **I ALMOST DIED!**"

6. Finally, end the story using the same verbal hook, then open the story up so the group can ask follow-up questions or better yet, ask whether they've had similar experiences. If you told a great story that got the group interested and engaged, they were probably already thinking of similar experiences. If you've really sold the story, the women might compete with each other by one-upping each other's crazy stories.

Putting it all together

The following story is 100% true, although it didn't have to be:

"**OH MY GOD!** You look just like this girl I dated last year named Amy. Actually, I had the **CRAZIEST** first date I've **EVER HAD** in my life with her, in fact **I ALMOST DIED!**"

I met this girl for the first time when some of my mutual friends met for dinner. We were totally into each other from the moment we started talking. During dessert, she told me she was going skydiving the next day, but her friend dropped out, and she wanted me to go with her. She seemed cool and I had never jumped out of a plane before, so, you know, why not?

So I went. Now, after four hours of instruction it was time to jump, so my instructor stayed on the ground to communicate on her walkie-talkie with me as I jumped. So I jumped and opened my chute, but she got me mixed up with another skydiver because we had the same color parachute. I didn't know any of this at the time, so I totally followed her instructions until maybe the last 1000 feet when I finally figured out I was nowhere near where I needed to land.

She kept yelling at me to "pull right" and "pull left," so I finally turned the radio off and tried to maneuver back toward the landing area, but it was too late to get over there. Instead, I was headed straight toward power lines and barbed wire fences. Luckily, I steered clear of the power lines, but I landed on the barbed wire. [Lift up your shirt for the group to see if the marks are still there.]

Man, it was insane, but I didn't get hurt, just shaken up. So that was the first date where **I ALMOST DIED.** So…any of you guys had a near-death experience?"

Stir the Conversational Pot

You can easily start to lose conversational steam after you tell a good story about yourself, so you need to be prepared to introduce a few topics that have nothing to do with you or the women in the group. But what are some good topics to discuss with women?

Think about what women read, what they watch, what they wear, and you already have your answer. In case you're unaware, women read magazines like *Cosmo* and *US Magazine*, they watch nighttime soap operas and celebrity gossip shows, and they most likely wear whatever young Hollywood is wearing. These are the topics that entertain the majority of women, so you need to pay just enough attention to bring up the same entertaining topics on which they've already "educated" themselves.

The following section details the main categories of topics you can explore with a group of women with a good chance of sparking their interest. If you misstep and they have no interest in what you're talking about, thank them for being different than the dozen other women you've talked to that night, and launch into a completely different topic.

Sex, Dating, and Drama

The only things guys seem to hate more than drama is talking about drama. Drama is gossipy and short on fact and forces guys to use parts of their brain they'd rather not, but women love drama. Drama speaks to women on an emotional level and lets them think about how they might react to situations in which they're not directly involved.

Since most men think logically, they have a lot of trouble thinking of emotionally charged questions—in fact they rarely know where to begin. If you spend a little time talking with women, you'll soon pick up on what they like to talk about. For instance: Would she stay with a guy who did x? Would she still talk to her friend if she did y behind her back? Would she ever hook up with a guy just because he had a huge z? I leave the specifics for you to fill in because it rarely matters what they are as long as they result in interesting, humorous, and engaging conversations.

If you've built some rapport and the group seems comfortable, you shouldn't be afraid to bring up stories and questions about sex and dating. If you mention sex though, it's best to leave out the raunchy details and talk about people who aren't with you. You should also avoid talking about your own sexual experiences unless someone specifically asks or they seem comfortable talking about their own experience, then share away!

Example Questions:

★ My two favorite co-workers are about to hook up and I think it's gonna end in tears. How do I convince them not to?

★ I went to [far away] for a girl and it was a complete disaster. Do you think long distance relationships ever work in the end?

★ I've never been out on an Internet date; they seem like a total crapshoot. How about you guys?

★ I've never cheated on anybody and to the best of my knowledge no one ever cheated on me. Do you think cheating and karma are connected?

Horoscopes and the Metaphysical

The average guy doesn't know much about astrology, runes, tarot cards, chakras, or any of the other pseudo sciences. You're probably blissfully ignorant of these topics and you would prefer to keep it that way, believe me, I used to be there. I still don't believe anything I can't see with my own eyes, but I'm at least a believer in the power of being curious about these subjects when talking to women.

Instead of reading up so I can pretend to be an expert on horoscopes and the like, I know just enough to be able to bring up the subject and tell her that I'm interested, but not yet convinced, which is true. Women understand that guys don't know about these things, but many are eager to explain what they do and don't believe in and why. A lot of women are very passionate about one or more metaphysical topics and love sharing something they feel deeply about. However, if you meet a woman who thinks it's all bullshit, agree, switch topics, and consider yourself lucky.

Example Questions:

★ My friend dated this girl for a week and then stopped talking to her, but said she placed a spell on him and now he says he's in love. Do you think spells really work?

★ My horoscope said I should be ready for an adventure, do you believe in that stuff? I think I only believe in fortune cookies.

★ One time this old woman with a freaky glass eye tried to read my palm, but she said she couldn't. Then she gave me my money back and pushed me out of the door. Would you ever leave the house if that happened?

★ I tried handwriting analysis one time and I purposefully wrote differently, but she still had me completely pegged. I guess I'm a believer now... Do you believe that the way you write is determined by your personality or the other way around?

Lifestyles of the Rich and Famous

Now, more than ever, women live vicariously through the lives of stars and starlets. It's not just bored housewives anymore, but perfectly intelligent college graduates who can tell you who is dating who this week and why it will never work out, or why a famous couple got divorced, or which starlet bitch-slapped another at a trendy nightclub. Situations like these are begging to be picked apart with wit and sarcasm. Whatever you decide to talk about, just make sure to bring it up in a humorous way so the group knows you don't take it seriously.

The obvious drawback to talking about these topics is that celebrities are idiots, their ups and downs are of little consequence to you, and these people wouldn't spit on you if your hair was on fire. However, the benefit is that it takes no more than five minutes to get yourself up to speed on their torrid lives so you can launch into questions or conversations about them. Without much effort, you can lob softball questions to a group of women who most likely will eat it up.

If you get stuck on the specifics, visit some celebrity gossip websites before you leave the house. If you're at the supermarket, pick up a copy of *Cosmo* or *People*. If you're watching TV, flip to the E! Entertainment channel and you should have more than enough gossip from which to choose. Just remember that women know that straight guys don't care about celebrity gossip, so add a little context like "this girl at my worked asked me/told me/won't stop talking about..." and then launch into the gossip of the day. If they profess not to care about celebrity gossip, wholeheartedly agree and move on to something truly interesting.

Example Questions:

★ This girl I work with keeps talking about how she can't believe *x* broke up with *y* just to go out with *z* because *z* is such slut and *y* is much classier. I think they're both pretty hot, what about you?

★ How many times is *x* going to get busted for drugs before people stop hiring him for movies? I know he's talented, but my nephew is totally into him. He's kind of a shitty role model, don't you think?

★ *X* needs the paparazzi just as much as they need *x*, so I think she's just a spoiled brat. What would you do if you had a bunch of cameras in your face?

★ One time I met *x* at a fancy restaurant when I was in New York. I always thought he would be a real dick in person, but he was super nice. Ever met anybody famous?

Psychology

Men aren't that interested in getting to the root of why someone did something. Whatever it is, it's done and has to be dealt with, but spending time discussing why seems pointless. However, if you're interested in holding interesting conversations with women, you should rethink your position. However, pop psychology isn't just useful for conversations—you won't truly excel at attracting women until you spend time trying to understand the psychological dynamic between the sexes. I'm not saying you will *succeed* in understanding, but you have to put the effort in. Plus, as an additional bonus, you will always have something interesting to talk to women about.

It's important that you never talk directly about yourself and your psychology or hers; keep things general in a "men do this, women do that" mode. This keeps things light and humorous because neither of you have to directly reveal how you do or do not fit the stereotypes, even though a lot can be learned about someone based on their opinions of men and women.

Example Questions:

★ Okay, get this, my niece is nineteen and she wants to get a tattoo of her boyfriend's name on her shoulder. I told her not to do it, but she won't listen to anybody. Are all girls like that? The more someone says not to do something, the more they want to?

★ Check out this text message [show your phone: I'm at nightclub *x*. Come buy me a drink and we'll have some fun!:)]. Is this how women flirt or does she just want someone to buy her some drinks?

★ My friend broke up with his girlfriend and then they got back together. Then she found a girl's g-string in his room and he lied and said it was his. Now she thinks it's sexy and makes him wear it. Do you women like that shit or is she just getting back at him?

★ I gotta get your opinion on this: my friend has been dating this really hot blonde for almost three weeks and they were getting kind of serious and then she finally told him she's a stripper. I think that's messed up. Would you wait that long to tell someone something so important?

Psycho-analyze the strangers around you

Look around at the people who surround you and find something interesting going on. Point something out and then try to guess what their dynamic is. Do they look nervous like they're on a first date? Do they glow like they've just had sex? Are their jaws clenched like they've been fighting? Speculate about whether they seem like a good match. Which one is dating out of their league? Talk about their body language, their outfits, or anything else that stands out. Picking apart people you don't know is fun and most women love it because you're saying what everyone else is thinking.

Conclusion

You can try to fake your way through some of these conversational topics, but most women will see right through you. The fact is you brought up a topic that they probably know infinitely more about than you do, so you have to be prepared to back up the questions you pose with thought-out responses of your own. Become as familiar as you can with at least one of these topics so you can talk about them in interesting ways. Remember that you're not trying to impress women with your judgments on these topics—you're just trying to bring something interesting and humorous to the table. Your goal all along is to gain approval from the group so you can then focus on your target.

Stay positive by not saying anything negative

Guys who don't have much experience conversing with women usually talk about the same things they might talk about with their guy friends or family members. Even though you may feel comfortable talking about these topics with your friends, it may cause a woman to feel distinctly uncomfortable. Most guys already know what topics to avoid, but for those who need to be told, stay away from anything that touches upon domestic violence, death, rape, or the harm of children or animals. I know, you're laughing, but some guys need explicit instructions every step of the way. In addition, although they may not seem negative in the classical sense, you should avoid talking about comic books, video games, sci-fi, pro-wrestling, politics, or any of your personal problems.

Some guys have been dealt a few bad hands in their lives and feel the need to share their misfortune and misery within minutes of meeting someone. Your goal is to be the best version of yourself whenever you're trying to attract someone, so rethink how whining and complaining plays into this goal. Surely you have some positive experiences to share that demonstrate how successful you can be or how happy life can be. Why spend even a second sharing negative stories about yourself or anyone else?

Should you stay or should you go?

By this point, you should have a good idea of whether you've Hooked her group or not. However, just because they enjoy your company and welcome your presence, doesn't mean it's in your best interest to stick around. Combined, the Open and Hook stages shouldn't last longer than five to ten minutes and since you included a time constraint early in your Opener, you should consider sticking to your statement of only having "a minute," even if they seem to want you to stay.

As long as you're going to be in the same vicinity, like a bar or a party, there is no harm in taking a break and leaving on a high note while everyone is still laughing and having a good time. By leaving, you're actually taking the value you provide (humor, positive energy, and sexual tension) away from them, not to mention away from the woman to whom you're attracted. While every other guy wants to talk about himself for as long as they'll listen, you'll leave a much better impression by quickly entertaining and charming them, then leaving them wanting more.

Depending on the situation, the woman you teased might eventually show up where you're hanging out to pick up your previous conversation. If she was attracted and intrigued by the way you held the attention of her group, she'll want to find out more about you. If you're in a bar, club, or other closed social situation, she'll have an opportunity to either approach you or make sure she's close enough for you to notice her again. If it's the latter, try to resist walking back over to her, but instead make eye contact and gesture her to come over and join you or your group. If she doesn't, stick your tongue out at her, and then ignore her. If she joins you, smile, and ask her whether she's always so obedient.

Number Close

Sometimes you'll realize that you need to Close immediately without ever building much attraction, usually because of time and location restraints. If this is the case, your only option is to get her phone number. There isn't a lot of value in getting a phone number at this point because they don't result in much success when it comes to picking up where you left off. When you call these numbers, it shouldn't surprise you if she's not interested in spending more time with you just because you entertained her and her friends for a few minutes. You may be funny and interesting, but you're also just some guy at a bar who was only a little more outgoing than the rest.

Ultimately, it's up to a woman to determine how comfortable she is with you, so if you have to get her number now, you should. There's no harm in collecting women's numbers. If you or her group have to leave, conclude by suggesting that you think it would be great to continue this conversation at another time and that you'll need her number to do that. For those of you who don't want to "ruin" the conversation by asking for her phone number, you really have no other option and your rate of rejection may run higher, but your rate of success by not asking is precisely zero.

The best way to wrap up a good conversation is to end on a high note and leave her wanting more, typically during a shared laugh. Don't wait for a pause after the laugh before telling her you have to go, because you don't want it to seem like you've run out of steam and *need* to leave. Instead, cut the laugh a little short and say that you've got to go. The basic structure is that you have to go, that you had a good time talking to her, and that you think the two of you should talk again. For instance, you could say, "Hey, looks like my friends are getting restless, I better head back over there...it was fun talking with you, we should definitely pick this up where we left off..." Then you can ask for her e-mail address or phone number or both (see page 339).

Disengage

Perhaps you decide to leave, not because you want to leave on a high note, but simply because you want to leave. Maybe your Opener didn't go down well or you just weren't able to Hook the group with high energy and funny stories. Or, just as likely, the woman you were initially attracted to turned out to be boring, bitchy, insecure, delusional, self-centered, desperate, or some other reason that causes you to start thinking about your exit strategy. Since you want to find your way out of the conversation and move on to Open another group, you don't want to waste too much time just to be nice, but you also shouldn't treat her or her group like crap just because things didn't go as planned, or because she wasn't what you were looking for.

When you know you're not digging a girl or the conversation, you should gently let her know that you have to work early the next day, you need to get back to your friends, your llama needs a haircut, or whatever comes to mind. You could be a dick about it, but what if you end up chatting up one of her friends later that night? Or maybe she'll invite you to a party she's having. Or maybe you have a change of heart after a few shots of tequila. It's best not to burn bridges just to make yourself feel better because it can hurt you in the long run.

Also, don't wrap up the conversation and leave just because you think you're going to get rejected—keep an open mind. If you like the woman you're talking to and you've put some time into it, go for the Close you originally intended. If it doesn't go your way, at least you tried. If you want to leave, do it because you found out what you wanted to find out—whether or not you two would make a good match—and now it's time to move on.

Conclusion

If you won't have an opportunity to re-engage the woman you've been talking to, typically because one of you are leaving the venue, you should get her number if you want it, or move on to a different group. In these circumstances, it's now or never, so if you're attracted to her, you should at least get her number. After you number Close her, you'll have to try to pick things up where you left them at some point in the future. Once you get reacquainted, you can jump straight into the Attract stage, because she wouldn't agree to hang out with you if she wasn't at least interested, if not already attracted.

On the other hand, if you decide to leave a woman or her group, but stay in the same venue, you'll have an opportunity to re-engage them some time later in the evening. As you just learned, jumping into a group with a lot of high energy and then taking it away helps elevate your social value. Because you brought and then took away such interesting and entertaining energy, some of the women you talk to will miss having you around, especially after having to hear a few pick-up lines from other guys. If any of the women in the group were attracted to you, they'll tend to find you again so they can flirt with you and vice versa.

Talking to lots of people and creating positive energy throughout the venue is the goal of the Open and Hook stages. Demonstrating your attractive qualities to as many groups as possible elevates your social value and can create competition for your attention and eventually, your affection. Don't hesitate to leave a group at the very moment when everyone is laughing and enjoying your company the most. If you decide to take a breather, just assume that you'll talk to the same group or at least one of the women in the group, before you leave. Use this time to mentally prepare yourself for the Attract stage, so you have an idea of what you might talk about and how you might transition into a strong Close.

Chapter 11

Attract

In this Chapter

★ Revealing why you have to break the touch barrier early and often

★ Mastering how to flirt with confidence and test her interest in you

★ Planning for the Close and how to transition to the Connect state immediately or in the future

Attract

The goal of the Attract stage isn't to directly impress or use logic to convince a woman of how attractive you are, or explain how insane she is not to want to be with you. Instead, in order to build attraction, you must focus on *demonstrating* your attractive personality during this stage. No matter how successful your Opener is and how charmed her friends seem to be, you have to demonstrate to the woman you're attracted to the qualities that she perceives to be of value to her. Women don't typically spend time thinking about how much value a guy can provide, but she definitely picks up on the way she feels when she's around you and it's that feeling that determines your value to her.

A lot of guys seem to think their mere presence and company is of some specific value to women, but it isn't nearly enough. If you have the face of a model or a muscular physique, your presence *can* be a turn-on for some women. She may like the way the proximity of your muscles or symmetrical face make her feel, so your looks can hold some value to her. However, even if your looks alone attract women, it usually wears off quickly if that's all you have to offer. In addition, instead of bragging about your possessions and status in life, you have to demonstrate specific desired qualities about yourself through stories, jokes, and in-the-moment interaction.

Demonstrating any of the qualities listed in the desirable traits section of Chapter 6, "What Women Want," usually works to your advantage when you first meet someone. Even if you haven't calibrated qualities to the woman you're talking to, there are some basic traits that almost all women like to see in effect. Any of the generic "desired" qualities are infinitely better than the "Here I am, this is the way I look (I'm sorry I'm not better looking), now please like me!" attitude held by most guys. That default attitude usually results in rejection and leaves guys thinking, *Oh, better luck next time, I'm sure someone, somewhere will like me...I hope.*

Before you start emphasizing your best qualities and building comfort and rapport by touching, flirting, and finally, breaking her away from her group so you can Close, you should work on frame control. Frame control involves dropping a few comments that convey the fact that you're someone who is comfortable around women, is used to being pursued by women, and is anything but needy around women because he, as well as most women, view him as a catch. By getting women to positively view you the way you view yourself, you'll have a much easier time breaking the touch barrier, playfully flirting, and pulling her away for some one-on-one conversation.

Frame Control

One of the most powerful ways to build attraction, beyond demonstrating social value and storytelling, is maintaining a strong frame of mind. Anyone who's even slightly self-aware has an idea of who they are, what they represent, and how people view the person they present to the world. Women are much more self-aware than the average guy and most spend an inordinate amount of time considering how their friends, family, and even strangers perceive them.

For instance, a woman might "know" that she's beautiful and her frame of mind is that men should be grateful for her company by treating her to expensive dinners, buying her clothes, and running her personal errands.

On the other end of the spectrum is an equally attractive woman who was an ugly duckling as a child and consequently has the frame of mind that she's never good enough. This woman seeks the approval of men by cooking for them, sleeping with them, and whatever else it takes to please them because she still views herself as an ugly duckling. To most people's eyes, these women are equally beautiful, but they view themselves and the world through a different frame of mind. If the ugly ducking changed her frame of mind and expected men to treat her with respect, she no doubt would get it.

People are quick to pick up on your personality and status by observing your body language and your attitude, and if you maintain a particular frame of mind, they begin to view you in the same manner you view yourself. For example, if Donald Trump were to visit a country where he was virtually unknown and visited a boardroom of people who had never heard of him, they would likely view him as someone who commanded respect and gets what he wants out of people. The Donald has always held the same frame of mind and it's constantly on display because it saves time and it works. If Andy Dick were to enter the same boardroom, he wouldn't get any respect and his demands wouldn't be met because he holds a drastically different, albeit equally strong, frame of mind.

I don't want to get too existential on you, but reality is what you make of it, there is no such thing as an objective reality as far as humans are concerned. We each view the world in different ways and while we generally see the world in the same way—blue is blue, the sky is up, sex is good—everyone holds unique viewpoints that don't always coincide, which is why we have different political parties, for instance. When you meet people for the first time, they have nothing to work with except your body language and your attitude, and they use these two factors to determine what kind of person you are and how they will interact with you.

When you walk up to a group with your shoulders slumped and half your body aimed away from them, it communicates that you aren't enthusiastic (shoulders slumped) and that you don't feel you should be talking to them (your body isn't committed to the interaction). If you move into their group with your head held high, your eyes locked into theirs, and your body squarely facing them, it brings a lot more gravity to what you're saying, because you appear to have confidence. At the very least, they will listen to your Opener because you act like they should.

State Breakers

Now that you've digested the psychology behind holding a strong frame of mind, it's time to apply it to the women you meet. As you've just read, women initially only have your body language and your attitude to determine what kind of person you are and how they should react to you. With that said, you want to make a conscious effort to convey a few things about the kind of guy you are and the way you are accustomed to being treated. Luckily, it only takes a few witty comments to jolt women into realizing that you're not like most other guys and won't tolerate being treated as such.

The term "state breaker" is used because most women maintain a default "state" of mind when dealing with guys who approach them, along the lines of "I'm a woman, you're just a man. From what I see, there isn't anything special about you. I'm going to end this conversation as quickly as possible because you're not in my league." Women will never admit to holding such a negative frame of mind, but it's patently obvious when you watch them interact with men they don't know. Therefore, the goal of the following example statements is to break a woman's default state of mind and either even the playing field or lower their status relative to yours.

Read the list below to get an idea of what you're trying to convey on the surface, such as "I've got high social value" and the meta-message you're indirectly communicating, like "I'm not sure *you* have high social value, so prove it." Women use these same tactics on men to quickly figure out whether they're dealing with a chump or a man's man, so don't be inhibited in the least when you use them. Pick a few, commit them to memory, and say them when most appropriate, otherwise they won't make any sense. For instance, if the woman you're attracted to says something silly, smile and loudly say to her friends "She doesn't get out much, does she?" Remember, with state breakers your goal is to be witty and perceptive, not sarcastic and rude.

I've got high social value: I'm not sure you do

★ You girls don't get out much, do you?

★ Those weird guys have been checking you out, I should go introduce you.

★ You're from *x*?! Oh man, my friend warned me about people from *x* because…

Women are attracted to me: I don't need to hit on women

★ Man, sometimes I get so tired of being treated like a piece of meat.

★ Could you please stop mentally undressing me?

★ Hey! My eyes are up here.

I'm hard to get: I don't sleep around

★ Women have to get to know the real me if they expect me to put out.

★ I swear…all you girls think about is one thing!

★ Don't think you're going to get anywhere with me just because you bought me a drink.

I have high standards: I'm looking for more than beauty

★ Is there more to you than meets the eye?

★ You've obviously got good-looking parents. Besides your looks, what's something about you that makes people want to get to know you better?

★ Did you go to school? Are you smart? I can't hang with dumb people.

I know you're into me: I'm a catch and you know it

★ Are you always this forward?

★ Hey, hands of the merchandise.

★ Yeah, if you're lucky!

Basic Kino

Kino is short for kinesthetics, which is just a big word for touching. Once you've started talking and everything seems to be going well—she laughs at your jokes, doesn't break eye contact, and squares her body toward yours— it's time to break the touch barrier. When you're ready to initiate a little kino, you have to remember one thing above all: touching isn't a big deal as long as it's done right. One of the first steps in making sure it's done right is to never act like you're doing something you're not supposed to. After all, it's no big deal, right?

Guys can get very uneasy when it comes to touching a woman they don't know, especially if they're attracted to her. For some guys, simply approaching a woman is a huge leap, so pushing forward and casually touching her seems nearly impossible. A lot of guys would rather wait until a woman touches his knee or grabs his elbow when she laughs so he knows she feels comfortable with him. However, if you wait, she may never make a move and if enough time passes without so much as a high five or a touch on the shoulder, her attraction to you may fade. With that said you *must* get over yourself and realize that people touch each other when they talk as a natural expression of rapport and comfort.

If you observe two female friends in close proximity to one another, you'll notice that they can't keep their hands off of each other. Whether sharing a moment of joy, sorrow, or anything in between, they platonically touch one another as a way of conveying that they understand one another, that they "get it." Casually touching reinforces a woman's friendship or furthers her bond to a new female acquaintance. If you want to further your bond with someone, male or female, touching is the fast track to making it happen. With guys you punch shoulders or high five and with women you touch their shoulder when they make you laugh or playfully swat at them when they're being bratty.

So now that you've Hooked the group and dropped a few state breakers, you have to find moments to casually touch the woman your attracted to without causing alarm. Start by touching her hand or elbow when you make a joke or want to reinforce a point you're making—just make sure it's done naturally by never looking directly where you're moving your hands. Always maintain eye contact and keep talking, laughing, or listening when you touch, because if you're looking around for something to touch, it's now a "big deal" to you and, if she notices, to her as well.

Unless she's already been touching you, I strongly suggest staying away from her butt and especially her breasts for the first few touches. Also, do not hold the touch for very long, just a second or two will accomplish your goal. Anything longer than that and she'll take notice, which you want to avoid. If she notices, she might think you're being too forward and put her guard back up or, even worse, her friends will notice and make a big deal about it, which can sometimes ruin any chances you have to pursue her further.

By touching her you are non-verbally saying that I like you and I might be interested in you beyond this quick conversation. By casually touching while you're in the moment, you're being ambiguous with your intent, just the way she prefers it. If your touch didn't seem to register with her, you've done it exactly as you should. You don't want a woman to take notice of you touching her, instead you want her to passively register that you're no longer strangers, but friends and potentially more.

As you continue through the Attract stage, you can continue with an occasional grab of her shoulder or clutch of the knee, as long as it's in context with your conversation and only for a moment or two. After she's given you multiple Indications of Interest and you eventually break her away from her group, you can escalate the type of kino you use by touching each other for longer periods of time and in much more invasive, but welcome, ways. Also, after you break the initial touch barrier, remember to wait until she is away from her friends to move past anything other than basic kino.

Is she interested?

Before you start thinking of how you're going to break her away from her group and where you want the interaction to lead, you should observe one or more signals that she's interested in you beyond the conversation you're having with her and her friends. Luckily, if a woman is interested in you, most are quite good at giving you all of the signals you need, you just have to notice them. Women live through meta-messages, which is their way of indirectly communicating without explicitly saying what it is they want to say.

I'm sure you've heard a woman lament about meeting a guy and giving him countless signals that she was really into him, but then he just ran off with his friends. Guys are cavemen and most of us need to get hit over the head with a direct verbal or physical declaration before we know "what's going on." Women will swear up and down that they make it quite clear when they're attracted to a guy, but from the guy's perspective, she gave absolutely no indication that she was remotely interested in him. Because most guys aren't naturals at picking up on these signals, you have to make it a point to pay very close attention to what she says, but even more attention to what she does, in order to find out whether she's attracted to you.

As you know, most women will wait for you to break the touch barrier first, which you should, but after that point you need to pay attention to see whether she demonstrates any interest in you. The ways a woman lets you know she's interested in you are different than your crude methods, so look for any of the following indicators; if you start to get a hunch that she's attracted to you, go with that feeling.

Table: Indicators of Interest

Conversational	Physical	Physical
She picks up on your conversation topic after you've stopped talking.*	She touches you or doesn't shy away when you casually touch her.*	She introduces you to her friends and insists you stay with them.*
She compliments you.	She moves closer to you.	She buys you a drink.
She asks if you have a girlfriend or talks about your girlfriend without knowing if you have one.	She leaves for a drink, goes to the bathroom, or talks on the phone and then comes back.	She whispers something to her friend(s) and they laugh, smile, or nod together.
She doesn't mention a boyfriend.	She looks you in the eyes when you talk.	On your way out, she stops to ask you where you're going.

Conversational	Physical	Physical
She asks your name, age, or other personal questions.	If she does something funny or embarrassing, she looks for your reaction.	She finds you on her way out to let you know she's leaving.
She tries to find common ground: music, restaurants, clubs, and anything else that you both like.	She repeatedly looks at you, sometimes just from the corner of her eye.	She interrupts a conversation you're having so she can join in or pull you away.
She disagrees with you or argues with you, but she's still smiling and laughing.	She plays with her hair or casually fidgets.	She overhears something funny you said to other people and laughs.
She playfully challenges something you say.	She brushes against you when she walks away.	Her friends leave her to dance or get drinks and she stays with you.
She talks to you more than her friends do when you Open her group.	She lets her legs touch yours when you're seated.	She waits for you if you leave for a moment.

*Most obvious signals that she's interested and expects you to take the interaction into the Connect stage, either now or in the near future.

Maybe she's not interested

It's easy to figure out whether a woman isn't interested in you romantically. Other than stating as much, she'll demonstrate behavior that's the opposite of any of the signals you just read about. For instance, if she moves away from you, flinches when you casually touch her, or insists on leaving with her friends to get drinks, she's letting you know she's not attracted to you. Since you should have picked a location with a lot of attractive women, just turn and find another group to talk to. The next day you can think back to what you might have said or done that turned her off, but for now, keep working the room.

Of course if you notice just one thing that could be perceived as an indicator of disinterest, you don't necessarily need to wrap up the conversation and move on. People do a lot of things without really thinking about them or because they've been conditioned in a certain way. If she pulls away slightly when you touch her, but displays many other indicators of interest, follow your instincts on whether she's worth further pursuit. It's far better to follow through on someone you're attracted to and face rejection than to give up because she inadvertently turned to look at something, for instance.

Flirting

One of the original goals of your Opener was to avoid telegraphing interest, which meant conveying that you're not out just to get laid, but to have a good time. However, now that you've got her attention, she's displayed multiple Indicators of Interest, and you've gotten to know her for more than just her looks, it's time to subtly convey that you're attracted to her now that you've gotten to know her a little better, assuming you have. Once she's shown you a few signs that she's interested, it's your turn to drop some little hints so that she sees you as more than just a friendly guy she met in a bar that she won't likely see again.

The point of a five-stage progression to meeting and attracting women is so you can avoid being viewed as one of millions of men who see women as a source of pleasure and not much else. By now, you've won over her friends and, through stories and teasing, you've shown that you're not like "all the other guys," but that doesn't mean you aren't a flesh and blood male. If a woman shows interest and seems attracted to you, you're fully expected to flirt and reciprocate with a similar amount of interest. Either that or you've decided that you're not interested, which means you should gracefully move on.

Now that you've got her attention and you're starting to think about where the interaction could lead, it's time to slowly but surely "react" to the idea that you're attracted to this woman, not just for her looks, but for her personality as well. By react, I mean that when you first approached her group it was because you were having fun and being friendly, but through her actions and her words, you found someone worth your attention. You were most likely attracted to her before you ever approached her group, but in order to quickly lower her and her friends' natural defenses, you had to use an indirect approach. Now that they've been Opened and Hooked and she now appears to be Attracted, it's time to bring more clarity to the interaction.

How to Flirt

Now that she's given you a few signals that she's attracted to you, it's safe for you to slowly unmask your intentions and flirt with her. Think of flirting as a means to indirectly compliment a woman without having to specifically mention what you're thinking and feeling. Because women are so much more emotional than logical, you have to flirt emotionally, not intellectually. What this means is that you have to *show*, not tell, her that you're starting to think of her less as a new friend and more as a potential love interest. As attraction increases, your flirting should move from subtle to overt as you start in the Attract stage and move into the Connect and Close stages.

Since most women are emotional rather than logical, your flirting should be designed to make her feel happy and attractive. You want a woman to associate these happy thoughts and feelings with you, which you can accelerate by touching her in a friendly manner as you flirt. For instance, if you make her laugh, touch her knee or her shoulder without drawing attention to it. You can connect everything you've learned about kino to flirting, so you can combine the two to increase the effects of both. Eventually, your touch will connect to her feeling happy and attractive, so that you eventually don't need to flirt as much because your mere touch will serve the same purpose.

Flirting isn't optional, it's a requirement, especially after she's already flirted and given you other indications of her interest in you. By flirting back, you can get a sense of how responsive she'll be to further advances, which in turns helps you decide how you want to proceed through the Attract, Connect, and Close stages. Remember, flirting is just a means to an end, because if you don't flirt, she may be caught off-guard if you ask for her number, or she might get confused about why you asked her to get coffee or go to a different bar. Flirting is how you first advance the idea that you expect to see her again.

Find something sexy about her

If you Open her or her group indirectly and you do it well, they most likely won't view you as the type of guy who says anything he has to just to get laid. When most guys flirt, they typically tell a woman she's sexy or that she has sexy legs, eyes, or just about any other body part he thinks she'll appreciate hearing about. When a guy starts complimenting a woman's beauty, this is a sign that he was just being friendly in order to get laid. It's not that he told her that she was sexy, it's *what* he told her he found sexy that she might find offensive. Instead of complimenting something she was born with, her looks, you should instead compliment her style or her energy.

One of the best ways to start flirting is to pick out something a woman is wearing and tell her that it's sexy. For example, "those boots are really sexy" conveys some interest and if she responds positively, she'll expect you to amp up your flirtation. Note that you're not telling her that *she* is sexy, but that something she's wearing is sexy. These types of compliments are indirect in the sense that you aren't admiring her God-given beauty, but her fashion and attention to style. After that, you're free to verbally admire her eyes, her ears, her lips—just about anything other than her ass or her breasts.

Use a deeper, sexier voice

When you first Opened her or her group, you had high energy and a lot of upbeat body language to convey how fun and friendly you are. Now you want to make it clear that you're interested in her as more than an acquaintance, so you have to slow things down and start talking to her less like a friend and more like a lover. However, that doesn't mean you should put on your best Barry White impersonation, because it will be seen for what it is—lame. Instead, think of a smooth operator like James Bond, who's every word seems to make women quiver.

After she gives you plenty of indication that she's interested in you, subtly morph your persona from high energy to smooth and laidback. You can do this by using a *slightly* deeper voice, talking at a slower pace, introducing strategic pauses as you talk, and speaking at a level that only she can hear. When a woman starts becoming attracted to a guy they start to pay attention to *how* he says things as much, if not more, than *what* he's saying. Transitioning to using a soothing, comforting, confident voice is one of the best ways to convey that you're thinking about her in a way that you weren't moments before.

Accuse her of being a player

Women think men are insatiable dogs who are only after one thing and if you say something that she remotely construes as "player" talk, it only reinforces her belief. A great way to circumvent that negative way of thinking is to accuse her of being a player before she ever gets the chance to think or say the same thing about you. Women are so used to being pursued by aggressive men that she'll not only be at a loss for words when you turn the tables on her, it will prevent her from thinking of you as a player because you called her on it first. Most importantly, it's very flirtatious to call a girl on something she's probably thinking, but far too demure to explicitly state.

It's fairly easy to turn the tables on her assumption that you're only interested in her body, as long as you beat her to it. Whenever a woman says something that can be misinterpreted as "too much, too soon," call her on it. For instance, if she asks you where you live or where you work, you can say, "Okay, I'll tell you, but you have to promise not to stalk me. You've got stalker written all over you!" Or if she asks you how to fix a computer or car problem, you can say, "What? Are you trying to get me over to your place already? You girls are all the same!" Women get a kick out of this and you would be surprised how many women will bring up your comment later on and ask whether you still want to help her install her cable modem.

Feel "used"

Most women are concerned about being used for sex, especially with guys they don't know very well, so you can create some sexual tension by accusing her of the very same behavior. As you know, women subconsciously test men to see what they can get away with as a means to learn whether a guy has confidence and maintains his boundaries. She might ask you to watch her coat while she dances with her friends, ask you for a drink, or countless other favors she probably wouldn't ask a woman she just met. For the most part, you should play around with these requests and rarely comply, but if she's shown some obvious attraction toward you, it's time to reward her behavior, but with a twist.

When a woman asks a small favor of you, like hold her seat while she takes a call, you can say, "Oh, I see...you're using me already! I bet you'd like to use me for a lot of things, wouldn't you?" If she has an adult's IQ, she'll laugh, partly because it's a funny role reversal and partly because there's some truth in what you're saying. This is a great way to subtly introduce some low-pressure sexual tension into your conversation and prompt her to think of the two of you in a sexual context. Always play the innocent who's put upon by aggressive women who seem to want only one thing from you.

Offer to "repay" a favor

When a woman starts to feel some attraction for you, she'll most likely become overtly nice, usually by doing all of the things she might normally test a guy with like buying him a drink, offering to watch his seat when he goes to the bathroom, and so on. This is a great opportunity to take notice of her generous spirit, but of course a straightforward "thanks" isn't going to cut it. If you've ever seen an old porn video where a pizza guy makes a delivery and his female customer doesn't have the money to pay for it, you just know that she's going to offer to pay him in "some *other* way." Almost everyone gets the premise, even if they haven't watched one of these cheesy sex scenes, so you can use the same concept *and* appreciate her favor at the same time.

When flirting with a woman and she does something that's obviously a nice thing to do for someone she barely knows, you give her some simple appreciation. Once she says or does something nice, say, "Thanks, that's really nice of you…" Then smile and say, "I'd like to pay you back…do you have any creative payment options in mind?" Start walking away and then tell her, "I'll give you some time to think about that one" and then go to the bathroom, have a smoke, or make a call outside. Notice that you've both appreciated her gesture and also offered to return the favor, but not in an overtly sexual way. Of course, it's not *that* subtle, because it allows her mind to drift toward more *interesting* possibilities without you pushing the issue.

Stereotype her as a sexual deviant

Both men and women are prone to asking boring interview-style questions. Some women are insistent on knowing what you do and where you live and when they ask these questions, they most likely have ulterior motives other than just meeting a great guy. So while there are some women who shamelessly ask these questions to divine your suitability as a husband and provider, the majority ask these types of questions because they're nervous, they're boring, or they just don't know any better. Since these questions usually get trotted out whenever a dynamic interaction starts to lose steam, it's the perfect time to break out some flirtatious comebacks. Since you've gotten to this point without exchanging boring biographical information, you shouldn't take offense if she starts asking for a little more detail.

As you start asking each other questions, at some point, she'll tell you where she grew up, where she likes to vacation, or what she does for a living and you'll have a perfect opportunity to stereotype her based on her answer. Start grinning or even laughing and then say, "Oh, man…you know what they say about girls from *x*, don't you?" She won't know, but she'll playfully demand an answer. Just be coy and say, "Well…I'm a gentleman, but let's just say I've been told that girls from *x* are a LOT of fun." It's a loaded response and she'll understand what you're inferring, but she won't disagree that she's a lot of fun, making it a hilarious way to turn a boring question into something sexually tinged.

Test Her Interest

One of the best ways to help you decide where you want to take the interaction once you break away from her group is to non-verbally initiate a small act of intimacy in which she either complies or resists. The key is to take a somewhat bold step in escalating the way you touch that also requires her active participation. You know by now that she's attracted to you, but in order to find out her "buying temperature," you need to take a "reading" and then proceed accordingly.

Compliance testing comes in many forms, but they all share the same basic requirement: a move toward light physical intimacy that gives her the opportunity to reciprocate or pull away. For example, if she's given you plenty of interest and you've flirted back with her, keep talking and as you do gently grab hold of her hand and place it on your knee. If you continue talking and she leaves her hand on your knee, even for just ten seconds, then you have a good indication that she's interested in getting more physical in the near term. If she casually pulls her hand away, you might just aim for a phone number, a simple kiss, or a move to another venue, but you probably won't be getting naked on this occasion.

You can run similar tests starting at this point in the interaction and throughout the rest of the other stages to continue gauging her immediate physical interest in you. Keep in mind that just because she keeps her hand on your knee, it doesn't automatically mean that she wants to have sex with you, but the odds are looking better. Even if you end up with just a phone number and a kiss, the fact that she was comfortable keeping her hands on you, someone she didn't know yesterday, shows that sex probably isn't too far away.

You can also try some of the following tests:

★ Take hold of her hand for a few seconds and then open your hand up. Does she hold on?

★ While you're holding her hand, give it a light squeeze. Does she squeeze back?

★ Casually put your hand on her knee and leave it there. Does she put her hand over yours to keep it in place?

★ As you take a walk around the venue, you intertwine her arm around yours. Does she keep it there?

★ If you're seated and she isn't, pat your lap with your hands. Does she sit on your lap?

★ While her friends are talking, pull her in closer so you can talk more intimately. Does she stay close or even lean further into you?

Remember, as with any kind of touching, it's never a big deal as long as you believe it isn't. At this point, she's probably already bought into your frame of mind, so unless you do something that embarrasses her around her friends or is in violation of her social and moral code, she'll most likely go along with it. The key is to treat these physical interactions as small gestures people do when they're attracted to one another, nothing more.

As always, keep your eyes locked onto hers, don't look nervous, and don't ask for permission or in any way point out what you're doing. Learn to get past that awkward feeling you used to get on a first date at a movie where you spend two hours just trying to touch each other's leg or hold hands. Don't attack, don't be timid, just be confident in doing something that feels good with someone to whom you're attracted. If she's into you and you've innocently crossed a line with her, she'll let you know and she'll most likely let you off the hook.

Plan for the Close

Now that you've got a sense of how attracted she is to you, it's time to start thinking about what might happen once you break her away from her friends. If she isn't with her friends, you should already be thinking about where the interaction could possibly lead in the next few minutes. In most circumstances you have two basic opportunities—get her number so you can

Buying Drinks

Never agree or offer to buy a woman a drink within the first five to ten minutes of meeting her. Most women won't admit it, but they have nothing but scorn and disrespect for men who do exactly as they're told, or have to use the offer of a free drink to secure a woman's company. Some women feel obligated to talk to a guy for ten minutes because he bought her something. Or they say "thanks" and disappear instantly because their only goal was to get a free drink. It seems harsh, but luckily there are pleasant alternatives to dealing with the situation.

Never ask a woman you just met if she wants something to drink and then leave her for five minutes, an eternity in a bar or club, to buy them and bring them back. Instead, *tell* her that you want another drink and that you're headed to the bar and then *ask* her whether she wants to go with you. If she likes you enough, she'll commit to walking with you to the bar. If it's crowded, don't be afraid to gently grab hold of her hand so she doesn't get lost behind you. If she follows and she holds your hand, you probably have enough signals of interest to buy her a drink without feeling used.

The best approach to take when a woman directly asks you to buy her a drink is to make a game out of it. Whether its thumb wrestling, hand slaps, or any other childish game, agree to buy drinks if she wins, but also insist that she buys the drinks if she loses. Alternatively if she asks you for a drink within just a few minutes of meeting her, instantly point to your lips and ask her for a kiss. If she's game, all the better and you can reward her with a drink. If not, she's the one who is forced to say "no," not you. Above all, it's a bold and confident thing to do.

pick up where you left off sometime in the future, or tell her you're going somewhere else and ask whether she's interested in joining you. "Somewhere else" usually means another venue like a bar, club, diner, or after-hours party, but it also includes taking her home, preferably hers.

So before you get too far ahead of yourself, now is the time to think about where the interaction might lead and how you want to go to facilitate it.

You Get Her Phone Number

If you think the woman you're talking to will accompany you to a café or somewhere else within a few minutes of meeting you, by all means, see what you can make happen. However, odds are that circumstances will prevent you from changing locations on the same day. If this is the case, spend as much time as reasonably possible to build Attraction and maybe even a Connection. If you put in the time and the woman you're talking to gives you plenty of Indicators of Interest, you should get her phone number (see page 339) so the two of you can pick up where you left off.

You Take Her Somewhere Else

If you don't have any time or location restraints, meaning you're not obligated to go anywhere else that night, your top priority is to continue escalating the attraction to see where it leads. Your goal is to get laid, is it not? It's nice to get attention, good to feel the attraction, great to get a number, and fantastic when her hands are all over you, but your goal all along is to have sex and *maybe* something a little more long term, like a booty call, a friend with benefits, or a long-term relationship. If she seems interested and has the time, you should think of nearby public places you can go to continue talking with the goal of building more comfort and rapport in the Connect stage (see page 299).

You Take Her Home

Sex (quality, frequency, and freakiness) is usually one of the major factors guys use in determining what type of relationship they eventually want to pursue with a woman. You shouldn't feel ashamed about your desires, especially knowing that men and women aren't much different when it comes to sex. Many women share your enthusiasm for great sex as long as they feel safe, respected, and perhaps a little special. With that in mind, you should aim for the stars and continue building trust and escalating kino until you feel a woman is comfortable and/or turned on enough to broach the subject of finding somewhere more private for a little nakedness (see page 369).

Transitioning to the Connect Stage

From the moment you found, whether before you approached a group or during, a woman you were attracted to, your sole purpose was to extract her from her group so you could talk more intimately. Of course, along the way you demonstrated social value, flirted, and teased, among other things, but almost everything was done as a means to get her attention, build attraction, and separate her from the influence of her friends. Now that you've both given signals that you're attracted to one another, it's time to make a move away from her group with the added benefit of having their complete approval.

If you hope to Close big with something beyond just getting her phone number, you almost always need to escalate the attraction *away* from her group. Once you're alone together, a woman typically feels more comfortable talking about sexual topics, overtly flirting, kissing, and more. Of course, you aren't talking her into doing these things—by this point, these are all activities she wants to pursue with someone she's attracted to, just not in front of her friends. Women are typically more reserved around their friends because they fear being labeled a slut, or they just don't want to make a scene that will come back to haunt them. Again, you should work within this reality, not against it.

When she's alone

Whether you go to cafés, bookstores, malls, or most other places, you can save a lot of time by approaching women who don't have a group of friends around to whom they look for approval on who they should and shouldn't be talking to. With that said, you still should have blended together elements of the Open, Hook, and Attract stages and now you want to transition to the Connect stage. Luckily, since she's alone, you only have to convince one person, not an entire group, that you're charming, interesting, and witty.

If you've just met someone and you've only spent a few minutes talking to her, you usually need more time if you want to Close in any other way besides getting her phone number. If your goal is to take her somewhere else or eventually take her home, she needs to feel comfortable with you, usually *very* comfortable. You can accomplish this by taking her somewhere within the same location or somewhere nearby. For example, if you're at a bookstore, you could take her to the in-store café where you can sit down and talk more intimately. Or, if you're at a club, you could take her somewhere with as few distractions as possible, like a diner or pizza spot.

By taking a woman somewhere else within or around the same location, she'll feel more comfortable with you because you both went somewhere together and didn't linger in the same place where you randomly met. It also helps her get a better sense of how a romance with you might feel with you taking charge and leading her on an adventure, yet keeping her safe and comfortable. Once you find a nice little spot, you can move into the conversational topics found in Chapter 12, "Connect," that allow you to build rapport and create a real connection.

Before you can do that though, you need to take the initiative and get the two of you moving toward somewhere with a little more intimacy and privacy. Since you've been flirting back and forth for a few minutes, you should try one of the following lines:

★ "Hey, you should meet my friend(s), let's go introduce you."

★ "I'm gonna go get a drink, come with me."

★ "Alright, it's time for a little adventure. Let's go!"

★ "I gotta get some coffee, let's keep talking."

★ "I wanna show you something really cool, let's go check it out."

The key is to avoid *asking* whether she wants to go with you, but to give her some context (meet your friends, get a drink, show her something) and then just *tell* her to come with you. Maintain your frame of mind as someone who is choosy, but now that you've chosen her, you *expect* her to follow you as if you didn't know any other way. It also helps to stand up and hold your arm or hand out as you talk, that way she can grab hold of you so you can whisk her away.

When she's with a group

If the woman you're attracted to is with her friends, you should have fully hijacked her group from her by entertaining them and letting them get to know your attractive personality. As you were doing this, you should have also been teasing, flirting, and keeping her off-balance as to exactly what your intentions are, which all serve to increase attraction. Since her group seems to like you and you've demonstrated a lot of social value, you shouldn't have much trouble breaking her away from her group, at least for a few minutes.

The best way to pull her away from her friends is to confidently *tell* the entire group that you're going somewhere nearby to talk to their friend one-on-one.

In most instances, you want to tell the group without ever consulting with your romantic interest. For the most part, if you've done a good job at teasing, flirting, and demonstrating value, she will happily comply, even if you catch her off-guard. If she perhaps wasn't ready to break away from her friends to spend time with you, she'll look to her group to help decide whether it's something they enthusiastically endorse or at least approve of—the reactions of her friends will help her determine whether leaving with you is a good idea.

In general, people follow the advice of their friends when it comes to social matters, but women are especially susceptible to thinking as a group instead of thinking as individuals—a fact that you can use to your benefit. Even if a woman is unsure or apprehensive about leaving her friends to talk to a guy she just met, she'll usually defer to their opinion above her own. This is particularly true if you've Opened big, told some interesting stories, and generally elevated their evening for a few minutes. If you accomplish this, you've essentially won them over as friends, so you shouldn't have a problem when you tell them you want to walk a few feet away and talk to their friend for a few minutes.

Make sure to engage her entire group shortly after you share a big laugh, then let them know that you're about to leave and that you'll be taking their friend with you. If you've built enough rapport, you should have no problem using one of the following lines:

★ "I'm going to borrow your friend for a second; we'll be right over there."

★ "Your friend and I are kind of into each other, are you cool with that?"

★ "Is it okay if I borrow her for a sec?"

★ "I like your friend, do you mind if I talk with her for a minute?"

★ "You know what, I think I've been ignoring your friend here and I'd like to fix that. Do you guys mind?"

Initially, her friends might need to be reassured that you're not a psychopath, so move only a few feet away from the group. Since your options are limited, just find a wall or a bar that you can lean against and allow the woman to face you. The best option is to find a quiet area within the same venue that allows you to sit close to one another, so you can escalate kino in relative privacy. Wherever you end up, stay within eyeshot of her friends, but not so close that they could hear what you're saying.

In a woman's mind, staying nearby is a lot less risky and it allows her to remain comfortable and concentrate on what the two of you are saying. You don't want her worrying about her friends leaving her or about what kind of person you're going to turn into when her friends are gone. Moving just a short distance is also a much smaller personal investment than moving to a different location, because if she finds she's not really attracted to you, she can quickly rejoin her friends. Your goal is to get one-on-one time with her, not necessarily alone time; that comes later after she's more comfortable with you and feels a connection with you, which you'll learn how to accomplish in the next chapter.

Conclusion

The purpose of the Attract stage is to focus on the woman you're attracted to in order to make it clear that, surprise, you're not just a guy who's entertaining and fun to be with, but also romantically interested in someone in the group. Until the Attract stage you were very indirect by telling stories, getting opinions, and generally having fun with people into you casually met without any specific intentions. Now that you've successfully defused the group's shields using an Opener, developed rapport using Hook material and developed Attraction through reciprocal flirting and teasing, it's time to create a real Connection, either immediately or at some point in the future.

The Connect stage always comes after you've isolated her from her friends. Because you both already know you're attracted to one another, you need to build more comfort, rapport, and trust. A woman who is attracted to you, who feels comfortable and safe in your presence and feels the two of you share a connection beyond the physical, will likely follow your lead when you're ready to Close. Chapter 12, "Connect," explains how to switch conversational gears once the two of you are alone, so she can start to see you as something much more than a guy she just met at a bar or in the mall.

Chapter 12

Connect

In this Chapter

★ Understanding how to build deep rapport beyond just basic conversation topics

★ Learning her "buy" strategy so you can capture her imagination and tap into her desired emotional state

★ Revealing how to accelerate her attraction to you so you can easily transition to the Close

Connect

The Connect stage comes after you've defused a woman's natural defense mechanisms using an indirect Opener, and isolated her from her friends with their approval. Before you pulled her away from her group, you observed some interest on her part and you flirted back, so now that you both know you're attracted to one another, it's time to develop some comfort and rapport. A woman who is attracted to you, who feels comfortable and safe in your presence and feels the two of you share a connection beyond the physical will likely follow your lead when you're ready to Close, which should be your goal from the beginning of the interaction.

Connecting almost always occurs at a different location than where you originally met. Whether you moved somewhere else in the same location, changed locations, or exchanged numbers and met days or weeks later, the act of going somewhere together is often integral to a successful Close. If you meet sometime in the future, expect to backtrack and start somewhere in the Attract stage, although not always, depending on how much time you initially spent together. If you transitioned out of the Attract stage on the same day you met, you should move directly into the Connect stage.

For most women, feeling a connection is an important part of allowing a relationship to escalate into something sexual. Of course things like money, fame, and power can mitigate the need for an emotional connection, but not everyone has such qualities working for them. If that's the case, you want to focus on creating a genuine connection by being or becoming someone with whom she feels she could share her life. Whether sharing her "life" means months, years, or forever is up to each individual woman, but it typically means that for the time she's with you, she's with someone who appreciates her unique style, outlook, inner and outer beauty, and most importantly, someone that makes her feel safe and secure.

At this point she has shown that she's attracted to you and she's been receptive to your flirting and kino, but you've only spent about ten minutes together, so you generally can only expect to get her phone number and maybe a kiss. However, if you have a different outcome in mind, like taking her to another location or even taking her home, you have more work to do. Considering that she just met you, you have to make her feel more comfortable by building rapport and trust and ultimately a connection that makes sense to her. To accomplish this, you have to introduce new types of conversational threads that allow her to further invest herself in the interaction and vice versa.

Build Rapport

You, not her, have to keep the conversation moving, which is a good thing since you can make sure it builds comfort and rapport instead of being boring and trivial. Unless she asks you a specific question about you or your thoughts, guide her so that she can tell you more about herself. You're doing yourself a disservice by dominating the conversation like every other overbearing guy she encounters.

Your goal is to encourage her to open up and provide you with material to keep the conversation moving in the direction you want it to, so you can reach the outcome you desire. A woman wants to be attracted to a man she sleeps with, but even more importantly, she wants to be understood by a man in a way casual acquaintances do not. You can accomplish this by listening and delving deeper into the topics that interest her most, not by trying to convince her of all your wonderful qualities.

Always allow a woman to talk freely and pay close attention to what she says to gain valuable insight on what makes her tick. Now that she's attracted to you, you want to find out whether she's the type of person with whom you want to spend your free time. As the conversation progresses, she'll also provide you with talking points you can use to build rapport throughout the Connect and Close stages.

Letting a woman do most of the talking also keeps her mind occupied. When she's talking, she isn't thinking of all the reasons why she shouldn't be talking to you—her friends may not approve, you live too far away, you're too old for her, and countless others. Imagine the old vaudeville act of plate spinning—you put plates on thin rods and she spins them and while she keeps the plates spinning, you add more and more so she concentrates on the here-and-now, not on how early she has to wake up the next day.

Keep the following conversational techniques—getting her opinion and asking open-ended questions—in mind as you move into the comfort and rapport-building topics covered in the next section.

Get her opinion

If you didn't Open by asking for her opinion, do it during the Connect and Close stages. Always keep in mind that getting a woman's opinion about things that she's truly interested in helps create comfort and rapport. Women fondly remember talking to guys who ask them about things they care enough to commit an opinion on, especially when you seem genuinely interested in listening and building on what they're talking about.

It's easy just to blather on about current events, for example, without digging deeper below the surface, so you aren't just two talking heads having a superficial conversation. You want to find out how she *feels* about what you're talking about. Start out with something simple that has nothing to do with either of you, then progress toward more personal topics so you're both revealing something personal, something to remember later in the conversation or the next time you meet.

Whether you agree or disagree, you can turn it to your advantage. If you agree, you have something in common and you can keep building on the things you have in common. If you disagree, you can playfully tease her about her opinion. Teasing leads the way to sexual teasing and innuendo, which keeps things fun and interesting. If a woman seems reluctant to divulge her opinions, it may well be a sign that she either isn't interested in you or she's boring—both are good reasons to move on.

Ask open-ended questions

When you ask a woman a yes/no question, especially when you first meet her, you shouldn't be surprised to get a terse yes/no answer. After all, you're still a stranger to her, so you shouldn't expect her to open up to you and reveal personal information just because you asked her a yes/no question. However, most women will open up and carry the conversation if you ask fun, interesting open-ended questions, questions that require far more than a single-word answer. For example:

Closed: "Where are you going overseas?"

Open: "Why are you going overseas?"

With questions that can be answered with just a word or two, you have little choice but to immediately follow up with either "that's cool" or another question. You don't want to ask yet another question because you'll begin moving toward an interview-style conversation, which gives people the creeps. Open-ended questions allow you to draw a woman into a real conversation which provides you with more information to play around with to tease her, build rapport, and generally figure out whether you really want to keep talking to her.

Comfort and Rapport-Building Topics

When you're talking to a group of women, it's best to keep things light, playful, and unsophisticated so no one gets upset and everyone can participate. It also keeps you from diving into some rabbit hole of a topic that prevents you from launching into something new and exciting. But now that you're talking to her directly, you want to up the conversational stakes by asking her about specific aspects of her life that aren't extremely personal, but have more to do with her own thoughts, feelings, and experiences.

By now, you've already built some attraction and gained the approval of her friends and you've spent considerable time doing so. Women perceive the time spent as your investment in getting to know them and their friends better and having done that, they're much more receptive to personal questions. In fact, if she's already attracted to you, she'll love that you're asking more interesting and personal questions. The following are some examples of the types of questions you can introduce to find out more about a woman in whom you're interested:

Personal tastes

Asking a woman about her personal tastes is usually the default for most guys, but they ask these questions within a minute of meeting someone—

hoping to find some common ground and then build attraction from there. In your case, you've already built some attraction, so don't be shy to ask about her favorite movies, music, books, food, and anything else for which someone can have a personal preference.

★ "Have you seen any movies/seen any bands/read any books recently? What types do you like? What's your favorite?"

★ "What kind of food could they not pay you enough to eat? What's your favorite dish? Do you have any specialties that you/your mom cook?"

★ "What books/people/events have had a major impact on you?"

★ "Where would you rather spend the night and why: a museum, a zoo, or an amusement park?"

What she does for fun

People always ask what you "do" and they're almost always referring to what you do for a living. That's a great way to find out the socio-economic status of someone, but unless they love what they're doing for a living, it's a rather boring and played-out question. Better to ask a woman what she does and then when she replies with a job title, say, "No, silly; not what you do for money, what you do for fun," Most people have precious few hours to devote to hobbies and other activities, so they relish a chance to discuss their passions.

★ "What's the craziest/most unusual/weirdest thing you know how to do?"

★ "What interesting things did you do this week/month/year?"

★ "What's the craziest thing you ever did when you were a kid? As an adult? If you were a kid again, what would you like to get away with that you couldn't now?"

★ "Do you roller blade/dance/play sports? If you didn't have to work and were ordered to have fun, what would you do all day?"

Her friends and family

You may have already asked her group how everyone knows each other, so hopefully you remember some of the stories and connections. Bring up some of those anecdotes and find out more about how she met them, where they like to go together, and what kind of trouble they get into. If you don't remember much about her friends or you never bothered to find out, ask about her family. Learning about a woman's family is another great way to get to the core of who she really is.

★ "Do you live with your parents? Do you get along with them?"

★ "Do you have any brothers or sisters? Do they get along?"

★ "What are your friends like? Do you have dozens of casual friends or just a small circle of close friends?"

★ "Do you like animals? Do you have any pets?"

Listen and Build on What She Says

Avoid agreeing with everything a woman says just because she's saying it and you want to seem agreeable. Doing so is needy, boring, and doesn't bring much dynamic to the conversation. Instead, really listen to what she's talking about, digest it, and be prepared to send it back to her in different and interesting ways. Sometimes you'll agree with her, but other times you'll disagree and need to offer a different, sometimes challenging, viewpoint. I know it sounds crazy to actually listen to someone after you ask them a question, but you only stand to benefit by being a good listener *and* being able to communicate that you're paying attention.

There isn't anything wrong with nodding as she talks, but you must be quick to keep these conversational plates spinning in the air with more than just "I know what you mean" or "Oh, really, I like movies too." You can build on the conversation by paraphrasing, adding specific insight, or simply teasing her about things you disagree with, all depending on the context.

Paraphrasing involves rewording her statement to make sure you fully understand what she means. Paraphrasing immediately communicates to her that you're truly interested in what she's saying and you're asking her to confirm that you're "getting it." Even though you're merely rewording her statement, it will seem as though you're expressing your own thoughts, causing her to subconsciously connect them to her own ideas, which helps build rapport.

Flowing versus Interviewing

Avoid asking a woman a bunch of disconnected questions that have nothing to do with one another. Questions in rapid succession, similar to an interview, are boring at best, creepy at worst. What you have to focus on is asking a woman a question, listening to her answer, and then building on what she says by asking a related question, hopefully with some authentic curiosity. A good conversation flows from one thing to the next without awkward pauses that give you time to think of something to talk about. If you listen to how a woman answers your question, you don't have to think too hard about what to ask next, as long as it leads her down the path of talking more personally and passionately.

Avoid interview-style conversations like the following:

You: What do you do?

Her: I work with animals in my free time.

You: Do you still live with your parents?

Her: No, they divorced when I was a kid.

You: Do you have any roommates?

Her: What's with all the questions?

You: Umm…

Her: See ya!

Instead, aim for a conversation that naturally flows through a single topic so you can lead her into talking about something she's passionate about:

You: What do you do?

Her: I work with animals.

You: [smiling] You mean your boss is a pig or you work with apes?

Her: [laughs] Noooo! I work at an animal rescue.

You: Ahh. So like pets or wildlife?

Her: Mostly wildlife…owls, raccoons…animals like that.

You: That sounds a lot more rewarding than working at The Gap.

Her: No doubt. There's just something about nursing a defenseless creature back to life and then sending them back into the wild. Sometimes they don't want to go!

You: Hey, if you brought me back to life, I wouldn't wanna leave either.

Her: [laughs] I see…

Conclusion

A lot of men become petrified when they have to hold a conversation with someone they're attracted to—usually because they just don't know what to say to someone they don't know. Above all, remember three things: ask open-ended questions, listen carefully to what she says, and then connect her stories, opinions, and beliefs to your past experiences so you can build enough rapport to continue. Along the way, pick up on information that you can use to screen her.

Screen Her

Screening is a way to convey that you have high standards with regards to the women with whom you spend your time. Since you view yourself as a catch, someone who has a lot going for him and doesn't need to accept just any woman who's interested in him, you have to casually let her know that looks alone aren't enough to get your full attention. If you properly qualify her, she'll understand that you're looking beyond her looks to see whether she's more than just a pretty face. Since she already knows you're attracted to her, the purpose of screening is to get her hoping that she's good enough to qualify as relationship material, or at least booty call material.

You don't want to seem blatantly obvious in screening a woman on whether she meets your requirements. Instead, you have to subtly infer that you have standards when it comes to women and she'll eventually realize on her own that you're screening her. Women aren't used to being screened because they assume that their exceptionally good looks, or even just their gender, are enough to capture the attention of just about any man, which is sadly true more often than not.

In your case, you're looking for more and you want to find out whether a particular woman is worth investing your time into. Sometimes you can witness a complete change in attitude once a woman realizes you're screening her. At first they're shocked, but eventually most come to appreciate a guy who requires more than just a hot body, whether or not you actually do. After they get over this reversal of roles, they usually play along by trying to qualify for your affection instead of the other way around. Whether women like it or not, you will seem different than most guys, so they usually want to see where the conversation leads.

Some of the best ways to screen a woman, without her thinking you're trying to make her feel screened, is to maintain a strong frame of mind from the beginning of the interaction and using some of the state breakers in Chap-

Never act overly impressed with her answers

Whenever a woman answers your questions, gives you her opinion, or tells her own stories, never respond with "Really!?! Aw...that's *really* awesome/cool/fantastic!" every time she says something. Fake enthusiasm is lame and it seems as though you're trying to gain her approval by believing that everything she's into or about is unequivocally great. Instead, pay attention to what she's saying and use the details to find mutual points of interest, tease her, or create new conversational threads.

Whatever a woman's energy level is, try to stay slightly more energetic, but don't overdo it by being excessively impressed whenever she reveals something about herself. Most women have become accustomed to this behavior and perceive guys who exhibit it as needy, insecure, and lacking in their own opinions and standards. In other words they think you're sucking up to them so you can get into their pants, which causes them to throw up their shields and turn you away.

Make her laugh

You may be wondering how many times you're going to read that you need to be funny and make people laugh, but once you start talking to your target one-on-one, it bears repeating: make her laugh. You may have chosen to take a humorous approach with the Opener and the conversations with her friends, but if you didn't, you need to make sure to include a few laughs when it's just the two of you, no matter what you end up talking about. Humor has great power to loosen people up and build comfort so they can open up and talk about the things that really matter to them.

You might not think of yourself as a funny guy, but you have to at least try so you can learn what makes women laugh out loud, giggle, smile politely, or shake their head in disapproval. You may have to go through some terrible attempts at humor just to calibrate what works and what doesn't. Remember, you can't tell jokes or in any way be perceived as someone who injects disjointed comedy into a conversation. Women can tell when you're resorting to something rehearsed, so try to relax, be your (best) self and make light of the world around you.

ter 11, "Attract." By this point, she already feels as though she's overcome some of your earlier disqualifications (It would never work out between us, etc.), but you weren't really screening her for specific behavior traits or value characteristics, so she correctly assumed that you were just teasing her.

The difference now is that she's shown some interest in you and you've revealed some interest of your own, so you're at least considering perusing something beyond this short interaction. You have to truly believe in your standards and she has to fully understand your need to qualify her without feeling insulted. Some examples of screening questions include:

★ "Do you cook/read much/give good backrubs?"

★ "Are you a passionate/adventurous/open-minded person?"

- ★ "Can you dance/sing/draw?"

- ★ "What are your three best qualities?"

- ★ "So…what are you all about?"

- ★ "What are some things about you that would make someone want to get to know you better?"

You can use the examples I've included, but you should also think about the qualities and traits that you are seeking in a woman, assuming you're not just looking for a quick hookup. It will be much easier for you to explain why you're asking these questions if you actually care about her answers, and they almost always question why you're asking.

For instance, if you ask whether she can draw, you can explain that you feel artists are really passionate people, that you consider yourself to be a passionate person, and you like to surround yourself with passionate people. Whether she can draw or not, she'll realize you're fishing for clues as to whether she meets your requirements, and then still actively try to meet those requirements—*if* she's sufficiently attracted to you.

Learn Her Buy Strategy

A woman's "buy strategy" is the thoughts and feelings she usually has to ascribe to a man in order to feel comfortable enough to be intimate with him, including sleeping with him. I say *usually* because alcohol and/or a heightened emotional state, like getting dumped or seeking revenge, can greatly diminish a woman's minimum requirements for intimacy. If you sense she's put her standards on the shelf for the night, her buy strategy involves ending up with a penis attached to someone who isn't psychotic.

Most women take great pride in their refined buying strategies, even when those unrealistic standards leave them alone and unattached for months, sometimes years. Because women hold tightly to these virtuous ideals of a "perfect man" or "dream guy," you need to find out what these ideals are. Even if a woman is attracted to you, she still wants and expects a man she sleeps with to meet certain requirements.

Just one of the problem in trying to meet a woman's requirements of her "perfect man" is that, of course, every woman is different. No two women have the same set of requires - each are shaped their upbringing and past relationships and have their own set of likes and dislikes. With that said, you can't assume that just because you're making all the right moves and saying all the right things that you're going to match her emotional needs, unless you specifically find out what those needs are.

There isn't an effective way to directly determine a woman's emotional needs, so you have to ask leading questions to get the responses you want without her thinking you're fishing for information. You should never directly ask a woman what her emotional needs are—if for no other reason than being an extremely weird and creepy question. Instead, bring up topics that allow her to talk about the traits she looks for in attractive men. While you may not possess the traits she thinks she wants, if you understand why she needs to have these in her life, you can find other ways to produce the same feelings, as you'll learn later in this chapter.

Remember to include context to your questions by telling similar stories from your own experience, or relating stories a friend or relative told you. Try not to directly ask a woman about the following topics, but bring them up casually as if they just happened to be on your mind. If you were to blurt out "What is your dad like?" a woman might be reluctant to tell you and understandably so. As long as you bring up these topics as part of a normal conversation, women won't automatically assume that you're using a shortcut to find out what they expect from their romantic relationships with men.

Below are a few topics you can introduce to find out what traits and qualities a woman seeks in the men she dates. Understanding how she feels when she's with someone who possesses those qualities will help guide you toward telling stories about yourself possessing those same characteristics.

Best and Worst Dates

Talking about your own best and worst dates is an easy way for a woman to jump in and reveal the activities and behaviors she seeks and avoids in men, at least when she first meets them. It also allows you to find out how she expects men to treat her, so you can determine whether she's high maintenance, self-centered, needy, or any of the other negative personality traits you want to avoid. It's always a good idea to start by reminiscing about the worst date you ever had, as long as it's humorous and you come off looking like the victim. If she doesn't start talking about her own experiences, ask her

Don't seek approval

The purpose of screening a woman is to impart that you expect a woman to possess more than just good looks before you consider spending more time with her. If you ask her whether she's having fun with you, whether you're her type, whether she's "into" guys like you, or any other question that essentially asks if she approves of you and your behavior, you undermine your efforts to screen her. Instead, you're seeking her approval by asking her to screen *you*, which she's perfectly comfortable doing. Keep her mind focused on your attractive qualities and whether she meets your standards. Never ask her to judge you or ask what her current state of mind is; she'll have an opportunity to do that later when you're not dazzling her with your charms.

as a follow-up question to your story. Most women will unknowingly reveal the guidelines you have to work within to be the type of guy she wants to be intimate with.

Traits She Likes in Men

Instead of directly asking a woman what she seeks in the men she dates, tell her a story about someone in your life who always has guy problems and use that as the basis for a conversation on what women, not her specifically, look for in guys. A woman feels much more comfortable talking about what women *in general* look for in men, but she will invariably use her own biases and experiences to reveal her personal likes and dislikes. For instance, you can talk about a niece who broke up with a bad boy-type a few months ago and said she would never date guys like that again, but only a month later she's dating another bad boy. Then ask her whether all women go through this stage and ask how women's taste in men matures as they grow up. A lot of women will go on to explain all of the phases they went through up to and including the present.

Her Relationship With Her Father

Finding out how a woman relates to her father or father figure can be difficult, but it gets right to the heart of what a woman truly wants from the "other" man in her life. There are a lot of psychological factors that lead most women to seek men who resemble, in looks and temperament, their fathers. If you can find out what a woman's father was like and whether they had a positive or damaging relationship, you will likely have all of the information you need to transition to the Close stage. Since there is a day dedicated to fathers, you can use that as the context for discussing your father as well as hers. For instance, you might be thinking of doing something really special for your dad this year and you want to run it by her. This will give you a good opportunity to ask her what she does for Father's Day and how well she gets along with her dad.

Desired Traits Into Desired Emotions

By now you should know some of the traits a particular woman seeks in men (tall, smart, confident, etc.) in order to find them attractive. However, if you don't happen to possess those traits, you can still continue to build a Connection by finding out how being with a man who has those traits makes her feel. It's not the specific traits she desires, but the emotions she has come to associate with those traits. For example, she may say she only dates tall men, but in actuality, she associates dating tall men with feeling safe and secure. If you were able to link yourself to feelings of safety and security in her mind, she'll likely abandon the physical requirement as long as her emotional requirement is being met.

At first it may seem like you're attempting to fool or even hypnotize someone into having feelings for you that don't really exist. What you're really doing is circumventing her social programming so she can see past her hard-wired assumptions and stereotypes. Your goal isn't to trick a woman, but create a situation where she can see you as someone who is every bit as capable of being safe and protective as someone who's seven feet tall. You shouldn't feel guilty because you took the extra step of finding out what emotions she values.

In many instances, women are their own worst enemies in finding someone who's right for them, at least initially. By handling a woman's objections (he's not tall enough, smart enough, rich enough, tanned enough, and thousands more) before she's even thought of them, you can overcome such shallow requirements. Whether a guy is pale or tanned, neither are a good measure of a man, so you must work around the notion that you must possess any particular characteristic in order for a women to feel attracted to you.

Once a woman describes a physical or material requirement she feels must be met in order for her to be attracted to someone, use one of the following phrases to prompt her to dig deeper into her statement so she can reveal an emotional requirement:

★ "What is it about guys who are/have _____ that you like?"

★ "How does it feel when you're with someone who is/has _____?"

The following examples illustrate how easy it is to ask a woman how she feels when she's with someone who possesses the traits she finds attractive.

After talking about relationships and what women look for in men, she mentions that women like tall men.

You: Oh yeah? So women like tall guys?

Her: Definitely.

You: So <u>what is it about</u> tall guys that all women seem to love?

Her: I don't know…I guess it's because they feel like he could protect her.

You: So when you're around tall guys, <u>what's it like?</u>

Her: Well, I guess I just feel **safe**…like nothing bad could happen when they're around.

Desired trait: Height

Desired emotion: Safe / Protected

In this instance, she stated that women want to be with tall men, but by digging a little deeper we find out that she feels safe when she's around tall men. So it's not a man's height so much as his ability to make her feel safe and secure that she finds attractive. Instead of feeling self-conscious about your height, you could tell her a story about how you helped your grandparents during a tornado, saved a child from getting hit by a car, or put out a huge fire in the family kitchen, for example.

After talking about Father's Day she talks about what it was like for her growing up with her dad, who was extremely smart and intuitive.

You: Yeah, my dad has always had his heart in the right place, but I wouldn't say he was a genius or anything.

Her: Well, I really wouldn't say my dad was a genius either, but it seemed like he knew what I was thinking about before I even asked him a question.

You: Interesting…so <u>what was it like</u> growing up with someone who always knew what to say?

Her: I really never thought much about it, but I guess I felt lucky, but mostly **proud** of him. He grew up poor, but he graduated from college and he never stopped learning.

Desired trait: Intelligence

Desired emotion: Pride

In this instance, she states that her dad was really smart, but by asking her what it was like living with someone so smart, we find out that his wisdom made her proud of her him. Assuming that most women look for men who share similar traits with their fathers, we can also assume she seeks similar emotional states in the men she dates. In this case, instead of worrying about how intelligent you are, you could tell a story about how proud your parents were of you when you won a competition, skipped a grade, or joined the Big Brother program, for example.

Capture Her Imagination

Now that you know what she prizes with regards to men and relationships, you can create scenarios that allow her to imagine you invoking the emotional states she desires most. Remember, women are mostly emotional, not logical, so you can't convince her that you're the perfect guy for her. Instead, you have to paint a picture, let her draw her own conclusions, then allow her to convince herself that you're more than just funny and attractive—you're the guy she's been looking for.

The key to capturing her imagination is to embed the values and emotional states she described (her buy strategy) into stories of you possessing those values or scenarios. Your goal is to briefly take her away from the here-and-now and transport her to a place where you can embody her notions of the "perfect man." You might actually be very close to her concept of a dream guy, but you probably won't be in a position to actually demonstrate it to her, nor can you just tell her that you're everything she's ever wanted in a man. Instead, you tell stories and let her decide what it means, although you should have a crystal clear idea of what you want it to mean.

The purpose of this type of storytelling is to get her to look past her immediate circumstances, which might be a bar or café, and imagine how great her life could be if she spent some of it with you. Again, you're basically accelerating what normally takes weeks or months of awkward phone calls, antiquated dating rituals, and clumsy attempts at intimacy, just so she can see what kind of guy you really are. Women are very visual, so most have no problem imagining how enjoyable it would be to sip rum drinks with you under a waterfall at sunset in Costa Rica.

The following are a few topics you can introduce to capture a woman's imagination and find out what drives her or what she fantasizes about doing with her life. Understanding what excites her can help you bring her into a similar state of excitement and connect you to those wonderful feelings.

Dream job

Every woman has at least one dream job she feels she would be great at, but many forget about those dreams once the crush of living in the real world sets in. Younger women still hold on to these dreams, as they should, and enjoy talking about how they might achieve their goals and what life would be like when they do. Women who are already well into their careers, or chose to forgo a career to be mothers still hold a special place in their hearts for what might have been. You can easily transition to talking about her dream job by bluntly asking, "If you could have any job in the world, what would it be?"

Winning the lottery

Much like landing a dream job, winning the lottery is something almost everyone has daydreamed about at some point in their lives. Most people have a few answers ready for what they would do with their winnings. What would be the first thing she would buy? Where would she live? Who would she give extravagant gifts? All these questions revolve around a form of wish fulfillment and it generally puts women in a good mood to talk about how great life would be if money were no object.

Favorite Vacations

Whether as a child or an adult, people take vacations and it's a time in their life where they can let themselves go and experience new and exhilarating things that stick with them forever. People in general love talking about past vacations or their dream vacation, so be prepared to paint a picture of your favorite trips and encourage her to do the same. Memories of great vacations bring people into their happy place—a great place for two people who barely know each other to be.

Future plans

Asking a woman about her goals, dreams, and ambitions conveys that you're interested in how compatible your lives might be. These are the types of questions women want to ask, but usually don't, so be proactive and find out where she's going in life and offer some insightful answers of your own. Guys who are interested in a woman's goals and have a firm grip on where they're taking their own lives can build a lot of rapport in a short amount of time.

Examples

The following two examples illustrate how easy it is to subtly ask a woman how she would feel if she had her dream job or took an exotic vacation.

After talking about your own aspirations, ask her what her dream job is.

You: Fashion designer, eh? That sounds like a lot of fun.

Her: It probably is fun, but I bet it's a lot of hard work too…I think I would work really well under the pressure though.

You: So what is it about fashion design that got you interested in it?

Her: I guess I just have an eye for what looks good, plus I know how to combine different fabrics and styles to create something completely new.

You: Sounds like you're really passionate about it. Imagine if you were giving your first fashion show and you were standing there with all of your models and the flashes were going off while everyone applauded you. What would that feel like?

Her: Wow, I get goose bumps just thinking about it! I would love to get **respect** as a designer because it's so difficult to break through.

Desired job: Fashion designer

Desired emotion: Respect

In this instance, she states she wants to be a fashion designer. By painting a picture of what it might be like to be a celebrated fashion designer, we find out she desires to be respected for her work. So even though you can't turn her into a fashion designer, you can help her imagine herself as one and all the good feelings that go along with it. You'll learn how to better connect yourself to these wonderful feelings in the next section.

After talking about your dream vacation to visit where your grandparents grew up in Ireland, you ask her where she dreams of going someday.

You: Costa Rica? I heard that place was awesome, kind of like Hawaii but with more animals.

Her: That's exactly why I've always wanted to go, I love animals.

You: So what is it about Costa Rica that makes it your dream vacation? Just the animals?

Her: No, it's more than that. There's just something about being away from all the noise and traffic of the city and being with the wildlife.

You: I can imagine you lying in some canoe in a river surrounded by monkeys and crazy- looking birds and all the sounds of the rainforest. What would that be like?

Her: It would be just the most **relaxing** thing ever.

Desired vacation: Costa Rica

Desired emotion: Relaxed

In this instance, she states that she has always wanted to go to Costa Rica. By describing a scene of what she might do there, you find out that it's not just the location she wants to visit, but to relax and get away from it all. For the moment, going to Costa Rica is out of the question, but by vividly illustrating what life might be like there, she can briefly imagine how relaxed she would be.

Link yourself to her desired emotional state

As you read this section, keep in mind that the act of linking to a woman's desired emotional state doesn't occur after you learn her buy strategy, or after you capture her imagination, but *during* these conversations. For the purposes of learning how to bring these emotions to the surface and how to link to them, it helps to learn each section individually. However, in practice all three sections should blend together because all of the concepts are interwoven and share the singular goal of accelerating a woman's feelings for you in a matter of hours, not months.

As you learned in the two previous sections, you should initiate conversations about your best dates, father figures, and dream vacations, for example, which typically prompts a woman to discuss similar topics. While she talks, she will invariably describe specific qualities about her father or emotionally rewarding activities at her favorite vacation spot. At this point, you can ask her how being with her father or enjoying her favorite activity feels; with very little prompting she will usually tell you at least one of her most desired emotional states.

To actually link yourself to a woman's desired emotional state, you begin by telling stories that describe situations where you invoke these emotions in other people, like your friends and family. For instance, if she likes tall guys because they make her feel safe, you could tell a story about protecting someone from a pit bull so they felt safe and secure because of your actions. Or, if she always wanted to climb Mount Everest because it would give her an exhilarating feeling, you could tell a story where you took your little brothers on their first roller coaster ride and witnessed the exhilarated look on their faces.

As you tell these vivid stories you can sometimes see her actually feel these emotions, however briefly. Women can be very visual creatures if they're allowed to relax and give in to their imagination, so she must be comfortable with you and the setting. Depending on the emotion you're describing, you might notice her keeping her eyes closed, sinking into her seat, and breathing deeply if she's relaxed. Or you might see her going wide-eyed, biting her lower lip, and stiffening up if she's excited. Either way, it's at this very point, when she's imagining your scenario and feeling her most desired emotional state, that you link yourself to that feeling.

Once you notice her imagining what you're talking about, slowly and gently touch her in the same place (her arm, shoulder, or knee) each time you bring up her desired emotion. After you do this a few times, you will usually create a subconscious connection between these emotions and your presence, voice, and/or touch. This is a very powerful tool to accelerate attraction in a short amount of time, but it requires shrewd listening skills and an ability to weave a woman's desired emotions into (hopefully) true stories that describe you stirring those very emotions in someone close to you.

After introducing the right topics, you have to be able to listen to what a woman says and encourage her to distill the events, activities, and characteristics she seeks into the emotions she desires to feel. The emotions she states are the keywords that should be embedded in the stories you tell, either immediately or sometime in the future. Since these keywords are so important to the stories you tell, you have to keep your ears open when she mentions them. With that said, some of the other emotions a woman might desire include feeling alive, happy, safe, proud, adored, desired, loved, respected, idolized, worthy, awed, independent, relaxed, comfortable, content, amazed, attractive, graceful, smart, intelligent, and interesting.

NOTE: Tactics like learning a woman's buy strategy, capturing her imagination, and linking yourself to her desired emotions aren't necessary for the majority of women, mainly because of the sorry state of the dating pool with which they have to deal. With most men bragging about their cars, asking inane questions, playing games and everything else you should avoid doing, you might seem like a catch just because you listened to her and made her laugh.

Accelerate Her Attraction

After you create an atmosphere that allows a woman to open up to you and tell you about the things that matter to her most and what emotional states she seeks and avoids, it's time to open up your own heart. When a woman starts to share her vulnerabilities with you, you should expect to do the same because it's the final step you need to take to create a lasting emotional connection, assuming that's what you want. By sharing and making a connection between her hopes, dreams, and fears and your own, it helps solidify the trust and comfort she feels for you, so you can then easily escalate your relationship into something more sexual.

If you've successfully progressed to this point, a woman can become disinterested in you if she bares her soul while you're still stuck on frivolous topics, like how fast your car can go. Everyone has vulnerabilities, but not everyone can embrace them and be willing to discuss them without being emotionally affected. Everyone gets it wrong sometimes, everyone gets embarrassed, everyone feels afraid at some point, but if you can swallow your pride and put genuine feelings on the line, you'll gain a woman's trust. When a woman finally trusts you, she feels emotionally safe and secure in knowing she can share things with you that she can't with any other man—a requirement some women need fulfilled before having sex.

Remember that the Connect stage takes time—sometimes a few hours or up to many months, depending on you and the woman you're interacting with. In some circumstances she may not be ready or willing to open up to you until you start revealing your emotional side. While it's always preferable to learn a woman's buy strategy and capture her imagination before you reveal any vulnerabilities, sometimes she'll expect you to show some emotional depth before she opens up to you. If you're really attracted to a woman or you don't have any qualms about letting someone get to know the *real* you, then by all means, take the lead.

When it's time to open your heart to a woman, remember not to feel sorry for yourself, get too angry, or act confrontational when she asks you questions. Even though you're baring your soul, try to stick to upbeat topics that are wholly uplifting or at least have a silver lining. No matter what you decide to reveal about yourself, treat it as if it's no longer a big deal to you, but that the events at one time had a profound effect on you and shaped who you are today.

The following are a few topics you can introduce to demonstrate your vulnerable side so a woman can come to understand the events that made you who you are today.

Embarrassing Stories

Everyone gets embarrassed, so it's a feeling that most people find universally relatable. Embarrassing stories are also usually funny stories, so they provide you with an opportunity to reveal something about yourself *and* show off how humorous you can be, as long as you can laugh about your embarrassment. If you aren't sure you want to invest too much of yourself into a particular woman, start by revealing an embarrassing moment from grade school and ask her what embarrassed her most as a child.

First Kiss or First Love

Stories about your first kiss or the first time you fell in love are perfect immediately after she talks about the traits she seeks in a man or her best and worst dates. You can naturally transition from her story to yours to connect her desired state to yours, increasing your odds of creating a real connection. First kisses and loves are almost always clumsy affairs rife with humor, so don't be afraid to explain how they affected you, but also what you learned by your childish mistakes and how you've matured since then.

Best and Worst Childhood Experiences

Unless she volunteers her own worst childhood experience, start with your best childhood experiences. You might be surprised how easy it is to make a connection with someone, not just women, by talking about these experiences, because quite often we share similar stories. Whether you loved your first day of school or the first time you rode a bike by yourself, everyone shares a similar moment of getting their first taste of independence. Themes of freedom, exhilaration, comfort, and learning your first life lessons are great ways to connect with people.

Secrets and Insecurities

If you find that the first few topics aren't bringing you the comfort, connection, and trust you would normally expect, you might have to dig deeper into even more personal topics. If a woman is willing to talk about her darkest or most cherished moments, she might expect you to do the same. Secrets and insecurities can range from addictions to fears to phobias, but be very careful when you delve into these painful issues and make sure you're at the point where such soul-baring is appropriate. You do *not* want to talk about your rampant sex addition after knowing someone for fifteen minutes.

Losing Someone Close to You

Nothing is more personal than losing someone close to you and if it's an important part of who you are, or a woman has just related a story about her own loss, it can be an appropriate topic that reveals emotional depth. Whether you lost a family member, a close friend, or even a pet, nothing else brings emotions to the surface as easily as talking about someone you lost that you can never get back. These kinds of topics shouldn't be brought up as a tactic, but because you feel you can make a real connection with someone who has also lost a loved one. Above all, make sure you're ready to talk about something so deeply personal—not just so you can get laid, but because you truly want to be understood as a human being.

Conclusion

If, after working through the entire Connect stage, a woman seems hesitant to taking your interaction to the next level, there's a very good chance that her interest has diminished or she's emotionally damaged and has extreme difficultly bonding with people. Either way, you just might have to make your move, let the chips fall where they may, and if you're not making the forward progress you want, let her know that you expect more out of a relationship and won't be seeing her anymore. It's always frustrating to throw in the towel after expending such great effort, but sometimes you find people who are completely unable to feel comfortable, make a connection, or trust anyone. After all, this is sex we're talking about and it shouldn't require a PhD in psychology to make it happen.

Connect ★ 331

Chapter 13

Close

In this Chapter

★ Learning how to handle rejection and turning mistakes into learning experiences

★ Discovering how to get a woman's phone number without even asking for it

★ Mastering how to initiate the first kiss and escalating towards something more sexual

Close

The Close doesn't always occur after working through all of the previous stages; once you've Opened, the remaining stages are optional as determined by the woman to whom you're attracted. As you should already be aware, you never know where a woman is emotionally when you first meet her. For example, a woman who was recently cheated on may need a minimal amount of attention and interest before she suggests you come home with her. On the other hand, an emotionally balanced woman who has dated many men probably has a clear idea of what she wants in a partner, and may require a sophisticated, protracted seduction.

Over time you start to get a sense of which women will require you to go the distance and which live in the moment and want something casual. By learning everything that it *might* take to convert a conversation into a sexual liaison, you can work within the entire spectrum of these women. If you're lazy and seek only woman of dubious virtue, a few killer Openers and a funny personality may be all you need to accomplish your goals. However, most guys eventually set their sights higher than the town dumpster, so they need to know all of the steps it takes to turn a virtual stranger into a vigorous lover.

You should always try to calibrate what you can feasibly accomplish in a single encounter because if you overreach, you may ruin any possibility of picking up where you left off. Appearing as if you *need* to make out, take her to another club, or take her home can come off as desperate, unattractive behavior. For instance, if you and your friends are going to another bar and you tell her she should come, respect her if she says she can't. Instead of whining, begging, or changing your plans to be with her, just tell her you had a great time talking to her and that you think the two of you should hang out sometime. Get her number, go with your friends, get ten more numbers, and then see where they lead later in the week.

So although all of the various outcomes are consolidated in Chapter 13, "Close," don't work your way through each stage if you don't have to, don't have time to, or just don't think a particular woman is worth the investment. If you're out with friends and having a good time, spend five to ten minutes with a woman to find out whether you're attracted to her and if you are, get her number and move on. Be the mysterious guy who was charming, interesting, hilarious, and socially adept, but left just when she was hoping you would stay. These are the women who answer your calls, who return messages, who show up on time with smiles on their faces the next time they see you.

There are literally thousands of ways to transition from a conversation to one of a few possible outcomes. As you know, you shouldn't care *too* much about the outcome because you don't have much control over it, but you need to have a specific outcome in mind, so you can conclude the interaction in the most advantageous way possible. If you want her phone number, be prepared to ask for it one way or another. If you really dug her and got the same vibe back, think of a nearby café or a nice bar and let her know you're headed over there. If she's giving you all the right signals and the night is coming to a close, let her know how rare it is for you to connect with someone the way you just have, and introduce the idea of having some nice wine at your place. You should have been indirect in the beginning and flirty in the later stages, but now you need to be direct in what you want to take away from the interaction—whether it's her number or her hot body, it's time to be direct.

You Get Rejected

There is no way around it, getting rejected sucks. But lots of things in life suck and you just get over it and try to do better next time. Getting rejected by a woman is no different than any other setback in life, except you haven't lost any money and haven't incurred any physical pain. Rejection isn't an event, but a state of mind, one that you must eliminate from your life. Rejections are lessons to be internalized and used the next time you Open a group, not a referendum on your manhood.

When you get rejected, and you will get rejected many times, just remind yourself that you're a catch and if she can't see that, she'll be missing out on some good times with a great guy. If it helps, take the elevator to the top floor of a tall building and just look at all the people below you. You'll see tens of thousands of people and at that point think about your last rejection and ask, *Why did I ever get hung up on that one girl, that one time, who never really got what I was talking about anyway? There are millions of possibilities out there and I'm hung up on just one of them!* Hold on to that moment and refer to it each and every time you get rejected and start to feel sorry for yourself.

I cannot stress enough that even though you bought this book to learn something, it's not meant to demystify every type of woman in every type of situation—the learning continues, or rather, *begins* in the field. You could read this book a hundred times and not get as much real-world knowledge as throwing yourself out there, saying whatever comes to mind to any woman who crosses your path, and paying close attention to the results. The only way to make this book work for you is to expect rejection or what I refer to as "your inability to let your best qualities shine."

Hopefully you've been rethinking some of the conventional wisdom you've been holding on to and now have a solid framework for how you can get out there and land some strange ass. The only way you can fill in that framework is to work through the states, allow for many rejections, and learn why approach x did not work for girl y in situation z. Learn to love rejection and then love to learn from the rejection. It's extremely difficult at first, but once you realize the next day that what happened in that one club that one time doesn't mean shit to anybody but you—you'll start asking yourself why it even matters to you.

You Become Friends

You did everything right or you did everything wrong, whatever, but she's still there talking to you or maybe laughing at you, but she hasn't walked away. Guys who are new to the "A" game usually don't know how to handle this—they look at picking up in terms of success or failure, when they should be looking at it like a scale, as in one to ten. Failure, as a concept, should never enter your mind because it's negative and unconstructive. Instead, look at your attempts to Close as degrees of success, leaving "failure" completely out of the equation.

If you totally flame out, that's a one on the scale, but if on the next attempt you get a smile or a laugh, but still no digits, that's a three and should be considered progress. Every interaction should be viewed as a learning experience if nothing else, but also an opportunity to make new friends and meet increasingly more and more women. With that in mind, making friends with a woman instead of bedding her should be considered progress, not failure.

Becoming friends with a woman you tried to pick up greatly ties in to Rule 5, *Keep an open mind*. Understanding that she may not be your type or vice versa, or one of the other countless reasons why things just didn't click, can still lead to success down the road. Maybe she's having a party the next week and it's destined to be full of her single girlfriends. However, you can't expect to build your social network if your sole concern for the night is to turn strangers into lovers and nothing less.

If you enjoyed talking to a woman, but things didn't work out, try to convert her soft rejection into a friendship or at least an acquaintance. As you already know, you should always keep an open mind toward meeting new people every day at anytime and at any place. This is especially true as you develop your pick-up skills, because once you've recalibrated your attitude and developed your "A" game, you'll be in a great position to pick up the phone, call all of the new friends you've made, and find out what's happening next weekend. Or, even better, plan an outing with your guy friends and invite all of these groups of women to go with you.

You must continually cultivate the bonsai plant that is your single life. This means allowing branches to grow without knowing how they'll turn out, then trying to give shape and form to those branches, and occasionally snipping off the ones that don't add up to much. So you thought she was cute and hoped more would come of it, but it didn't, so work with what you *do* have, which could be a friendship with a cute girl who has cute friends. Something fantastic could come out of meeting her friends and if not, snip that branch and move to the next one. Keep an open mind to the possibilities and always look a few moves ahead, instead of solely on the here-and-now.

You Get Her Number

Before diving into the details of getting a woman's phone number, you must be reminded that getting a woman's phone number is not a success story in and of itself. Unfortunately, phone numbers are sometimes just the beginning of a frustrating game of phone tag, clumsy initial conversations, and if all goes "well," an expensive date filled with awkward silences. Once you get a better understanding of how the game is played, by both men and women, you'll soon realize how many numbers you need to get in order to find one woman who remembers talking to you, remembers that she *liked* talking to you, and now that she's thinking clearly, will talk to you again, one-on-one, during an antiquated dating ritual. Plus, consider how many of those dates will produce a quality woman that you will want to talk to again.

Although the numbers-getting game isn't considered an actual Close, you should still aim to get a woman's phone number if you're attracted to one another and you can't take the interaction any further that day. Getting a woman's number is especially important when you've just started to learn and incorporate elements of the "A" game, because it shows progress and builds your confidence. Most importantly, it creates opportunity, no matter how slim the odds are. Any opportunity to better your conversational and flirting skills is welcome, even if it doesn't lead to much success.

A lot of guys have a problem when it's time to ask a woman for her number. More often than not the problem stems from a mindset of knowing that they have to ask, but don't fully expect to get a number. If you don't think you deserve to get a woman's phone number, they pick up on it through the words you use (I was wondering, if you don't mind, would you be interested in…), the tone of your voice (unsure, hopeful, nervous) and your body language (head down, hands in pockets, moving away from her). Women subconsciously notice these signals and then they wonder to themselves whether they should give you their number when you act as though you don't deserve it.

The entire act of asking a woman for her number can betray your frame of never needing to chase women because they often chase you. If you've portrayed yourself as a catch, someone who chooses the women he spends time with, it's incongruent to sheepishly ask someone for their number. So even though you want her number, you don't want to appear as though you *need* it. The best way to avoid a situation like this is to never directly ask a woman for her number; instead ask her why she hasn't tried to get your number.

By inquiring why she never asked for your number despite her obvious attraction to you, you can accomplish many things. Beyond just avoiding being needy or unsure of yourself, it can also take a lot of pressure off a woman from feeling she has to give her number to a stranger. It's also a good way to screen women, meaning that you expect women to be mature and sexually confident enough to call. If they never call, you've simply saved yourself time in having to learn that she's insecure and possibly a host of other negative traits.

Women who do call usually have the mindset that they're good enough to date you and view you as their equal. Since you've put a woman in the driver's seat when it comes to calling you, she'll typically feel much more relaxed when you next meet up. That comfort typically extends through future interactions up to and including sex and it takes the pressure off of you when it comes to deciding when to call. Instead, whenever she calls you, you have the benefit of knowing she's attracted to you and interested in doing more than talking.

So how do you turn the tables so a woman understands that you expect her to get your number and call you, otherwise it will never happen? Instead of directly asking for her phone number, you start out with a different question. You should lob the following question at her in the middle of a good conversation, not after you've run out of steam and you're confronted with uncomfortable silence.

"Hey, I gotta ask you an indiscreet question, but if it makes you uncomfortable in any way, just flip me off and I'll let it go."

This approach works well because it shows you have the confidence to ask an indiscreet question, and the fact that you used the word "indiscreet" can command a woman's attention so she listens intently to what you're about to say. You also show some consideration for her feelings and emotional state by letting her know that you understand she might be made uncomfortable by your question.

The kicker is the little bit of humor you throw in to let her know that even though you want to ask her the question, you won't be shattered if you don't get an answer. You should be smiling when you tell her she can give you the finger and it should make her smile or laugh too. If it doesn't, you should consider how insecure or uptight she is to take herself and someone she just met so seriously.

If she does start to laugh or gives you a big smile, ask her **"Are you single?"** and you'll almost always get one of the following responses:

"Why do you ask?": Because she couldn't answer a simple, straightforward question and it must have made her self-conscious or uncomfortable, respond with "Oh, I'm just curious…" Curiosity isn't cause for a woman to be alarmed, so she should be able to relax and feel comfortable again. Plus, you aren't defaulting to needy male behavior by apologizing or justifying your question— you're just curious.

"No": Respond with "I figured someone like you wouldn't last long in the dating pool." It may have taken you ten minutes to get to that point, but it isn't time wasted because you demonstrated value to everyone around you by getting her and her group to focus on you. Consider concluding by asking for her opinion, disagreeing with her, and then bringing her into another group using her "crazy" opinion as your next Opener.

"Yes": Respond with "Great…so when are you going to ask me out?" Make sure you're smiling, but also serious in asking her when she planned on asking you out, or why she hasn't asked you yet. Tease her by saying she doesn't really seem like the shy type.

By asking her when she's going to ask you out, you're trying to accomplish a few things. First, you're trying to find out whether she has a sense of humor. Second, you're testing her insecurities as a female by finding out whether she truly believes it's a "man's job" to pursue a woman. You may want to spend time with a woman who subscribes to traditional roles, but most guys are tired of contorting themselves to match a woman's ever-evolving ideas on what dating, courtship, and manhood should be.

Note: Sometimes a woman will say yes, even though she isn't single and she's talking to you for validation, because she isn't getting enough attention from her significant other or her relationship is on the decline. If you don't have any moral objections, keep talking to her, because she might be looking for an "out" and you could be in line for some rebound hate sex. However, if she says she's single, the assumption should be made that she's truly single, otherwise she wouldn't be spending one-on-one time talking to you.

Typical responses to "When are you going to ask me out?"

She laughs

Laughter is the usual response and it's a good sign because she probably "gets it." Women laugh because deep down they know there's truth to what you're saying. After all, she's single, out to meet guys, attracted to you, and here you are, so why *hasn't* she asked you out? Most women are still too shy to step up, so some explanation might be required:

"You know, some women are just looking for a career guy so they can bring him home to Mom because he's a doctor or an architect. Or they want a really good-looking guy they can show off to their friends to make them all jealous. But you seem like you might be different...like you have a little more heart than that..."

With those three sentences, you've now turned an ambiguous question into a direct challenge. By telling a woman she seems like she "might have a little more heart than that," you're really asking her whether she would pursue a guy she's really attracted to by asking him out. Often, she'll still be laughing at the circumstances and how you were able to put her on the spot, but you shouldn't be offended.

Women laugh because they're nervous and aren't sure of themselves in situations like this. For a lot of women, this is uncharted territory, especially with a guy they've only talked to for ten minutes. Allow her to calm herself and collect her thoughts, but you should still expect her to ask you out. If she doesn't laugh and acknowledge that you turned the tables on her, you might get one of the following responses:

"It's usually the man's job to pursue the woman."

If you get this type of response, it usually means she's old fashioned, which might be exactly what you're looking for. However, when a woman in a major metropolitan area spits out antiquated rules of "how it should be," you need to ask yourself whether you're prepared to meet such expectations. Some guys are past being old-fashioned because they've spent years being "equals" with the women they've dated. You've taken the interaction this far, so feel her out for what she means and see if she might make an exception.

"I don't ask men out" or "I don't call guys."

This is an inflexible variation of the previous response and usually means she expects or demands control in her relationships. Often, these women have very specific "rules of engagement" and they expect you to know what they are, even though they vary from woman to woman. It's up to you, but I usually smile, hand them my card, and say "Rules are made to be broken, so if you change your mind, you know how to reach me." Most women are so taken with your confidence that you eventually get a call or a text message.

They just don't "get it"

This response can come in many forms, but the takeaway is they don't understand that you've playfully turned the tables on them. The fact that you think a woman should at least be open to the idea of calling a man she's attracted to is a concept they just can't comprehend, as if you've hit a glitch in their social programming. If she gets confused and you have to explain and defend what you're saying, you're probably dealing with someone who can't or won't follow her heart. Instead, she chooses her relationships based on what the world expects of her (career guys for mom, good-looking guys for her friends) rather than pursuing someone she's passionately attracted to. You might want to consider finding someone less shallow and more mature to get involved with, or see what you can make happen in the short term.

You Ask For Her Number

If you're not ready to be so bold as to question why a woman hasn't asked you out yet, you can always revert to asking for her number. However, through all of the previous stages your attitude and behavior has been significantly different than what the majority of men do when they meet attractive women. With that said, you should continue to be different and challenging and that also includes the way in which you ask for her number. In fact, if you've led the interaction up until this point, you shouldn't *ask* for her number, you should *tell* her to give it to you.

Since you've presumably spent some time in the Attract and Connect stages, you have every reason to believe that she'll want to pick up where you left off at some point in the future. By asking for her number, you're working under the assumption that you aren't sure you just had a good time together. You think you might have, but you aren't sure, which shows a lack of confidence on your part. In fact, your success rate at getting phone numbers greatly increases by *telling* a woman that you'll need it if the two of you ever hope to talk again. In effect, you're telling her to give you her number, but also what you plan to do with it after she gives it to you.

One of the best ways to tell a woman to give you her phone number is to ask her whether she has an e-mail address. By now, everyone has an e-mail address, so it's hard for a woman to lie and tell you she doesn't. Since you already know she's going to say "yes," you should have pen and paper ready so you can swiftly lay the paper on a nearby surface, hand her the pen, point to the paper, and tell her to write it down. If she asks why, tell her "I'm going to need it so we can continue our little conversation next week" or something similar.

While she's writing her e-mail address say, "You know, just go ahead and put your number below your e-mail address—I don't always check my e-mail." Strangely enough, since she already has pen to paper and is in the middle of writing down her e-mail address, she'll almost always comply with your instructions. If she protests or simply doesn't include her phone number, she must have her reasons. As long as you have one piece of contact information, even just an e-mail address, you can still get to know one another and work toward meeting up sometime in the future.

In some ways writing an e-mail is much easier and allows for a greater rate of success than a phone call, especially if you're nervous when you make these types of calls. E-mails allow you to write whatever you want without getting tongue-tied or running out of things to say. You can write an e-mail whenever you want and she can respond when it's convenient. E-mail also allows for multiple exchanges before you meet again, giving you more opportunities to build rapport before you see her again. Of course, calling a woman shows a lot more confidence than writing an e-mail, so if you really want to hook up with someone sooner rather than later, calling is your best option.

Always remember that at no point should you offer too much detail on why you want her contact details, and if she doesn't want to give you all or part of this information, don't whine or complain about it. Again, since you're outcome-independent, you don't *need* her information because you presumably have many other women from which to choose. Her perception of you should be that you're a confident man who doesn't feel insecure about getting a woman's phone number, and if a woman doesn't want to provide it, it's not a big deal to you.

Putting Phone Numbers to Good Use

A phone number isn't just contact information that you use to call a woman so you can ask her out on a date. Instead, a phone number should be considered a rain check that you use to pick up on the conversation you were having, or at least dive back into the stage you were in when you concluded your original interaction. Often a woman will give you her phone number before she feels comfortable enough to see you again, so you have to know how to talk to women on the phone as well as in person, so they'll feel comfortable enough to meet with you again.

Just because a woman was initially attracted to you doesn't mean she will instantly agree to see you again—most likely because she didn't get to know you very well or she doesn't remember much about you. If you can pick up on your in-person conversation and continue displaying your attractive qualities—at least verbally—you can greatly minimize the number of flakes and dead-ends you get when following up on phone numbers. With this in mind, you have to focus on building or even rebuilding enough attraction, rapport, and comfort with a woman over the phone before she'll agree to hang out with you.

Calling, texting, and e-mailing a woman are all ways to reinitiate your conversation so you can ultimately see her again. If you spent a considerable amount of time building attraction when you first met, you can usually get reacquainted over the phone in just a few minutes before asking her out. If you only had a few minutes to Open and generate some interest, you sometimes have to be willing to call a woman a few times and continue building attraction and rapport as if you were meeting for the first time.

A lot of guys get nervous when they have to call a woman and ask her out. Just like when men worry about what they're going to say to a woman when they first meet her, they get nervous when they call a woman for the first time. Some men will call and talk as little as possible before asking a woman to go out with them, which can alarm some women because they wonder why a guy they barely know is so eager to see them. Other guys ramble on with meaningless small talk until a woman gets bored or frustrated and tells him she has to go. Both approaches can turn women off and cause women who were initially attracted to a guy to flake on him or stop answering his calls.

Your goal, even before you get a woman's phone number, is to see her again so you can build the kind of trust and rapport that advances a relationship into intimate territory. That goal, getting her alone so you can talk, flirt, and escalate kino, still holds true when you're on the phone, but when you first call her, you must completely forget about getting her alone. You have to avoid getting ahead of yourself and instead focus on picking things up where you left them as casually as possible and follow the "A" game as you normally would if you were seeing each other in person. At the very least, you have to spend time in the Attract stage and get her laughing and playfully flirting with you again. Only then should you bring up the idea of getting together and enjoying the same kinds of conversations in person.

Before diving in to the details of how to conduct a phone call so you can set up a time to meet again, there are some basic questions that most guys ask about when to call, for how long, and what to do when a woman doesn't answer her phone. The following Q&A covers the basics on calling a woman and what to do when her roommate answers or you get her voicemail.

How long should I wait to call?

Every guy has his own theory on how long to wait to call a woman after getting her number. You can wait two days so you don't seem too eager, later that night so she remembers you well, or a week later so you appear to be busy and in demand. For the most part, it doesn't really matter how long you wait as long as you call within a few days. Most women give you their number because they're interested in learning more about you, but that interest wanes very quickly if they don't hear from you. In general, it's better to seem too eager than to call a week later and talk to someone who doesn't have the faintest idea who you are.

Of course, if you hit it off and had a really good conversation, don't hesitate to call or text her ten minutes later to tell her so and then mention that you'll call her later. Or, if you parted ways, but you're still in the same location, like a bar or club, you can tease her by texting "Stop staring at me" or "Come save me." If you were only mildly interested in someone, just put their numbers in a pile and call them all at once when you have the time. Start by calling the women you were the least interested in so by the time you get to the most promising numbers, you will be well-practiced and relaxed after talking to so many other women.

When should I call?

Again, the exact time of day doesn't usually matter as long as you reasonably expect her to be available to talk to you. If you meet someone over the weekend, Sunday evenings are usually a good time to call because women are almost always at home relaxing or preparing for the upcoming week. On a weekday, you should call a few hours after a woman gets off of work if you know she has a typical nine-to-five job. These are basic rules that apply to the majority of women, but if you know she works odd hours or doesn't work at all, just call when it's most convenient for you.

More important than the time of day or night that you call is what kind of mood you're in when you call. Always make calls when you're in a really good mood, because women can pick up on your state of mind even if you don't explicitly state how you're feeling. If you aren't in a good mood, but know you should make a few calls, you need to find ways to pump yourself up and lift your spirits. For example, jog in the park, talk to women you know will answer your calls, or think about the last time you talked to a woman and it went really well. Do whatever you have to do to bring energy and excitement to your phone calls and then start dialing.

How long should I talk?

A woman may remember a few things about you or even specifics from your conversation and she may have had a really good time with you. However, just a few days later, most women will remember very few details other

Directly After You Get Her Number

Once you get a woman's number, don't leave her in the lurch as if your only goal in talking to her was to get her number. A lot of men view the exchange of phone numbers as the end of the interaction, because that's seemingly the high point, at least for some guys. Women don't view the act of giving a near stranger their number as a high point, so you should stick around for a few minutes and continue through the Attract or Connect stage. There's no harm in sticking around for a few minutes to continue talking so she feels more comfortable about what she's just done. It also greatly increases the odds of her responding to your call.

than whether she made out with you. Because of this, you have to be willing to put in just enough time on the phone so that she's again comfortable being alone with you.

Women know that if they gave you their phone number, you must have been reasonably attractive, but it doesn't mean she remembers why she found you attractive. When you call her for the first time, you should demonstrate your attractive personality quickly and then spend as much time as you need to telling stories, teasing, and flirting until she remembers why she was originally attracted to you. Stay on the phone for as long as you seem to be enjoying talking to each other.

Although some men feel it's better to be the one who says "gotta go," it really doesn't matter who wraps up the conversation and ends the call first. Anytime you feel the conversation is about to run out of steam is the time to end the call. As long as the woman you're talking to seems interested in keeping the conversation going, don't feel as though you have to end the conversation because of some arbitrary rule. The more you talk with a woman on the phone, the more material she is likely to give you to use when you finally meet in person. Most women think nothing of how long they spend on the phone or who ended the call first, so you shouldn't either.

What if someone else answers?

Most women prefer to give a guy their cell phone number instead of their home number, if they actually even have a home number. However, you should be prepared for those occasions when someone else answers the phone. Unless it's her boyfriend, whoever answers the phone is likely someone to whom you should demonstrate social value. For instance, if another woman picks up the phone and you find out it's her roommate, you want to spend as much time as possible charming her, so she is sure to relay the fact that you called, as well as letting her roommate know how cool you seemed over the phone.

Whenever you call a woman, you typically introduce yourself and then ask to speak to the woman you gave you her phone number. If the person you're talking to is someone other than who you assumed would answer, automatically act as though you were calling for them. Ask for her name and then tell her you've heard a lot of good things about her, or ask whether her and her roommate want to go out with you and your friends. After a few minutes of chatting, whoever you called will eventually ask whether you want to leave a message, but just ignore her.

Much like you would act if you approached a group of her friends, use the same material that you would in the Open and Hook stages. After you feel you've "won over" her friend, roommate, mom, sister, or whoever else might have answered, try to get off the phone without leaving a message. The best approach is to say, "It was a pleasure chatting with you, but I need to get going...bye." Again, if she asks whether you want to leave a message, just say, "Thanks, but no message." If you do your job well, her roommate will not only find out that you called, but also how charming and funny you were. With that kind of praise and the mystery of not leaving a message, she'll most likely call you back as soon as possible.

What if I get her voicemail?

If you really impress a woman and then call her within 24 hours, you can reasonably expect her to answer your first call, as long as she's available to answer. Otherwise, you should never be surprised to get a woman's voicemail on the first few calls. It's a simple fact that people are busy and attractive women get more than a few calls from guys every day. They aren't being rude, just practical, and again you have to work with that reality instead of against it.

There are a few good reasons to always leave a message on your first call. First, almost everyone has caller ID, so a woman will know that you called her and how many times, so you don't want to seem insecure or even rude because you refuse to leave a simple message. Second, by leaving an interesting message on her voicemail, you can gauge how interested she is in you by how quickly she returns your call. If she never gets back to you, that doesn't mean you have to give up, but it usually means you have your work cut out for you if you hope to see her again.

Instead of worrying about what you should say on her voicemail, always have a few little quips ready to go that can work for any woman you call. Your goal is to leave a short "open loop" message that only says enough to pique her curiosity. You want to say something that gives only a small part of a potentially exciting story, so she'll feel compelled to call you back. As long as you use a playful tone and high energy, most women will want to find out what you're so exited about, especially if it involves them.

The following are a few examples of open loop statements that you can use:

★ "Oh my god! You're *never* gonna believe what just happened…"

★ "I heard the *craziest* thing on the radio today and it made me think of our little conversation…"

★ "I was taking a shower this morning and I could have sworn I saw you watching me from out the window…"

★ "I just had the most amazing idea…I've got to tell you about it…"

★ "Hey, brat, I just saw something about [conversation you had] and I wanted to ask you something about it."

★ "You are soooooo busted!"

Try to end any of these statements with "I'll talk to you later…" but never "Call me back." This is partly a face-saving technique so you can call her again even if she never called you back and you won't seem needy. After all, you told her you would talk to her later and you're simply living up to your word. Never ask a woman to call you back or any other variation, just tell her what you plan to do—talk to her later—and then follow through. Also, you can use any of the open loop messages you just read, but you should have stories from you own life that fit the context of the message. When a woman asks why she's "busted," you need to have a fun answer ready to go.

Making the Call

Asking for a traditional date is of course "nice," which means it should be avoided, at least initially. To many women a date means dinner and a movie and the possibility of being trapped for up to four hours with someone they barely know and might not know much better after two hours of eating and two hours in the dark. You're doing a disservice to women and yourself by being nice and asking a woman to go on a traditional date with you. So, after you get her number, play coy, and conduct your phone calls in the same way you behaved during the Hook and Attract stages.

Since the location where you originally met most likely wasn't very conducive to building rapport, your goal should be to arrange to meet a woman somewhere that you can build more comfort so you can eventually Close her. Good places to build more comfort and trust are usually quiet and secluded, yet still public places, like lounges and cafés. Other good comfort-building locations/adventures include:

★ Produce shopping at a farmer's market

★ Fun errands like dog walking or test driving cars

★ Your living room for wine, appetizers, and a DVD

★ A scenic drive down the coast or through rolling hills

★ Shopping at the mall for clothes or presents for female relatives

★ Hip upscale bar on a slow night—dark and with comfy booths

Beginning

Before you start dialing, remember to use a confident tone of voice and keep an outcome- independent frame of mind. When a woman answers the phone, introduce yourself by saying, "Hi, this is [*your name*]. Is [*her name*] there?" If she answers the call herself, as opposed to a roommate or friend, launch into a high-energy story or use a relevant Opener and skip any pleasantries or re-minders of who you are. If she interrupts you to ask who you are, tell her "Brad Pitt" or something similar, and then keep talking. Eventually she will figure out who you are based on your attitude and what you're talking about.

Start by telling her a funny or interesting story like you normally would and get her laughing and involved. Don't ask whether she's busy or what she's do-ing and never remind her who you are or where she met you. Talk confidently and don't rush through your conversation just so you can quickly ask her out and get off the phone as soon as possible. You aren't on the clock and you don't have to be the first to end the conversation, so relax and talk slowly.

Don't expect a woman to hold up her end of the conversation, at least not for the first few minutes. You have to build your own momentum using the attractive qualities of your personality. Keep using material from the Hook and Attract stages until she starts to chime in and build on your stories. Your goal is to come across not as just "some guy" but a guy she already knows, has history with, and feels comfortable talking to, even if she doesn't.

Middle

Avoid using any small talk and don't expect a woman to carry the conversation by saying things like "So what did you do today?" or "So, how was your day?" As with an in-person conversation, you choose the topics and drive the conversation, so you need to have an idea of what you're going to say before you call. In a way, if you're prepared to talk to someone for ten minutes without them ever saying a word, you'll be able to handle your initial phone call with no problem whatsoever.

Keep the charm flowing and bring her back to the flirty mood you hopefully left her in. Again, stay outcome-independent and don't introduce the idea of going out together for now, just focus on demonstrating your attractive personality. In some cases you will have to re-attract her as if you had never met, so be prepared to tell the same stories and introduce similar conversation topics just to jog her memory. By keeping the pace and directing the conversation, you can avoid any uncomfortable silences and you won't give her any opportunity to wonder why she's talking to you or why she shouldn't.

If you spent a considerable amount of time together when you first met, you can usually pick things up right where you left them, assuming you called her within a reasonable time frame. Whether you were at the beginning of the Attract stage or near the end of the Connect stage, take one small step back from where you left off and then drive right into building more attraction or comfort as if no time had ever elapsed. Consider the phone just another comfort-building location and ignore the fact that you might be miles apart, because when she falls back into the same stage you left her in, you won't be apart for long.

End

After about five to ten minutes of conversation, asking her out should be fairly easy and straightforward. However, instead of directly asking her out on a traditional date, you matter-of-factly mention that you have something you have to do this week and thought she might like to join you. With enthusiasm, talk up some errand you have/want to do, like going shopping or walking your dog, and then *tell* her that she should join you. If she still seems hesitant, tell her it's going be a lot more fun than whatever she's currently doing. Just remember not to pressure her if she declines, otherwise she'll *never* agree to see you again.

Some examples of how you might initiate a meeting include:

"Hey, I'm about to head out for some coffee…you should join me. I'm way more fun that whatever you're doing now and that's a scientific fact!"

"My dog is going crazy over here...he probably needs a walk, so I better go. You like dogs? You should help me walk him, he's a handful. I'll pick you up."

"I gotta get my niece a birthday present and I have no idea what to get her. I think I'm just gonna go to the mall and wander around. You should come help me out."

If she doesn't accept your invitation and she doesn't have a good reason why, just interrupt her and say, "Hey, you're the one who is missing out" or

"You know, never mind. I guess you don't like having fun." These are simple no-pressure tactics that encourage a woman to break out of her immature comfort zone and act like a women instead of a little girl who's too scared to get coffee or go shopping. If she says anything other than "I'm just not that into you" or something similar, you have every right to tease her and even guilt her into hanging out with you. After all, it's not a big deal to go shopping or walk a dog.

Alternate End

If you built a lot of attraction and comfort before you called her, you probably want to arrange something a little more interesting than coffee or shopping. Instead of inviting her to tag along with you, casually say, "Let's get together this week" or "What's your schedule like?" and then let her talk. At this point, most women will recite their schedules and let you know when they have free time. Pick a date and time that works for both of you, but don't tell her what you're going to do together. It's very rare that a woman will flake on you after you arrange to hang out when she knows you know she's available, so work with her schedule, but take responsibility for the activities and keep the details under a shroud of mystery until you call back to confirm the date and time.

If she claims to be too busy to get together, ignore it and dive back into your conversation, so you can try to build more comfort and rapport and then try again by rephrasing or using a slightly different approach. If that doesn't work, you can end by asking her to hang out with you right then by saying something like "Let's go get coffee/ice cream/smoothies. I can pick you up in x minutes." If she still isn't interested, it's time to let her go with a simple "Nice talking with you, I gotta go." You can try to call her again in a few weeks, but you should probably put her number into the trash.

Typically, if you put a woman in the right mood and pick up on some of the topics you originally discussed, you shouldn't have a problem arranging to hang out with her. You don't always have to do all the work to make a meeting happen, especially if you invested a lot of time in the original interaction. Sometimes, if you impress her or she was already very attracted to you, she'll introduce the idea of getting together before you do. When this happens you can usually jump right into the Attract or even the Connect stage when you meet her, without having to backtrack.

You Make Out

You may have accelerated her interest in you intellectually and emotionally, but if you feel it's time to take the interaction into the bedroom (or bathroom stall), you have to accelerate her *physical* interest in you. After all, you didn't come this far with someone just to make a new friend, but to make a new *naked* friend. Accomplishing what you've learned in the last few chapters in a matter of days, instead of months, is hard work and you deserve to be rewarded, as does she.

Just about everyone wants and needs to have sex, so you should strike the idea that you're tricking someone or getting away with something by converting attraction into sexual intimacy. Guys always seem to wait for women to take the lead, especially when it comes to intimacy, largely because they don't want to get rejected, or feel like they're pressuring a woman into doing something she doesn't want to. Unfortunately, women actually expect men to take the lead and appreciate it when they do. Women are attracted to men who can show their capacity to take them through a seductive journey that leaves them breathless.

Most women, especially after going through the Connect stage, have no appreciation for a guy who asks permission to kiss them. It demonstrates a real lack of confidence in your supposed understanding of her, who she is, and what she's about if you can't detect whether or not she wants to kiss you. It's true that it can be awkward deciding when to kiss someone for the first time, but if you find yourself asking whether you should kiss, the answer is "yes, right now." Typically, if you're thinking about it, she's already two steps ahead and wondering when and if you're going to grow a pair and show her how you feel.

You should have already found a secluded spot that's ideal for making out away from the public eye. If you're still in plain sight of many people, find a hallway or doorway where you can find at least a few seconds to spontaneously kiss without embarrassing her in front of friends, family, or complete strangers. Even the biggest sex kittens prefer making out in private, sometimes for the increased intimacy or for the opportunity to move beyond kissing. Most women just like the privacy because they feel safe and more comfortable, so it shouldn't slow you down much to oblige her, especially since you may be in line for a significant "reward."

Making Your Move

You know that feeling you get when you can't read her signals and you have no idea whether she's *truly* interested in you? If you've ever let this nagging feeling prevent you from kissing someone, you have to change your frame of mind. If you've worked though all or even just some of the stages, you have to make a leap of faith and assume that she is *of course* interested in you. Men and women are similar with regards to the uneasy and anxious feeling surrounding the need to know just exactly what's "going on here," but it's up to you to eventually make your feelings crystal clear.

In the beginning, when you first met, there was a definite need for ambiguity, but before she gets completely frustrated and throws in the towel, you *have* to make your intentions clear by kissing her. The length of time between meeting and kissing can take minutes, hours, days, but hopefully not weeks or months. It depends on the particular woman and the circumstances, but if you haven't kissed her by the third time you've met, at the very latest, then you're likely spending time with a new friend instead of a new lover.

If it helps to boost your confidence, you can look for a few signs that indicate whether a woman is ready to be kissed. I strongly recommend *not* waiting for any signals and just going with your instincts, before she feels she has to give you a signal if something intimate is ever going to happen. Always try to stay a few steps ahead, but if you really need to know for certain that she won't reject your advances, look for the following signals and if you get a few of them within a few minutes, it's time to act immediately:

★ She puts gum in her mouth and/or offers you some.

★ She puts on lip gloss or licks her lips a lot.

★ She stares at or seems distracted by your lips.

★ She moves closer to you so that you're constantly touching.

★ She puts her head on your shoulder.

★ She moves her face extremely close to yours.

★ She twinkles her eyes a lot while smiling at you.

Whether you waited for some signals or not, you're now ready to go in for a kiss. As you already know, you shouldn't ask her for permission to kiss her and you don't want to alarm her by kissing her without warning, so you should give her some indication of what you're about to do. If your first kiss seemed "magical" to her, you're in line for much, much more, but if it's lousy she might start to second-guess whether the connection transcends mere conversation. In other words, in the absence of alcohol, women prefer a first kiss to be memorable, if not outright electric.

You can rarely create this electricity if you jump in and kiss her like a sniper, so you have to indicate that you're going in for a kiss just seconds before you do so. It's not that you're asking her or giving her time to reject you, you're simply giving her a few seconds of anticipation where she can prepare herself, both physically (moving toward you) and emotionally (I'm going to make this kiss mean something). If she doesn't know a kiss is coming, you could miss her lips, bump heads, or catch her mid-sentence, all of which can be cute, but why not aim for kismet?

Use one of the following phrases about five seconds before you lean in for a kiss:

★ "Come here, I want to kiss you."

★ "I think it's time we kissed."

★ While she's talking put your finger to her lips and say, "Shhh…"

★ "Aren't you ever going to kiss me?"

★ "You want to kiss me, don't you?"

After you throw one of these lines out, don't wait for her response, even if you seemingly asked her a question. These lines are only meant to let her know what you're about to do so that she's not caught completely off-guard. Of course you are giving her enough time to pull away or otherwise object to your advances, but she has every right to do so. In a way, you're telling her that you're about to kiss her and you're giving her just a few seconds to either lean in and respond positively or lean away.

Beyond the statement you make, consider the actual act of moving in for a kiss as a non-verbal question, similar to kino compliance. If she moves in and closes her eyes, she's saying "yes" and if she pulls away, obviously that's her way of saying "no." Typically, if you've gone this far and she feels safe and comfortable in your presence, she shouldn't have any hesitations about kissing you. However, if for some reason she pulls away, puts her hand up, or asks "What do you think you're doing?" you should at least be prepared with a dignified response.

Most guys, who may have even observed some apparent "buy signals," get extremely defensive when they finally put themselves on the line and get rejected. Instead of whining, "But you were giving me all the signals" or "You know you want it," just apologize and tell her, "You know...I really enjoy talking with you and I just want to find out what it would feel like to have that connection with you." She might reconsider or you might never see her again, but at least you took a chance and tried to make something happen with a woman you were attracted to, instead of waiting for something that might never happen.

The last thing you want to do is not take a chance and then go home and ponder for hours about what you could have said or done. If everything works out, you'll continue to learn through your successes. If things don't go as planned, spend a few minutes thinking about how you could have done things differently, and then forget about her completely.

Even though you should temper your desire to get as hot and heavy as soon as possible, it doesn't mean you shouldn't go in for a kiss. If your first kiss goes well, meaning she doesn't push you away, ask why you kissed her, or give you a dirty look, more discreet kissing is completely acceptable *and* expected. Since many women like to tease men with their sexuality, you should aim to do the same. Kiss her for a moment and then playfully push her away and say, "Okay, time for a drink." It throws women completely off balance when they think they're giving you what you want (guys only want one thing...), but you playfully deny them. When you seem to live by a different code than most men, it confounds, intrigues, and excites women to no end.

You Take Her Somewhere Else

Most guys are familiar with getting rejected, making new friends, scoring a phone number or two, and possibly having a one-night stand. However, a lot of guys fail to consider taking a woman on a "mini-date," which involves taking a woman that you've just met to a different location, so you can get to know each other better without any break in the interaction. As your "A" game improves, your confidence and strong frame of mind will enable you to attract women in such a way that they get wrapped up in your world and will follow you to a different venue because of their attraction to you.

A mini-date usually starts at a bar, club, or restaurant in the evening where you met a woman and after a great conversation, she seems open to going to a different bar or club with you. By bringing her along, you can bounce to a few different venues so she can get to know "your world" and by going places together, even on the same night you met, it seems like you're on a date, not a random hookup. However, despite the term "date," it definitely does not mean taking her from a club to dinner and a movie.

There is a lot of psychology at work when it comes to explaining the mini-date and why it can accelerate attraction so quickly. To sum it up, most women have mental and social barriers that prevent them from arriving with their friends at a club, meeting a guy, and leaving their friends to go home with a guy. For most women, disappearing with strange guys is taboo when they're with their friends unless it's been agreed upon beforehand and then all of them will be working to pull guys home, which is seemingly rare these days.

Why wouldn't a woman who is dressed to kill and dancing like a stripper have any interest in putting those skills to immediate use? To put it bluntly, a woman's social network is the most important thing she has, along with her family, and she will never tarnish her image in the eyes of her friends just to go home with you. Within that statement you can probably zero in on how to circumvent those barriers.

Moving in Too Soon

Instead of being too nervous to make a move, some men are either so nervous or overconfident that they make a move before a women is comfortable with them. If you've shown a lot of confidence and you've led the interaction up until this point, chances are good that she won't reject you and she'll allow, and even participate in, some heavy petting. However, if your goal is to move past kissing and into something more carnal, you should be aware of some of the drawbacks of a shortsighted make-out session.

Most women can separate a drunken public make-out with a stranger and a smoldering seduction that keeps her on her toes with a mysterious new man. In other words, these types of guys are mutually exclusive—you're either one or the other, but rarely both. With that in mind, you have to consider whether you think you want to see a woman again before you start groping each other in the middle of the club. Groping may even lead to sex, but a woman will compartmentalize the event and consider it a moment of spontaneous lust, something she probably won't want to revisit again, at least not with you. If all you seek from a particular woman is a one-night stand, this is the perfect situation. However, if you want to see her again, you should reconsider public groping and grinding.

Once you make a move and you start kissing, always be the one who slows things down, who doesn't want to get too heated up, who suggests the two of you will have plenty of time for passion. When you do this, most women will hold you in high regard, mainly because it's virtually unheard of for a guy to try to slow down sexual intimacy. The kicker is that after you gently push her away and tell her to slow things down, she'll completely agree with you, but just minutes later she'll feel extremely comfortable because of what you said, so comfortable that she'll be all over you despite your protestations.

In order for a mini-date to work well, you have to take a woman with you somewhere as if it were a date you had planned out in advance, although you just met. You need to arrive somewhere together, without her friends, and slowly but surely introduce her to your world by taking her to your favorite bars and/or clubs. By packing a week's worth of courtship behavior into three or four hours, you can melt those barriers so she can find it perfectly reasonable to do all the things she doesn't want her friends to know about.

It sounds lame in description, but in execution it can escalate a five-minute conversation into a wild, wonderful night. For those who believe this is yet another form of pick-up trickery, you have to believe you are simply creating the circumstances that allow a woman to express her sexuality without being judged for it. Guys don't have such problems, in fact it's quite the opposite, but it's extremely important to understand why she has these barriers and objections so you can whisk her to an environment where those objections seem immature. There is no trickery, just a girl and a guy with none of society's rules standing in the way of a good time.

If you have the time and desire to continue an interaction beyond the Attract stage, you have to break a woman away from her group, assuming she's with one, so you can spend some alone time together. Or perhaps circumstances didn't permit much more than a kiss and an exchange of phone numbers. In either case, you need to pick a new location so you can build enough comfort and rapport to help escalate your relationship toward more sexual intimacy.

The entire reason you move to or meet at another location is to create a connection, because by this point it should be well established that you're attracted to one another and you've proven as much by flirting, kissing, and possibly more. Going somewhere together is a powerful way to build comfort because you're doing something together, not randomly running into one another as you probably did when you met. Going somewhere together also gives a woman an opportunity to focus on the two of you without the distractions of a loud club, her friends, or other commitments.

Move to a New Location After You Meet

If you're in the moment and you want to continue talking, you have to start thinking about places the two of you could go. In some circumstances, you have to think about places that both her friends and your friends can go, or perhaps one of your groups already has a destination, like an all-night restaurant or pizza shack. Since it's your job to lead the interaction, at the very least you should suggest a place that might logistically work for all involved. In some instances a woman is out alone or she doesn't mind ditching her friends, in which case you can pick the nearest quiet spot to grab a bite or just start talking.

If She's Alone

If it's day time and you're in the moment and want to keep talking to a woman, you could say something like "Well, I'm on my way to get some coffee and you're probably on your way somewhere too…you drink coffee?" You can use the same context for most locations as long as you tell her that you're on your way to doing something, you understand she is as well, but if she's into whatever you're about to do, she's welcome to join you. Notice that you haven't asked her to go with you, but you *told* her you were doing something and you *told* her she could join you. It shows more confidence when you're on your own path and you decide that you wouldn't mind her company, but don't need it.

Nearby daytime locations, when a woman is on her own, include:

* A park with open space and benches

* A simple restaurant with outdoor seating

* A café without an extreme amount of foot traffic and noise

* Any trivial errand, like picking up dry cleaning or stamps

* A walk in any highly trafficked area like a beach, mall, or city street

If She's With a Group

If it's night time and she's with her friends, you have to assume she's go-ing to leave with them. The chances of her leaving her friends on a whim with someone she just met are slim, so consider locations that both of your groups wouldn't mind going to. A few minutes before you're about to leave, say something like, "You're a pretty cool chick…my group's heading over to [wherever you decide], you should come with us." She'll probably have to consult with her friends, which is a perfect opportunity to introduce her and her group to your friends. In the event that the two groups have to go their separate ways, get a rain check by getting her phone number.

Nearby evening locations, when a woman is typically with friends, include:

* A greasy diner

* An after-hours party

* You or your friend's pad

* A noodle house or pizza joint

* Anyplace where you're on the guest list

Remember, whenever you propose changing locations, your delivery should be smooth, effortless, and outcome-independent. Women will ques-tion your intentions when someone they barely know asks them to leave, especially at night. However, by telling her that you and your friends are going to get some grub and she and her friends are welcome to join you, she feels more like a tag-along and not your sole focus of attention, which is your goal. Keep the mindset that you're just about to walk out the door with your friends and it doesn't affect your night whether she joins you or not.

You Sleep With Her

Most women assume that one-night stands are the sole objective of every male on the planet. This is especially true if a woman sees this book or similar books on your bookshelf. She most likely labeled you a player and gave you a lot of grief for making a conscious effort to meet and attract women, presumably with the intention of sleeping with them. Frankly, that's a woman's jealously shining through, because you decided to turn the tables by expecting the same options with women that women enjoy regarding men. You have nothing to feel sorry about and nothing to apologize for.

The thing is, most guys aren't interested in one-night stands or at least they aren't *solely* interested in them. Meeting a woman, at least a woman of quality, and taking her home the same night you meet her is either a testament to your skills, the stars aligning in your favor, or a little of both. For most guys, it's simply hard work and we all know how much we hate hard work. Most guys want to sample what's out there, refine what kind of women they like to be with, and eventually settle down with one. If women ever complain about your attitude or behavior regarding meeting and attracting women, use the disclaimer you just read, because you have every right to seek out what works for you and what doesn't.

Hard work aside, the fact of the matter is most guys who can cultivate and execute one- night stands will usually follow through and never look back. At the very least, taking a woman home the same night you meet her isn't usually considered a bad thing except maybe by her friends. One-night stands are always a possibility, especially if that's your focus, so it needs to be addressed. Now that your conscience has been soothed and you've been absolved of feeling like you're using someone if you have casual sex with them, you can learn how to handle such situations when they arise.

By now you've gone through all the stages or maybe you skipped a few, but now it's time to decide whether she wants to sleep with you. It's a pretty important question and one you should put some thought into before you start making assumptions that could destroy the comfort and trust you've worked hard to develop. Unfortunately, since every woman is different, one may exhibit what you consider to be extremely forward, sexually-tinged behavior, while it may just be her way of playfully flirting with you. With that said, you can still observe her behavior for "buy signals" that indicate she's not only attracted to you, but comfortable enough to let that attraction escalate into sexual activity.

New relationships rarely progress from the Attract or Connect stages directly to sex unless your "A" game is up to speed or alcohol is involved. Typically, you have a few make-out sessions somewhere within the Attract and Connect stages, which can happen either when you first meet or on subsequent outings. Eventually by building a connection while also escalating the sexual nature of your relationship, you build enough attraction and comfort to progress to sex. The majority of women aren't looking for a purely sexual relationship, especially with someone they don't know very well. So despite how well everything has gone up until this point, you have to pay attention to her signals before you make a move that can lead to ecstasy, but also disaster.

With women typically waiting for a man to advance the sexual nature of a relationship and men fearing pushing a women too far too fast, how do you know when it's the "right" time to start unbuttoning her jeans? As you know, every woman has a different timeline and some exhibit different types of behavior to indicate they're ready to get naked, but most will make it clear using the same basic signals. You may not always get it right, but it's better to observe some "buy signals" *before* you invite her to your bedroom. If you blindly make a move without any consideration of her comfort level, you may end up getting your face slapped instead of slapping her ass.

She touches you a lot

From a guy's perspective, kino is a big part of building attraction, but when a woman continually takes the initiative to touch you, especially in a sexual manner, she's giving you a clear sign that she's willing to do more with you. If you initiate kino and she responds in kind, you're definitely on the right track. However, if she starts making bold moves of her own, such as caressing your inner thigh, running her hands through your hair, or even touching the bulge in your pants, you should immediately start thinking of where you can go to get more privacy.

She talks about sex

Under most circumstances, you shouldn't discuss hardcore sexual topics, especially sex between the two of you. While it's acceptable to joke around about sex or even talk about your "friends'" sexual escapades, you should let your actions do the talking when it comes to sex. However, many women will take the bait when you indirectly bring up sexual topics including how bad most men are at sex or how long it's been since she's been laid. More often than not, these are direct challenges to you to resolve the "problems" she's experiencing.

She gives you sexual compliments

You shouldn't directly compliment a woman's body unless you've developed enough rapport to give her an honest compliment she can truly appreciate. But again, women aren't bound by such rules and if they start to compliment your body instead of your style or your humor, they're telling you they're interested in seeing what's under your clothes. When a woman is sufficiently attracted to you, she'll start to compliment your butt, your chest, your hands, and virtually anything else she might fetishize. Accept the compliment and allow her a better view or greater access, but only for a moment and only if she's being "good."

She invites you home

An invitation to her home or asking how far away you live is more than a signal; it's usually an all-access pass. If a woman starts hinting she needs a ride home or if you're already giving her a ride home and she invites you up for coffee—she's already made up her mind about you. Once it's clear she wants to have sex, it's up to you to make it happen. Whatever barriers either of you feel might impede your nakedness need to be handled with little to no involvement from her. The last thing you want is a woman who is ready for sex thinking about the logistics of how you're going to get there, how she's going to get home, how far away you live, and anything else that might cause her to reconsider.

She wants you, now what?

When sex seems imminent and you haven't yet come up with a plan on where it should take place, you have to quickly decide where you can go to make it happen. Obviously you shouldn't wait until you're inundated with "buy signals" because your options by then might be limited to cars, alleys, bathrooms stalls, and other less-than-desirable locations. There is absolutely no excuse for neglecting the details of sex—if you've put in the effort and she's ready to ravage you, don't leave the location for your naked romps up to chance.

Her Place

Generally, given the option between going to your place and going to hers, you should opt to take her to her own home the first time you have sex. While it's not always possible, it's definitely preferred to allow a woman to take you to her place, mainly because she'll be much more comfortable in a known environment. Even when a woman is attracted to you and feels comfortable around you, when it comes time to go to your place she might start asking herself how well she *really* knows you, especially if she's never been to your house before.

Always keep in mind that once women are away from their friends, it's entirely up to them to protect themselves from any worst-case scenarios, meaning they don't want to be found in a dumpster the next day, or end up as a lampshade. Given these realities, if she doesn't recommend going to her place, gently suggest it before offering other alternatives. Even if you don't eventually spend the night at her house, she'll feel more comfortable knowing you were willing to.

Your Place

If a woman really connected with you and she feels comfortable and safe when she's alone with you, she most likely won't have a problem going home with you, especially if you initially offered to go to her place. As you learned in Chapter 4, "Preparing Yourself," your house needs to be appropriate for female company *before* you bring her home. If you've been making out up until this point, the last thing you want to do is set her on the couch for five minutes while you clean up your room. Make sure everything is ready for her stay *before* you arrive so you can head straight to the bedroom without tripping over your porn DVDs.

If you didn't progress to sexual intimacy in one evening, you most likely got her number and made plans to see each other again. Since dinner and a movie is such a lame idea for a date, you should opt for dinner and drinks at your place, followed by a DVD on the couch. This should inevitably lead to some hot and heavy make-out sessions and with your bedroom only a few feet away, there are no obstacles to nakedness. Plus, since you're on your home turf, you can set the music and temperature, light the candles and incense, and orchestrate just about every other aspect of your environment to help set the mood.

Friend's Place

Whether you live with your mom, you're homeless, or you're concerned a woman might be a stage-five clinger, sometimes your friend's couch is the best or only option. The younger you are, the more feasible it is that you're visiting someone in college, going to a friend's house party, or just a bum living on a couch. If you're living a drifter lifestyle, you have to learn how to make the most out of the spaces you have available to you. Although it's rarely a big deal, it's always a good idea to ask your friend whether he cares if you bring a woman home.

If you're in your early twenties, the type of women who go home with guys they just met rarely care whether they're in a bed, on a couch, on a futon, or even a bare floor, usually because they're drunk and eager for sex. For the most part, you want to keep the specifics of your living situation to yourself and let her find out for herself what spending the night entails. Don't give her additional objections to work with because if she's drunk, she's been making out in public, and you end up screwing in your friend's bathroom, she's probably used to these situations.

Hotel Room

Sometimes people are eager to have sex, but they have absolutely nowhere to make it happen—either because they're away from home, unwilling to go home, or the situation merits the charms of a secluded room you can walk away from. Depending on the woman, a hotel could infer a distinctly unpleasant connotation, so it can help to add a little context after you've exhausted the possibility of going to either of your homes. Consider telling her you know a really nice hotel nearby where you attended a wedding or bar mitzvah, so she'll understand she's not headed to a fleabag motel with crusty sheets.

As with most of the interaction leading up to this point, you're not only in control of the situation—you're responsible for making it happen. That means if you sense you need a place to get naked and you know you have no options other than alleys and bathrooms, excuse yourself and make a call to a nearby hotel to book a room in advance. Also, when you get to the hotel, you have to take care of the room without ever involving her. In fact, you should consider sending her up with a bellman while you take care of the room charges—no splitting of the bill. You don't want to be cheap at such a critical moment, especially if you think this moment of passion could turn into a regular occurrence.

Other—Car, bathroom, closets

If you're relegated to any less-than-romantic locations, there isn't much in the way of guidance to be given. For whatever reason, you don't have a bed to go to, so you have to make the best of what's probably an alcohol-fueled situation. The best advice that can be offered is to spend a minute or two thinking of all the places you could possibly go and then choose the one that will incur the least number of interruptions, which is hopefully none at all. Even though a woman who is willing to have sex in a bathroom probably won't be alarmed by other guys taking a shit, why chance it?

Conclusion

By now you have a solid framework to guide you when approaching and meeting a woman, demonstrating attractive behavior, making an emotional connection, and finally transitioning those feelings into a solid Close. The past five chapters are meant to give you a five-act structure to work within so you know where you're at and how far you have to go when you meet and attract women you want to sleep with or otherwise build some form of relationship with. Other than the ten rules you read at the beginning of the book, there are no other absolutes when meeting and attracting women.

The information you've learned is a guideline, not a script to which you must slavishly adhere. Always remember that attracting women is dynamic and rarely follows a consistent path, but you can build on the basics in this book by *always* approaching and *always* looking at every woman you're attracted to as an opportunity to learn more, whether you succeed or fail. If you always maintain this frame of mind, your game will continually improve. Your goal is to build on the foundation provided for you in this book until you develop your own custom game plan that works for you time and time again.

Although you probably have just as many questions as you have answers, if you followed closely and remembered most of what you read, you have enough information to confidently approach and Open any woman. Always remember that the "A" game provides you with a map, but the terrain and your journey are both unique and won't always go according to plan. While the circumstances may not always be in your favor, if you find yourself getting stuck in one of the stages more than a few times, you may have a sticking point that needs to be addressed. The next chapter troubleshoots some of the common issues many guys encounter, even after they've read and applied what they've learned.

Chapter 14

Troubleshooting

In this Chapter

★ Understanding why a woman might not want to talk to you and why it's nothing personal

★ Exploring typical "sticking points" that prevent men from successfully working through to the Close

★ Getting to know types of women who seek sex and how to spot them when you're off your game

Troubleshooting

Even the most charming men have trouble areas that cause them to ruin an otherwise successful courtship. If you find yourself making similar mistakes over and over again, don't beat yourself up about it, but try to isolate and improve those areas of your game. For some guys, the biggest problem is how they present themselves before they even open their mouths. Other guys can successfully Open and navigate an interaction through all of the stages, but can never Close. You might fall into one of these categories or you might have a different reoccurring issue, but at the very least you understand you have a sticking point.

More often than not the problem lies in your attitude—typically some remnant of just being yourself and blaming others when things go wrong. If you're having problems with one or more of the stages, read through the problem descriptions in this chapter and see whether any apply to your own attitude or behavior. Try to internalize the suggested remedies and really focus on modifying your behavior the next time an interaction is about to enter into one of your problem areas. Over time, you should be able to fix the problem by thinking positively and staying outcome-independent.

Sometimes the problem isn't a trouble area, but just a stretch of bad luck because the last few women you approached were in a bad mood or otherwise unavailable. Some women simply aren't interested in talking to you, not because of what you said or who you are, but because of their own personal situations. Before assuming that you're the root of your problem, read the reasons why women may not want to talk to you, as well as what you can do to work around their objections, if possible.

If, after reading this book and adjusting your technique based on the tips in this chapter, you still aren't having much success, you might need to temporarily adjust your expectations. Certain types of women may normally be considered less than ideal, but when times are tough, you should consider aiming lower just so you can have a little fun and bolster your confidence. The last section of this chapter is your "Plan B" for when nothing seems to go right despite your best efforts, but you don't want to go home alone.

Why She Might Not Want to Talk

Throughout most every day of their adult lives, beautiful women get hit on. Because of this they have to spend a ridiculous amount of energy developing ways to block out the vast majority of men hitting on them. It may not sound like a big deal, but when a woman hears the same thing over and over again, fully realizing there's an ulterior motive to even the simplest of conversations, she gets bored, then frustrated, then finally, she gets angry. But despite all of the hassles women have to put up with, they still wake up and make themselves beautiful all the while hoping that someone will find their mind as attractive as their body.

Knowing that beautiful women are inundated by men hitting on them, how do you manage to approach her without being lumped in with the dozens of guys who tried to get her attention that day? Let's start by examining some of the specific reasons why a woman might not want to be approached, and how you can work around it without having to spend too much time breaking through her defense mechanisms.

She Wants to be Out With Her Friends

Just like guys who like to get sloppy drunk and cause trouble without having to deal with female drama, women love to go out with their girlfriends with no intention of dealing with any bullshit from guys, at least for one night. Women seem to really get a kick out of dressing to impress, getting men's tongues wagging, then having a good laugh at all the clueless guys as she shuts them down one by one.

What you can do: There is no harm in testing the waters even if you feel intimidated by a bunch of hot women dancing their asses off. Whatever the situation is, wait until they've got some dancing or laughing out of their systems and they're starting to relax into their evening. If they're smiling and drinking and having a good time, you can drop an opinion Opener and they'll subtly let you know whether they're entertained or interested enough to keep you around.

Another approach is to walk by, act as though their energy just caught your attention, and then tell them they look like they're "having a really good time" or "up to no good" and ask what the occasion is. You can also ease tension by joking with them about how you know they're having a ladies night out so you better get out of there before they body slam you with all their girl power.

She's Heard it All Before

"Don't I know you from somewhere?" "Do you come here often?" "Can I buy you a drink?" If these sound familiar to you, how familiar do you think they sound to the woman in the bar waiting for her friends to show up? Even if you think you have the greatest, most original pick-up line, it's still going to come across as a pick-up line, something almost no woman appreciates. Pick-up lines rarely work and most women will tell you they are a bad way to try and strike up a conversation.

What you can do: Although you might think it would be flattering to get approached by guys all day, most women view it as repetitive and annoying. With this in mind, you should strive to be original if you want to catch her attention and give her something to remember your conversation by. For most women, as long as you're original, interesting, and sincere, she won't lump you in with lame guys who repeat the same lines over and over again.

Also, depending on the circumstances, if you see an attractive woman who just got hit on and she instantly sent him packing, you now have something to use as your Opener. "I was headed over to my friend's table and I couldn't help overhearing that lame pick-up line. Do you mind telling me how someone like you prefers to meet a guy?" If she's interested, she'll tell you how to pick her up and more often than not, it works like a charm.

She Knows What You're After

Don't be surprised when you approach a woman at a club or a bar and she doesn't buy into your notion of having an intellectually stimulating conversation when you try to make plans to "hang out" later in the week. When confronted with a stranger, good- looking or not, a woman wants to quickly categorize men so she can set her emotional, sometimes physical, defenses accordingly. If you stride across the bar and walk straight toward a woman and then act as if your only interest is in making a new friend, she'll know better and think you're creepy. Women look for sincere guys, whether they're out to make new friends, hook up with someone, or looking for genuine romance, they want to know what your intentions are.

What you can do: Essentially, be a man or at least act like one. Don't pretend to befriend a woman when you really aren't interested in making a new friend. It may seem like you're just being polite and nice, but in a way, you're trying to trick someone into thinking you're friendly when your true intention was to find someone to make out with. Women are smart and when it comes to the male/female dynamic, most women are smarter than men. Unless you aim low and seek out only the most air-headed bimbos, chances are high that women will see through your "friendly" act.

Most men and women go out to clubs and bars to have fun and maybe meet some new people to distract them from their boring weekday lives. You have friends and she has friends, so you're probably both out to find someone worthy of more than just a platonic friendship. At some point after the Hook, you have to start letting a woman know you're interested in her beyond the immediate interaction and you're interested in her as more than a friend. Don't feel ashamed for having and sharing your intentions, because the longer you wait the more confused or distrustful she'll become when you do make a move.

Other Men Have Ruined it For You

Regardless of whether you're approaching the hottest woman in the bar or the homely wallflower to the side; you have to recognize she's been hit on before by guys who didn't know what they were doing. These guys have done nothing to help you out by touching women when they didn't want it, making out with a woman after they just made out with someone else, or picking them up and then treating them like trash when they were done with them. Because of this behavior, we now have books that teach guys how to approach and talk to women because it's no longer straightforward and intuitive.

What you can do: Since women have been approached by assholes since they were in high school, they know what to look for and how to rid themselves of jerks in short order. Women know the look, the attitude, and the lines to watch out for. To avoid bearing the brunt of her fury against all the men who wronged her, focus on being genuine and original. This book can help you hone your originality, but it's up to you to be a genuine person who doesn't use people.

Original may seem like a tall order, but it really only involves employing some basic techniques like using opinion Openers over pick-up lines, getting to know her friends before isolating her, and finding out what she values instead of bragging about yourself, to name a few. After reading this book, these techniques might not seem original, but they will to her. However, being genuine isn't a technique; you're either genuine or you aren't, so your best bet is to know the difference between saying what you want to say or what you *think* she wants to hear and then trying to correct yourself. If you can stay original and genuine, chances are she'll make an exception for you despite all the other guys who "ruined it" for you.

She's Apprehensive Without Her Friends

Some women need the security of having their friends around, or they may be too shy to handle a one-on-one conversation with someone they don't really know. In some cases, you may have moved too quickly or didn't develop enough chemistry. Regardless of what leads you to an awkward conversation, you can sense it as soon as the two of you are alone. Whether there are long awkward periods of silence or she just seems distracted or distant, you usually know when a woman isn't comfortable talking to you.

What you can do: For some guys, the natural reaction to a stilted conversation is to acknowledge how uncomfortable the interaction is, kill the momentum entirely, and move on. However, you can quickly turn a negative situation into a positive one by concentrating on making her laugh. Laughter releases chemicals in the brain that relax a person, especially if they were stressed out to begin with. If you focus your energy on getting a woman to laugh for a few minutes, you'll find she often warms to your company.

Avoid making jokes that have anything to do with either of you and the tense situation you're currently in. For a few minutes you want her to forget that her friends are no longer with her and that she's with a guy she barely knows. You can accomplish this by making light of what other people are doing, or trying to guess what people are saying to each other. If you work together to try and find humor in your environment, she'll generally start to relax and open up.

Mistakes men make when approaching women

Whether you're at a bar, shopping at the mall, or having coffee at a café, acting in three seconds and working through the stages you've learned about takes practice. Initially it can take a lot of mental preparation to effortlessly move from Openers to stories to teasing and beyond. It's easy to be so caught up with all the things you think you have to do that you lapse into some of the same mistakes that prompted you to read this book in the first place. With that said, the following sections detail some of the most common mistakes men make before, and even after, digesting the tips and tactics they've learned throughout this book.

Before You Open

Your expectations are too high

After learning a few new tips and techniques, some guys think they've found the Holy Grail to making out with every woman they approach, without ever putting in the time to make the techniques work for them. Every guy has strengths and weaknesses when it comes to attracting women, so just because you have an understanding of what attracts women doesn't mean you'll be good at it, at least not until you practice. The key is to have a good time and stay outcome-independent, meaning whether you get her number, take her home, or get rejected you know you'll have fun learning something you can use later.

You're not confident

Even the best seducers in the world get a tinge of doubt right before they're about to approach a woman. No matter what, you'll always be just a little apprehensive about taking a chance approaching someone when you don't have control over the outcome. The difference between guys who never build their confidence and those who do is that they try, even when they're unsure of how things will play out. Over time, taking risks, which aren't really risks at all, build your confidence, making it easier to approach every time you do it. Instead of worrying about what *might* happen if you approach, think about what will *never* happen because you didn't approach.

You don't have a game plan

Until you build the confidence and experience to effortlessly approach and Open anyone, anywhere, anytime, you need to have a plan for each step of your "A" game. In fact, it's a good idea to write down your plan so you have a few Openers, a few stories, and a few jokes to refer to when you go out. For some guys it helps to mentally picture themselves successfully Opening a group of women, hooking them in, attracting the one you're interested in, and then Closing her. Visualizing success can help you realize the same sequence of events you were imagining only hours beforehand.

You approach every woman you see

When guys start to experience some success, they tend to want to show off as much as possible. It's understandable that you want to show off to yourself to reinforce the new direction your life is taking, but success could be short-lived if you don't hold yourself back. By holding yourself back I mean not approaching every woman you can after you've already Closed a few women at the same location. If you're just practicing getting numbers, it's okay to try to learn as much and as quickly as possible, but if you actually want to see a woman later in the week, don't let her see you getting other women's numbers.

You take it too seriously

While some guys have no game plan, others have a very rigid plan and expect reality to closely match it, otherwise they get frustrated. Guys can take themselves and their circumstances far too seriously as if they were proposing marriage. If she doesn't laugh at your joke or she just doesn't understand what you're talking about, don't get frustrated and quit, instead recalibrate and try to learn from your mistakes. Women are turned off by guys who act as though getting a number will save the planet from certain doom, so don't take yourself, your interactions, or her responses too seriously.

You aren't enjoying yourself

Whatever her or her group's general attitude is, your mood has to be a little more upbeat than theirs. If you're in a bad mood because you've been rejected or there aren't any interesting women around, it shows, even if you don't realize it. If you aren't in a good mood, a woman will know it before you ever open your mouth, which doesn't encourage her to find out what you're about. If you're having negative thoughts, shake them off by smiling, giving high fives, dancing like a fool, or whatever it takes to get yourself pumped up.

Open

You use pick-up lines

Nothing destroys an approach faster than a lame, unoriginal pick-up line. It's nothing specific about a pick-up line that annoys women, but rather the concept that you've used the same line on other women many times before. A woman is less-than-flattered when it seems as though she's not worth the time to think of something original to say to her. Next time you consider laying a pick-up line on someone, think about how you felt the last time a woman gave you a lame, unoriginal brush-off like "I have a boyfriend" and you'll have an idea of how she feels when you use a line on her.

You don't value first impressions

When you're meeting a woman for the first time, she has to quickly figure out what kind of person you are and whether or not she should be talking to you. All a woman has to go on to make this determination is your appearance and the first few sentences out of your mouth. These two things are all you have going for you to make a good first impression, so you have to make them count. If you look good, you feel good, and others tend to feel good around you, therein lies the power of first impressions. If you don't value a good first impression, chances are high that you won't make one and your success with women will suffer. Prepare yourself both mentally and physically to make a great first impression by reading Chapters 3 and 4, "Adjusting Your Attitude" and "Style and Grooming."

You don't have high energy

Whenever you interrupt whatever a group of women are in the midst of doing, you have to bring a slightly higher energy level into their group. Your goal is to spread some of the same infectious, good-time energy to their entire group, so they view you as an asset to their fun evening, not an obstacle. It only takes a few seconds to recognize whether you've introduced enough positive energy into the group based on how they react to your Opener. While you normally shouldn't focus solely on how women react to what you say and do, for the first minute or two of the Opener, it's critical to note whether you're brightening their evening or dimming it. Have fun and bring the fun with you and make sure the women you're interacting with are having a great time while they're with you.

You don't recognize external variables

When some guys get rejected they tend to lay 100% of the blame for their lack of success squarely on their own shoulders. While it still holds true that "it's always your fault" for not successfully Opening someone, it's not always your fault if that Opening doesn't lead anywhere. Always keep in mind that you don't know someone's circumstances before you approach them, and an individual's circumstances can have everything to do with why she wasn't interested in you. Whether she's having a bad day, she's got a boyfriend, she's a lesbian, or she's busy at the moment, don't let a few rejections cause you to believe no one is interested in you. Assume they were too caught up in their own situation to fully notice how attractive you are. In two words: her loss.

You don't feel you're in a woman's league

Some guys like to believe the majority of beautiful women are only attracted to guys with the looks of a model and the wealth of an investment banker, giving them an easy excuse for not approaching them. These guys think because they don't have any of the materialistic or superficial qualities they think women want in a guy, they shouldn't bother finding out what she's really attracted to. Most women, beautiful or otherwise, are attracted to the strong male role models they had while growing up. Those role models may have been fat, skinny, bald, pale, short, or a combination of these traits and because of this, you might be exactly the physical type she finds attractive. Since you view yourself as a catch, you decide who's in your league, not the other way around.

You make false assumptions

Almost as bad as believing all beautiful women are out of your league is the belief that a beautiful woman must already be taken, or that she's high maintenance. These are just a few more justifications guys use to excuse themselves from approaching women. Almost everyone has read an interview with a model or actress where she complains she goes to bars and clubs and never gets approached. The complaints are so frequent they can't be taken for granted and should allow you to shake off your doubts about whether to approach someone, even if they are drop-dead gorgeous. Every time you make one of these false assumptions as an excuse not to meet someone new, you've wasted an opportunity to meet someone who could really be into you.

Hook

You act like a pig

Some guys just don't know how to act around attractive women, or they intentionally sabotage their chances with someone because they're nervous. Whether you say something tacky or crude, keep your eyes transfixed on their asses or touch them inappropriately, you're likely to be called a "pig" at best or kneed in the balls at worst. Remember to tease women like they're your little sister or niece, and keep reminding yourself of that every time you find your eyes drifting toward a woman's chest or you're thinking about grabbing her ass. Anytime you think about doing something inappropriate, give them a concerned look and accuse them of wanting to do that same inappropriate thing to you, then smile and tell them you're not that kind of guy...until after midnight.

You concentrate too much on women's reactions

It's easy to forget about what you're saying or doing when you focus solely on women's reactions to you. Women quickly pick up on needy behavior and interpret it to mean you don't have a personality of your own, that you filter yourself so you conform to whatever you think they're interested in. In turn, they reason that you aren't confident and lack conviction in what you say and do, which aren't attractive qualities. Instead, focus on what they're saying and use it to build comfort and rapport. In the end, why waste your time with people who aren't interested in you? Be your best self and if they're not interested, move on.

You brag too much

Nobody likes a braggart, especially groups of women, most of whom wait for guys to slip up and say something stupid so they feel justified in giving them the cold shoulder. Guys who like to boast about themselves usually have low self-esteem and most women know this, even if the guy doesn't. There isn't much more of a turnoff for a woman than a guy who feels he has to convince her he's worthy of her attention by constantly singing his own praises. You can just as easily imbed your best personality traits and accomplishments in witty stories that allow people to draw their own positive conclusions about how accomplished and interesting you are. The only form of bragging that seems to attract most women is when you've bested her at a silly game like thumb wrestling or hand slaps.

You give up too soon

It may seem like you're not winning the hearts and minds of the group you're talking to, but unless they walk away, turn their backs, or tell you to leave, you have no reason to give up. You must have been interested in at least one of the women in the group if you Opened them and continued interacting with them, so allow them to decide whether you're good company instead of deciding for them. Some guys like to desert a group in the middle of the Hook stage because they don't feel they're making any progress. Even if you aren't making much progress, you aren't going to learn how to break through the Hook stage unless you power through it and never give up. As long as you keep at it, you'll continually try new things to Hook the group, but if you give up, you'll be stuck Opening forever.

You don't respect a women's personal space

Just because you think or *know* that you're a nice, interesting, attractive guy, doesn't mean women will feel the same way, despite your best efforts. It's important to keep this in mind through the first few stages, especially during the Hook stage where you're attempting to gain a group's approval. With this in mind, maintain a respectable distance and try to keep your hands from flailing around as you talk. Women traditionally keep their guard up when meeting a guy for the first time; you don't want to create an additional burden on yourself by making them so physically uncomfortable by your presence and mannerisms they never lower their guard and listen to what you have to say.

You interrupt when women are talking

When women talk, they're virtually handing you the keys to the castle, giving you all of the information you need to push through the Hook stage and on to the Attract stage. Throughout the entire interaction women will provide you with plenty of material to work with to keep a fun and interesting conversation going, but not if you talk over them. Nothing you have to say is nearly as important as the things they're saying to you and especially to each other, so smile, laugh, high-five, swat at them, bump hips, but never interrupt them. The only exception to this rule is when you're teasing the group, during which case you can break right into whatever they're saying, so you can let them know how bratty, silly, drunk, or high-maintenance they're acting.

Attract
You don't find out whether women are single

Naturally, your success with women is somewhat dependent on whether the women you approach are single or not. It's discouraging to spend ten minutes talking to a woman only to find out she's got a boyfriend or she's married, so try to find out what her status is as soon as possible. With that said, a successful Opener almost always involves using indirect reasons for wanting to talk to a woman, so avoid directly asking her whether she's single. Instead, keep your eyes and ears open for indications that she's involved with someone else before you move into the Attract stage. Most women are very upfront about their status, so expect them to let you know in the first few minutes or observe them as they put their hand up, palm inward, to casually show you a wedding ring without directly telling you as much.

You try to convince women to like you

Just because you successfully Opened her group, hooked her friends, and isolated her doesn't necessarily mean she's attracted to you. Sometimes this realization results in a guy using logic to convince a woman why she should be attracted to him and why she's crazy if she's not. Your job is to *display* your attractive qualities through your actions and stories, not *explain* your best features and traits as if you were on a job interview. All you can hope for is that the qualities that make you interesting, funny, and unique are the same qualities she's attracted to, because if they aren't mere words will not create attraction where there is none. If you aren't getting any indicators of interest from her, try to make her laugh, let her know that it was a pleasure to meet her, then move on.

You insult your ex-girlfriend or women in general

You could be the most interesting, intelligent, humorous guy when you're trying to attract someone, but the moment you say something negative about women in general or your ex-girlfriend specifically, expect to get rejected. Even if she's never met your ex and probably never will, women take offense when you badmouth your former partners. She could just as easily end up being your ex and assumes she would be insulted in the same way you insult your other ex-girlfriends. Insulting an entire gender is equally inexcusable, even if you're trying to tease her. Teasing is supposed to be lighthearted and should be specific to her and the situation, so anything that mocks women, including their driving skills, insecurities, PMS, mental or physical short-comings, or lack of logic should never be discussed.

You talk about sex too much

The Attract stage is where you take the ambiguity out of the interaction and in ways small and large indicate you're interested in her romantically, not as a friend or acquaintance. If you've built enough rapport and comfort, subtly steering the conversation toward sex is only natural when you're trying to attract someone, but don't take it too far. Also, if she's clearly uncomfortable talking about sexual topics, you should drop the subject, but don't apologize for bringing it up. Some women are sex fiends once you get them alone and into bed, but up until that point they seem very skittish about the topic, possibly because they don't want to be perceived by the general public as sex freaks. A good way to segue into sexual topics is to tell a woman her shoes, boots, earrings, necklace, or outfit are sexy and gauge her response for how to proceed from there.

You don't treat women as equals

Most women enjoy it when a man displays flashes of chivalry, but for the most part they expect to be treated as equals—no more, no less. It's natural to confer wonderful qualities to someone you're interested in, but it's best to tease your praise out in small batches instead of all at once during your initial conversation. Try not to place too much value on someone just because she seems interested in you. In fact, try to wait until she starts to feel you might not be that interested in her, then drop a little indicator of interest on her. For instance, if she moves a certain way to your liking, ask her to do it again and then say, "That's perfect, thank you." She'll ask or wonder why, but don't tell her, let her figure out your flirtatious behavior on her own.

You're afraid to touch women

It's difficult to move from the Attract stage to the Close until you instigate a little bit of touching. It doesn't need to be much, simply touching her shoulder when she makes you laugh, or swatting at her with a napkin when she says something outrageous is enough to get things started. If a woman is attracted to you, she'll sense something isn't right if you never break the touch barrier. Whether she thinks you're not attracted to her or that you're too intimidated to touch her as a friend would, she'll find her attraction waning to the point where she's hesitant to take things further. Often, a woman understands the pitfalls associated with a guy touching a woman he barely knows, and she'll take the initiative to touch your knee or your shoulder. View this as an invitation to respond in kind and possibly escalate the tone and frequency of your touching.

Connect
You don't ask the right questions

A lot of men never fully switch gears from asking simple questions in the Hook and Attract stages to more personal, rapport-building questions in the Connect stage. You can typically expect a phone number during and after the Attract stage, but if you haven't developed much trust or comfort, you shouldn't be surprised if she's hesitant or even offended when you assume there's more comfort than actually exists. Whenever you've isolated her from her friends or met up with her at some point in the future, spend a few minutes in the Attract stage and if that goes well, consciously progress toward the Connect stage.

You complain about your life

Just because you talk to a woman one-on-one doesn't give you permission to tell her your sob stories or complain about how unfair life is. The purpose of the Connect stage is to bring up topics that create comfort and trust on *her* part, not necessarily yours. Even when women agree with your whining and complaining, it doesn't mean she's more attracted to you. In fact, you're likely to ruin any comfort you developed because you introduced negative topics, while she's just out to have a good time. If you start to complain, you shouldn't be surprised if she finds a reason to rejoin her friends or mentions an appointment she suddenly has to make. If you ever catch yourself complaining, drop it immediately and think of something fun to talk about to clear out the negative vibe you created.

You don't act like yourself

Instead of emphasizing the positives and downplaying the negatives of your personality, you lie and act like someone you're not. Most women are experts at sniffing out liars, so while you might be able to fool a few naïve girls, it won't be long before you're caught and embarrassed because you lied about something trivial. Instead of lying, be your *best* self and show some confidence in who you are. Lies are sure to sabotage any short-lived success you might have, so stay true to yourself and believe that you're a catch. Women will appreciate your confidence and honesty even if they ultimately aren't attracted to the *real* you. At the very least you'll be able to carry your confidence and dignity into the next interaction.

You don't read her body language

A woman's body language is your personal barometer for how well the interaction is going and, during the Connect and Close stages, what she physically expects the two of you to be doing. A woman will rarely initiate the first kiss and will, in fact, expect you to initiate most other aspects of physical intimacy. However, once you break a particular barrier, most women become comfortable with it and no longer require you to initiate it. Just remember, from the first kiss to pulling off her jeans, you're expected to lead the way, so you have to pay attention to the signs she gives you. Both Chapters 12 and 13, "Connect" and "Close," detail "buy signals" you can look for so you can act without worrying that you're moving too fast.

You screw up compliments

Compliments are a very delicate matter during the Connect stage because you want her to know you're interested in her romantically, but you don't want her to think you're trying to gain her approval by showering her with compliments. A good compliment at this stage should be designed to make her feel really good about herself in a way others rarely notice. They should also be as unique as possible by using details that tailor the compliment directly to her, so she doesn't view it as a generic line. For example "I noticed you from the moment you and that little yellow sun dress walked in here. It wasn't just me either, I looked around and everyone perked up when you brought your positive energy into the room. Did you notice it?"

You attempt to create more connection than necessary

Chapter 12, "Connect," attempts to provide you with a complete set of tools to turn attraction into something intimate, but it doesn't mean you *have* to use every tool each time you meet someone. In fact, throwing everything you've got at a woman just because you know how can completely backfire, because not every woman needs to feel a connection with the men she sleeps with. While you're asking about her father she might be itching to get back to your place, and by the time you've finished linking to her desired emotion she feels completely psychoanalyzed and turned off. Avoid steam-rolling over the needs of a particular woman by working through every aspect of every stage of the "A" game just because you can. Instead, pay attention to her indicators of interest and her general body language, then calibrate your game accordingly.

Close

You get too drunk

Although inebriation can affect virtually any stage of an interaction, drunkenness frequently torpedoes your chances to effectively Close, whether it's getting a phone number or taking her to a different location. For most men, alcohol is the crutch used to feel more social and start speaking freely without fear of consequences, which is why it's commonly referred to as "liquid courage." It may seem like a good way to unwind a bit, but more often than not two drinks lead to six and by then you might have difficulty delivering an Opener, much less working through the stages and Closing the way you would like to. If you're of age, pick nights you want to drink and just have fun drinking and then choose other nights where you limit yourself to an appropriate amount of drinks spaced out so you can still follow your game plan.

You make out in public

If your goal for the evening is to make out with a bunch of women and you've accomplished this, you really don't have a problem with Closing. However, some guys want to make out, get a phone number, and then initiate something in the future. After making out, they soon find the woman is reluctant to give her number or if she does, she's reluctant to answer or return a phone call. Women are quick to categorize a drunk make-out session as a onetime event, something she's not willing to follow up on, so consider whether it's a single slobbery make-out session you're after, or something longer term that involves actual nakedness. The same holds true for dancing; keep your humping and grinding within reason if you hope to see what other moves she's got.

You don't make a move

Sometimes a little bit of success can scare a guy from going the final mile and Closing an interaction. It may be that they're worried they'll get rejected and they want to stay in a happy place where everything seems to be working for them. Or maybe they just don't know what to do when it's time to start kissing and beyond. As with any sticking points during any of the other stages, Closing is something you have to work through and then deal with the consequences if and when things don't go as planned. In fact, if you're able to successfully take a woman through the initial four stages, she'll likely go along with whatever approach you feel comfortable with that takes your relationship into more intimate territory.

You burn bridges

Guys who burn bridges typically never leave the house to have a good time. For whatever reason, some men feel as though women owe them something for the time they spent trying to get to know them and they get upset when they don't get the results they expect. If you find yourself lashing out at a woman because she wasn't attracted to you, you either need to meditate on being outcome-independent, see a therapist, or stop trying to meet women. When things don't go your way, you have to laugh it off and try to learn from it. It's never a woman's fault because she didn't find you attractive. Be mature and end interactions that aren't going anywhere with a simple "Pleasure to meet you."

You take rejection personally

Regardless of what your status is in life, how good you look, what shape you're in, or how much money you make, there are, at a minimum, thousands of women who could be attracted to you if you just Opened them. These thousands of women may be spread around the globe, but if you take rejection personally, you'll eventually stop creating new opportunities for yourself to meet them. Even the best players in the world deal with large groups of women who never spend any time with them past their Opener. If you're looking for a serious relationship, someone you might marry and grow old with, you have to take this aspect of your life seriously. Your long-term happiness is at stake, so understand that women who reject you were never good matches for you to begin with, and move on to the next woman until you find a good match.

You don't learn from your mistakes

Although you're about to discover a few alternatives if you can't seem to learn from your mistakes, you're failing yourself if you have to continually aim low just to taste some success. For some guys, meeting and attracting women comes naturally, but the majority of men have to make a conscious effort to attract the kind of women they think they deserve. Anytime you want to try something new, you have to expect to endure a learning curve, short for some guys, longer for others. You have to accept that you're going to make mistakes and you're going to get rejected, but if you have any hope of improving your success rate and attracting the women you want to, you have to be honest with yourself about what is and is not working for you. If you aren't willing to try new things and change bad habits, you'll be stuck in the same situation you were in before you read this book.

Plan B – Women Who Seek Sex

Sometimes a guy just needs to clear his mind by finding a less-than-ideal sex partner for the night. She might be older, less than beautiful, perhaps even a little crazy, but for one night, she'll do. If you want to have some fun without using any advanced techniques from this book, you have to learn what traits and characteristics to look for in women who enjoy sex with no strings attached. The following section details seven distinct types of women you can look out for, so you can quickly determine whether they're on the same page as you and whether they'll be sharing the same bed as well.

The types of women you're about to learn about reject the traditional social programming of "saving themselves" and view sex as an enjoyable, healthy activity, much like men do. Instead of treating sex as a prize to be bestowed on men who navigate their convoluted and drawn-out dating rituals, they follow their libido. Some women are just out for a good time, temporarily forgoing their usual standards and practices so they can get laid, while others are on the lookout for new conquests and adventures. By learning about women who seek sex, you can start to pick them out of a crowd and if you ever find yourself down on your luck, you can still manage to have some fun for the evening.

The Out-of-Towner

Out-of-towners are away from home, whether for business or pleasure, and open to no-strings-attached good times. Out of her area and away from her social circle, she's free to flirt and screw anyone she pleases without regard to how she might be perceived. Women act remarkably like men when left to their own devices and without the need to keep up appearances. If you can find a good Out-of-towner who frequents your town often, you can develop a nice long-distance booty call on a regular basis.

Sales reps and stewardesses are common Out-of-towners who might also work with a group of Out-of-towners, so they aren't even worried about keeping up appearances; they're looking for a good story to tell when they get back home. If this is the case, be prepared for a wild night. For business Out-of-towners, hotel bars and lounges are your best bet—the closer to the airport the better. For Out-of-towner tourists, try hotels near the attractions in your area. If you're lucky enough to live in a resort town, like Palm Springs or Aspen, go directly to the resort bars and offer your local color and your take on the best things to do in town, including yourself.

The Cougar

Cougars are older women who have previously been married or in some cases, still are. Whether they were left for a younger woman or their current husband prefers golf to sex, Cougars take it upon themselves to go out and pick up guys. Given their circumstances and their difficulties in finding satisfaction, most Cougars are open and direct about their motives, if for no other reason than to save time.

Most Cougars lived very structured lives from elementary school to high school on to college, then a few years into their career until they got married and had children all before they hit thirty. Because they played life "by the book" they rarely lived for the moment and now they're ready to make up for lost time.

Cougars are out to enjoy life and have a good time with younger men who still find them attractive and skilled between the sheets. You can spot Cougars anywhere you find someone dressed like a teen in a bar filled with twenty-somethings. They're often smokers who wear too much makeup and die their hair unnatural colors, all in an effort to look like anything but a soccer mom.

If you want to snag a Cougar or rather get snagged by a Cougar, you need to look good and look young. Cougars are after younger men because they're eager to please and don't bring any baggage into the bedroom. Since Cougars are direct in their approach and make no apologies for it, you can't act coy or intimidated, just match their confidence level and let your hands do the talking.

The Rebounder

A Rebounder is emotionally vulnerable due to a breakup with a long-term boyfriend or husband, so while they may seem similar to a Cougar, they're actually much more timid and unsure of themselves; at least until you come along. Rebounders may seem initially very shy or standoffish, but if you take a little time to charm and humor them, they drop their pretensions and their panties in no time.

Rebounders rarely go out alone and in fact were probably dragged out of the house by their girlfriends. Her friends should become your friends because they want their girlfriend to get laid, or at least pre-occupied with something other than her breakup. If you please her friends, they will do most of the work for you, including buying her drinks, talking you up, leaving the two of you alone, and if you've done a really good job, driving off without her.

Like Cougars, Rebounders probably lived very structured lives, but haven't quite realized that their dream of living happily ever after with the love of their life is over. They haven't quite come to the conclusion that they can now do whatever they want when it comes to men and sex. However, if you can help unlock this untapped sexual potential, she'll aim all of her hate sex in your direction, if only to get back at her ex.

If you're in the mood for a Rebounder, you have to focus on making her feel sexy by giving her more compliments than you would normally. If she feels the need to talk about her ex, let her know it was his loss and then offer her a drink and a dance. Keep her mind off of her ex and reaffirm how hot and bothered she can make a man. If you can keep this up, she'll want to follow through on how hot she can make you.

The Bachelorette Babe

Bachelorette Babes are women that are part of a bachelorette party with the exception of the actual bride-to-be. Bachelorette parties are meant to be fun, the kind of fun that a newlywed may no longer be able to experience. Since the bride-to-be is committed to domestication, it's up to the friends to go crazy and let their friend live vicariously through their misadventures, including of the sexual variety.

Some bachelorette parties involve strippers or a visit to a male strip club, which only serves to whip a crowd of women into a frenzy. With their appetites whetted, they hit the bars or the casino floor or anywhere else they can find some action. This is the point where you come in and because bachelorette parties stand out from even the most crowded bar, they are easy to saddle up to and befriend.

To find the bachelorette party, look for a veil or sex props or even a tattered wedding dress, sometimes covered in Lifesavers that can be purchased and "sucked off." Always be game to buy and suck off one of the Lifesavers and if you're feeling bold, break it off with your teeth and ask one of her friends to help you with it. Even if she's not ready to make out with you in front of all her friends, she'll know who to look for when she is.

You have to have very high energy and if you aren't as drunk as they are, you need to be able to go along with their squeals and slurs so you're part of the fun. Make friends with the bride by buying her some champagne or whatever she wants and ask which of her friends is single. Help them take pictures and include yourself in some of them with your tongue out and your hand cupped over someone's breast. Even though it's a girl's night out, most women are willing to break the rules given enough drinks and a reason to celebrate.

The Adventurer

The Adventurer is a woman who wants or needs to experiment sexually—usually a college girl who left her small town and has recently had her eyes opened to life's possibilities. Although, sometimes it's a woman who missed out on the traditional college era "finding yourself" stage because she was career or marriage-minded, but for whatever reason is now ready to wave the freak flag.

Whatever a woman's reasons are for discovering or rediscovering her sexuality, you can easily find yourself in the role of teacher to her student, as long as you can live up to the title. These types aren't playing around—they feel they don't know all they need to know compared to their girlfriends and want to catch up as quickly as possible. Not only do you need supreme confidence in your sexual prowess, you also need to be able to vocalize it and deliver on your promises.

Too much confidence can intimidate even the young Adventurers, so it needs to be wrapped in a bit of mystery. In addition to discovering more about herself, create a situation where she's also discovering you. Let it be known that you're worldly, open-minded, and non-judgmental and allow her to take the bait.

If an Adventurer is interested in the mystery you present, she'll find ways to be around you, to touch you, and more. Since they're somewhat new to all of this, their clumsy attempts are pretty obvious to spot. Don't make light of their efforts, just go with it and don't be afraid to tell them exactly what to do, including positioning their body however you like.

It's difficult to put a finger on how to locate Adventurers; instead you have to find the places where they're likely to frequent. Since most adventurers are still in college, you have to go to college parties, cafés, libraries, and campus events to find them, at least during the school year. If you decide to frequent these places, try to have a legitimate reason for being there—don't be the lecherous old man who preys on young women.

The Insatiable

Similar to the Adventurer, an Insatiable woman is sexually open and enjoys all kinds of sex, except she's not new to it, she just loves it. There are sexually open women everywhere, but the problem lies in where to find them. You may have hit the jackpot by chance, but if you want to increase your odds, you can start by taking some yoga classes.

Yoga classes are almost completely filled with women, limber women, many of whom are very open minded and free spirited. In addition to stretching out with lithe beauties, you'll also discover an entire community of new age women who not only take yoga classes, but also classes on sexuality, including masturbation, sex toys, fellatio, Tantric sex, and more.

You might not want to be so bold as to just ask the girl next to you about sex classes, but you can usually find a cork board filled with items for sale, apartments for rent, and yes, classes on sexuality given by community colleges, sex shops, or extension classes from the yoga studio. Grab a flier and ask the front desk about it and act as shy and curious as possible so you don't give the impression that you're a sex fiend on the prowl.

If you can accomplish all of this, your work is mostly done. Just show up at the classes, listen intently to what you're being taught without eyeballing everyone else, then stick around after class and ask follow-up questions and make some new friends. For instance, talk about how you plan to incorporate some element of your yoga training with what you've just learned and some women will just key in to what you're saying. Be forewarned that some of the women who attend these classes have partners, so find out what you're getting yourself into before you find yourself in an awkward situation.

The Lucky

Once your game is up to speed and you've been focusing solely on the most attractive women in the room, sometimes you just want to turn the dial down a bit and lob a few sincere compliments at a woman and see where it takes you. With the right calibration, you can brighten an otherwise average woman's dull day and find yourself rewarded for the effort. There is absolutely no harm in doing a little charity work for women who might otherwise spend the evening watching reruns and eating ice cream from the container.

The world is full of perfectly nice, normal, friendly women who may not win any beauty pageants, but still want to be appreciated for their looks. By giving her a few honest compliments, helping her feel attractive, and giving her attention that other men don't, she's likely to be "appreciative" as long as you're respectful of her feelings. It's entirely possible that you will have a better time with an average woman that appreciates your charms than a stuck-up hottie.

So even though you might not immediately notice her when you walk into a bar, club, or party, keep your eyes open for women with potential who aren't getting any male attention. You never know, she may have a very attractive personality, but she came there with a friend and doesn't know anybody. She might seem apprehensive at first, wondering why you suddenly walked up to her and treated her so nicely, but don't acknowledge it, just keep talking.

Conclusion

While it's impossible to provide a comprehensive troubleshooting guide, the pointers in this chapter should benefit the majority of men who find themselves repeating their mistakes. For those of you who still can't seem to overcome your difficulties, consider seeking out a mentor or finding other people who want to better their game. A good support system can go a long way in smoothing out any problems you're experiencing.

If finding a mentor or going out with a group isn't possible or desirable, you can always try falling back on Plan B. While attracting sexually accessible women doesn't always go smoothly, if you focus on these types of women, you will find that your rate of success increases significantly. If you feel you're doing everything right with women you're really attracted to, don't despair. Instead, aim a little lower—you won't likely end up going home alone and you'll get a bump in confidence that might make all the difference the next time you go out to meet and attract women.

Epilogue

If you read, practice, and thoroughly apply what you've learned in this book, it could very well change your life forever. Changing men's lives for the better, specifically when it comes to meeting and attracting women, is why I spent the last few years of my life learning, writing, and refining *Secrets of the "A" Game*. I've toiled endlessly on the Internet searching for new techniques and tactics, been on hundreds of disastrous dates, spent thousands of hours in bars, clubs, and malls meeting women, and worked through a lot of painful trial and error to figure out what works and what doesn't, all of which evolved into the concepts and strategies you've just learned. Now that you have a head full of knowledge, you MUST take the initiative and use this information and make it work for you in the real world.

Success with women isn't like riding a bike, you *will* forget what you've learned unless you constantly practice and learn not just from books, but from personal experience. Every man is different and one book or particular viewpoint isn't going to be a perfect fit for your lifestyle and the types of women you want to meet. You must continue to learn and grow by taking what works and discarding what doesn't until you've developed your own unique "A" Game. Initially, you might find yourself easily discouraged if you don't achieve instant success, but you must never give up because you WILL get better.

When learning how to play a musical instrument, you might not achieve anything remotely resembling a song for weeks, even months; the same holds true when it comes to meeting and attracting women, especially if you've had very little experience to begin with. However, by practicing, visualizing your success, and never giving up, you'll suddenly realize that you're not only playing a song, but you're on your way to becoming a virtuoso.

Just imagine what your life would be like if you were a master with regards to attracting women. See this goal in front of you, and then be your goal. It may sound simple, but it isn't and you'll have to keep this in mind for the next few months. Be willing to make mistakes and embrace them as learning experiences that may initially hurt your ego, but vastly expand your knowledge and increase your confidence.

Also keep in mind that small victories don't automatically translate into unqualified success. Just because you were able to Open a group and even Hook them doesn't necessarily mean you'll be successful in Attracting and Connecting with a woman. This might lead you to continually Opening groups of women and then never following through, because you stopped trying to advance the interaction or forgot how to do it. When you start having a lot of dead-end conversations that lead nowhere, refer back to the book and brush up on the areas where your skills come up short. Just because you read the book cover to cover, doesn't mean you "know it". When you stop thinking about what to do next, when conversations automatically flow through the five stages, when women are eager to advance your relationships physically, only then are you beginning to "know it".

So, my friends, I wish all of you the best on the journey that's in front of you. The supreme satisfaction of turning book smarts into street smarts is yours for the making, but you have to want it. Whatever physical or materialistic limitations you think you might have are illusions—you have the power to design your own life and blaze a trail to your own unique version of happiness, whether that's finding the woman you want to spend the rest of your life with, or finding a girl for every night of the week. Start by setting realistic goals for yourself, making time to practice as often as possible, keeping a positive attitude and above all, having fun. When it comes to meeting and attracting women, ALWAYS HAVE FUN!

-Logan